sand
in my
eyes

Christine Lemmon

BOOKS BY CHRISTINE LEMMON

Sand in My Eyes
Sanibel Scribbles
Portion of the Sea

sand in my eyes

AN OLDER WOMAN GROWING FLOWERS,
A YOUNGER WOMAN CAUGHT UP IN THE WEEDS

CHRISTINE LEMMON

PENMARK PUBLISHING
FT. MYERS, FLORIDA

SAND IN MY EYES

ISBN-10: 0-9712874-7-3
ISBN-13: 978-0-9712874-7-1

Penmark Publishing, LLC
www.penmarkpublishing.com

First Trade Printing: March 2009

Cover art by Chris Tobias
Editorial & prepress production by Windhaven Press, Auburn, NH
(www.windhaven.com)

Printed in Canada

10   9   8   7   6   5   4   3   2   1

THIS STORY WAS WRITTEN FOR MY THREE CHILDREN
JACOB, MICHAEL, AND JULIA

AND DEDICATED TO
MY MOM

ACKNOWLEDGMENTS

I want to thank my husband, John for the positive motivation he has given me during the writing of my three books. Through morning sickness, sleep deprivation and many of life's hectic moments, he has cheered me onward in my writing. It was hard at times writing about a "not-so-there" husband in *Sand in My Eyes*. My own husband is absolutely there for me and our children, and we are blessed to have him! He is my best friend.

JUST WHEN THE CATERPILLAR THOUGHT
THE WORLD WAS OVER, IT BECAME A BUTTERFLY.

— PROVERB

prologue

BELVEDERE

Dear Marjorie,

After we talked, I hung up the phone and stayed awake, thinking of you, of all that is stressing you at college. I'm writing to tell you how proud I am of you, studying the way you are, and the grades you are getting. You are an ambitious woman and will achieve great things in the world. But more importantly, I hope you live a life that you love. There is nothing a mother longs to hear more than that her grown daughter is living a life she loves.

This is not to say life is meant to be an everyday beautiful walk in the park. It's not. But as you journey into adulthood, you will hear all kinds of advice and things said about life, and will experience them for yourself. In case you're wondering, here are a few of the things your mother has heard, a few of the things she has experienced for herself:

1

Life is brilliant, life is dull. It's easy, it's hard. It's about reaping wealth, about giving to others, about living passionately, about doing what one must to survive. Life is joy. Life is suffering. The bigger the better, less is more. It's a world of abundance, a world of scarcity, a beautiful world, an ugly world, a world moving toward peace, a world headed for destruction. People are good. People are bad. Ask for help. Do it yourself.

I hope you rake through that which you hear about life. Some of the stuff, keep, but some, bag up and burn. As you work your way through this world you will see that everyone has something to say and is an authority on "life." Me? I can relate to most everything I've heard. It depends on the morning I'm having.

I stopped writing, then folded and dropped the letter to my daughter into my purse. My writing it was the act of a loony mother bird, one whose baby has left the yard for the first time. It had me awake at five, pacing the floor of the hotel room, unable to sleep, worrying whether I had taught her everything she needed to know about survival and the world—how to find food, water and shelter, and to fly, of course, but more importantly, how to soar; had I taught my daughter how to soar through life, so her journey is not all demanding, but breathtakingly beautiful, too?

"I don't think I taught her that," I mumbled to myself as I picked out a bouquet of flowers from a kiosk in the hotel lobby. "But if I pick her up and bring her back to me, she'll only want to leave again. That's where she's at in life. She's flown the nest."

As I unlocked the car I had rented for the week and got in, I had to start accepting it, that it was my time now, and to focus on the very present and the trip I was on—the trip that was mine—the trip to southern Indiana!

They *say* convertibles are the best cars for women suffering hot flashes, but after opening the hood, trunk and gas door I found myself sweating profusely by the time I found the button that makes the top go down. It made me want to pull out the letter I had started to my daughter and add a P.S. to it, to tell her that life is frustrating, that, well into my fifties, I had wanted by now to have mastered the basics and to be going about philosophically, spending my mornings sipping green tea in profound thought; not wasting precious time struggling to get the top down on a convertible!

But, oh well, it was a five-mile drive from my hotel to the nursing home and Indiana's crisp autumn air had me forgetting my frustrations and thinking instead how wonderful life can be—until I picked up speed and my hair whipped across my eyes, making it hard to see the colorful corn stalks out in the fields.

"This is *not* the best car for me," I muttered under my breath, questioning the guy who worked at the rental car agency, and all the other so-called experts of the world. "Who are they and what are their credentials?"

And because I didn't want to miss the corn drying, and the crimson maple trees, and the big white birds headed south for winter after a summer spent in the Midwest, I pulled to the side of the road to buy a cup of apple cider and slices of fudge, and to tie my hair back with the silk scarf I kept in my purse, the one I typically wore around my neck to hide the telltale signs of my age. I then took my sunglasses off and put my reading glasses on instead. I had taped the directions to the nursing home to the dashboard and would soon need to look at them.

I was on my way and feeling older than I did the last time I rode in a convertible—twenty years ago, through a wildlife refuge in Florida; a forbidden ride I have never told anyone about, my romantic secret that only the tri-colored herons witnessed, and I'm sure they haven't told. And there were a few other birds looking down at us that day, but I can't remember what they're called, the ones that seem to be wearing golden slippers. Their name was on the tip of my tongue, lingering with all the other words I had been forgetting lately.

As I continued along the winding country road, I worried that if I was forgetting things at my age, what if the friend I had flown all this way to see wouldn't remember me? I was the frazzled mother of three who lived next door from long ago. She was the elderly widow who, by way of her garden, lent me a unique way of looking at my life and the world. After all these years, I've never forgotten her and I hope she hasn't me.

Serendipity is what helped me in tracking her whereabouts when, recently, I turned on the radio and listened to a national story on butterfly gardens cropping up throughout the country, at campuses, schools, museums, zoos and institutions. I was captivated by the interview they did with a resident of a nursing home, by what she had to say and, to my astonishment, I knew before they gave a name that it was her, my neighbor from long ago.

"It's the life cycle of the butterflies that gets me to thinking," she told them when asked whether the newly instated garden had increased her quality of life at the facility. "I'm old and frail," she went on, "but like those butterflies need flowers, I need people. I crave the company of others."

I glanced at the directions taped to the dashboard, the ones her son—Liam is his name—had given to me. After hearing his mother on the radio, I tracked him down and called. I had met him back when I was living next door to her, and it was he who took me on that ride in his mother's convertible, the ride that gave the birds something to chirp about.

"Remember that silly little story about flowers?" I told him over the phone the day I called, the day I booked my flight. "The one I started way back when I lived next door to your mother?"

"The one you wouldn't let me read?"

"That's the one," I said. "Well, I've been tinkering with it on and off for years now."

"And you're done?"

"Not quite," I said. "That's why I'm calling. I need to see your mother. I need her blessing before I move forward with the story, before I send it out into the world. After all, she's the inspiration behind it, and so are you to an extent."

"Is this story of yours fiction or fact?"

"A little of both," I told him.

"Should I be worried?"

"It was a long time ago. You shouldn't be. I've changed the names and made up a bunch of stuff. It's hard to remember everything the way it happened."

"How many years has it been, twenty?"

"Around that," I told him. "I'm better off not doing the calculations."

"Well, my mother is in a nursing home in Indiana—sharp as a whip mentally, but physically, she's touch and go. I don't know how much longer she can go on."

I glanced over at the simple three-step directions he had given me to where his mother was living, and felt remorse over the friendship I had let wither away—silently retreating over differing points of view one day—and for having lost touch, and for showing up now, after all these years of not making a simple phone call or sending a single letter. I had been feeling this way lately about several past friendships I had let fall by the wayside. It happens at a certain age. We question ourselves regarding things we once did and said, and more so over the things we didn't do or say. It's why I flew all this way to reunite with her and tell her, "I'm sorry, please forgive me," for the ending we had.

Only then would I be able to write an appropriate ending to my novel and move on, by asking if she had any of the tidbits she used to share with me—ideas for how a woman my age might go about re-landscaping her current life and the dullness setting in.

"This is the day," I declared out loud as I turned into the parking lot of Belvedere Nursing Home. "This is the day for change in my life."

chapter one

As I got out of the car with the bouquet of flowers, and a canvas bag with the manuscript strung over my shoulder, I wondered whether my friend liked where she was living and, other than watching butterflies, how she passed her time, all those hours in a day. And could she recall the details of the life she had lived, born at the turn of the century and now living out the New Millennium in a bed on wheels, a bed operable by remote control?

I stared at the two-story white brick nursing home, wondering whether I had it in me to live as long. I always assumed I might die before getting so old, but now, thanks to health care advancements, I knew I needed to start brainstorming ways I might go about living productively for another half century on Planet Earth. Others my age were talking optimistically of the future, and were content with the present, but I had been living in the past, walking in my mind the halls of the old house, hearing the voices of my children when they were small, and wanting to know that the years I already spent living mattered, that they were significant.

I've got years, decades—at least two, probably three, and hopefully four—I figured as I walked up to the main entrance, before I need to think about assisted care housing options, nursing homes or living in a place other than my own home. Then again, in the last year alone I had gone to the funerals of an older first cousin, an aunt and a roommate from college, so there's no telling whether or not I would make it so far. I only knew that it felt like yesterday when I was thirteen years old and my junior high teacher had us volunteer at a facility like this and then write a paper about it.

I turned and rammed my behind into the large, silver, square wheelchair button that is supposed to automatically open a door and, when it didn't open, I rear-ended the button several more times, trying to remember what I wrote in that paper, or the grade I got for it. But I couldn't open the door with my butt, nor remember life lessons from my nursing home experience. All I remembered were the stenches that had me running out the door, performing cartwheels with my girlfriends in the parking lot.

"That's not the button," a woman looking to be in her twenties and jogging effortlessly up the stately steps told me. "Here," she said, pushing a silver button I hadn't seen. The doors opened instantly.

"Whoops," I said, pulling my reading glasses from my purse, putting them on and taking a better look at the button I had been ramming. And when I read that it was a plaque of dedication for the building, and knew that my eyes had failed me, I felt far removed from the junior high girl I once was, the youthful me intoxicated by a sense of invincibility and the belief I'd remain forever young. I should laugh at myself, I thought as I hurried inside, at my hormones for playing tricks on me. They say laughter is the best medicine. Then again, they say convertibles are the best cars for women with hot flashes.

As I stepped up to the reception counter, I didn't feel like laughing. I didn't find me funny. All I felt was nervous at the thought of seeing my friend, and how the years and disease would have had their way with her. I knew from her son that her health had been rapidly deteriorating in recent months, and that the progression of her type 2 diabetes and complications associated with it had been one reason for her children switching her from the assisted care facility she had been living in to this one.

I picked up a pen and did what the sign-in form instructions told me to do, writing my name, the time I arrived, and the person I came to see.

As I wrote her name—Fedelina Aurelio—on the line, I felt overtaken by emotion regarding this lady I knew from my old street, at a time when I had been feeling entangled by life and its pestlike frustrations and was hardly seeing all the beauty that was there. I was balancing three children, a marriage in crisis, financial distress, a house in need of repairs and, lastly, myself, and I had been feeling as if I were the only woman in the world struggling, juggling, with it all. And because we had recently moved, she was at that time the only friend I had.

It was through our chitchatting here and there that I learned to identify the weeds that were pulling me down and getting in the way of the significant. She never spoke in the form of a lecture, nor did she sound like a preacher. And she wasn't a clinical psychologist. I never paid her a co-payment. All I did was open my door when she came a knocking, or stopped by her garden when I saw her watering roses, or waved when I spotted her looking out her window at me and my children going by with the wagon.

Fedelina shared with me the insight I needed to rake through my mess. I don't think it was her intention to do gardening on me then and I don't know whether she knew that, one by one, our small woman-to-woman talks were helping me pull the ugly from my life, so that beauty, peace, simplicity and contentment could sprout forth strong and free. We were two females gabbing away. She was the older widow out growing flowers and I was the mother of three caught up in the weeds.

And I'll never forget the letters she shared with me—letters her mother once wrote to her—words I let sprinkle down like slow-release fertilizer, inspiring me long after we both went our separate ways. But it bothered me through the years that I never had the chance to tell her of the profound impact she had on my life. It's why I bought tickets and flew all this way to Indiana, to let her know her life mattered, that it meant something significant, at least to me, and to thank her for sharing with me her knowledge of flowers and of life.

"You don't have to fill that column in," the girl working the reception counter said. "You can skip that, the purpose for your visit."

I stopped writing and crossed out what I had written so far. "Good," I said. "It's enough to fill a book."

"You're here to see Fedelina Aurelio?" she asked, reading the clipboard.

I nodded.

"Down the hall, seventh door on your right."

chapter two

The hallway was long and sterile. It smelled of ammonia and I was glad for my friend's sake that the floor was clean. Fedelina once told me she kept her floors so clean that her children, when they were young, could lick butter off them. It was her children who found her this place. Her son said they visited a dozen before settling on the one that smelled, felt and looked the best.

When I found myself at the heels of a woman with a hunchback inching along, it made me feel younger than any jar of antiaging cream ever could. I switched to the fast lane, passing her by and stealing glances into rooms with open doors as I went, catching glimpses of women passing time propped up in beds, sipping through straws, dressed in nightgowns and living by way of the television. One was talking out loud, having a lively conversation, but there was no one in her room.

The sights I was seeing lent me a sense of urgency. Life is as long as it is short. And despite it feeling like yesterday that I turned sweet sixteen, so too could it be like tomorrow that I would be a resident of a nursing home. The place also had me feeling young, and grateful. A sense of youth was oozing from my pores. Throughout the halls and in the rooms were women no longer fighting, hiding, or masquerading their physical age, and it had me reconsidering the cosmetic procedures that, in recent months, I had been researching, looking into for myself. Does it matter how we age if, in the end, this is where we all end up? Then again, yes, all the more reason to postpone those wrinkles as long as I could. I would purchase, as soon as I got home, a jar of serum to reduce my age spots, RSVP for that seminar on preserving youthful brain activity, and order the supplements I saw on the late-night infomercial, the ones that promise to extend life. What a breakthrough it is, modern scientific intervention!

But for now, I felt peace as I looked at the faces of these old women, and acceptance as they looked back at me. I felt temporarily removed from all that is culture, a refreshing respite from that antiaging movement of which I was becoming a patriotic member. Within the walls of this place, I no longer felt like a criminal. And what a crime it is in the world today, a shame at least, for a woman to look older than she is. Women are ambushed for how they look, thrown into vans, driven to talk shows and made over to look like the women they need to become. I didn't know what I was supposed to look like. I didn't know who I was now that my children were grown and I was entering this new phase of life.

I stopped outside the door with Fedelina's name beside it. Her door was opened a crack. I almost knocked, but stopped myself and checked the time on my cell phone instead. It was too early in the morning to come barging in for a reunion. I should wait an hour. Who knows what her mornings were like? I didn't want to disturb a nearly one-hundred-year-old sleeping, bathing, eating, dressing, or television-watching old woman, and so I pulled out the letter I had earlier started writing to my daughter. With the stationary held up against the corridor wall, I added a little more.

Some say life changes in the blink of an eye. Others say it changes with a mere thought. Chaos theorists claim the whole world changes with the single flap of a butterfly's wings, and that the ripple it sends out could spawn a hurricane. I don't think you know this about me, Marjorie, but my life changed long ago, with a knock at my door, or rather, it changed with the opening of that door.

I folded the letter and put it back into my purse, and softly but confidently began knocking, this time on her door, on the door of the woman who two decades earlier showed up early in the morning knocking at mine.

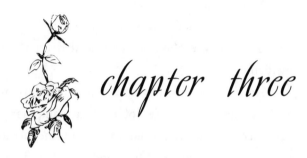

chapter three

When no one answered, I slowly pushed the door open and walked in. There, lying in bed, her eyes closed, was an older version of the woman who once claimed she had no secrets with regard to raising children, marriage, and living life. Her hair, the natural red resource she was born with and later kept red by way of a box, was drab and gray, and her once powdery white skin with faintly pink cheeks and nose that glowed from beneath the awning of her floppy gardening hat now had a dull matte look. She no longer looked like the fairy godmother I thought she was, but the grandmother of a fairy godmother. In other words, she looked old, and less colorful than I remember. And tinier, too!

There was a thin blanket pulled to her neck, tucked along her sides, and her body looked more like that of a child, no plumpness left to it. I was expecting a bigger person, a giant. Over the years, and through my writing, I had turned her into this larger-than-life character in my mind. I could see now that she was just old, really old.

"Amazing, with the illness she has," I commented when a male nurse walked in. "How do you think she did it? How did she make it so far?"

"I don't know," he said.

"Oh, come on. She's got to have a secret."

"Good genes," he said. "That's probably it."

"She always said, always believed, she'd live to be one hundred."

"Well, she's almost there!"

"You think that's her secret, believing?"

"Yeah, maybe," he said, and headed for the door. "That and modern medicine."

I looked around the room. There were as many photographs on the wall as there were pieces of medical equipment, and I wondered which sustained her more, the equipment or the pictures. I recognized people in the pictures—her children and grandchildren, older than when I saw them last, when she used to pull photos out and brag about them to me. And then my eyes stopped at a sketch of a woman standing in what looked like a mangrove forest. I recognized the mangroves in the background, and the bay and I knew then that it was me—that her son had sketched me! No one else would know it was me. He did a good job of making me more beautiful than I ever was—although I felt beautiful the day I stood there posing for him—that day a long time ago in southwest Florida, on Sanibel Island, at the wildlife refuge.

But there were no flowers in her room, no butterflies, and other than the sketch of me at that refuge, the only color that caught my eye was a lavender sock lying on the floor. I bent down and picked it up, carrying it with me as I walked over to the foot of her bed. Liam had told me over the phone that the diabetes had damaged the sensory nerves in her legs, something that had started years before, and this had been the reason for her unsteady walk. And it was a nail she stepped on in her garden one day, an injury that went unnoticed due to poor circulation, he had explained, that left untreated became infected, destroying layers of her skin and creating a hole that went all the way to her bone. The bone, too, had become infected, and that was why doctors had to take her foot, and that was another reason why her children had talked her into moving into the nursing home. She couldn't walk.

It was cold in the room and I wanted to help the woman who once helped me. I never helped her the way I could have. She had been the one living alone, grieving her husband while caring for a house, lawn and, most challenging of all, caring daily to keep her health under control and to prevent or delay the disease's destruction. And through it all she was the one bringing me gifts from her yard, leaving me optimistic toward life.

"Good morning, Fedelina," I whispered, waiting for her to stir, or open her eyes, but she didn't. "It's cold in here, don't you think?" I clung tightly to the sock in my hand. "I found this comfy, soft sock on the floor. I could put it on your foot, if you'd like. I'd be happy to." She didn't move but I could still hear her voice from years ago telling me mornings would come to mean a million different things to a woman through her life. I looked around at all the medical equipment, wondering whether she ever imagined her mornings would come to this.

I crossed the room to the window and opened the curtains. A glimpse of the good old outdoors would do the trick, and sunlight would wake her kindly so she would open her eyes and see that I was here. But it had turned into a somber, sunless day, with no flower boxes out her window, only a view of the asphalt parking lot and my rental car. I closed the curtains and sat down in a chair facing her.

"Fedelina," I tried again, needing for her to open her eyes and look through my rhinestone-studded glasses and know that it was me. "It's been a long time, but I had to see you. I hope your son told you I was coming."

It was then that her eyes, a brilliant blue like the petals of a morning glory, opened—only to look right through me, as if she didn't know me at all. "It's me—Anna Hott!" I said desperately, to no reply, and went on. "I look different than when you saw me last. My eyes are no longer puffy from sleep deprivation, and my hair is showered and styled. I have all the time in the world now for putting on makeup, and look, my nails are manicured, but it's still me."

She blinked countless times and closed her eyes again, but then licked her lips, which were dry and cracked and said, "It's good to see you, Anna."

"You, too," I said on the edge of my seat. "I've been remembering lately all the good talks we used to have. It's why I'm here. I felt like talking with you one more time."

"One more time?" she asked, "What do I look like to you? A woman on her deathbed, a flower with no petals left?"

"That's not what I meant. I guess I'm nervous," I admitted, as if talking to a shrink.

"I know," she said. "I know what you meant. How's the family, the kids?"

"Great—the boys are well into college, planning semesters abroad, and my daughter, well, she's a freshman now. I moved her in a couple of months ago."

"And what are you doing now?"

"Looking around for a town house is all," I told her, not wanting to pour it all out, the details of my empty nest syndrome, of how all I do is saunter around my house, which is hauntingly quiet since my youngest left for college, wondering how to pull myself out of the gloomy, childless hours, those after-work hours that, without kids, feel like nothing more than flat, boring patches of soil. "My house, it's too big, and too much work. I don't need it anymore."

"And what about that husband of yours, how is he?"

"Oh, I'll tell you all about it," I said. Her mouth was opened slightly but she didn't say anything and I feared she wasn't in the mood for all this talk. I could see that her gums had pulled away from her teeth, exposing a part of the root.

"My son tells me you've been writing," she said.

"Same old story all these years," I confessed.

"I remember that about you—that you loved to write. Is it good, your story?"

"I'm too attached to know."

"Well, Liam tells me you want to share it with me."

"That's right," I said, wondering whether he had mentioned that the story was inspired by her—by knowing her! And when she didn't say anything further, and her head rolled to the side as if she were falling back so sleep, I asked, "Are you tired? Would you like me to come back later?"

"That's a good idea," she said. "Why don't you enjoy the fall colors and come back tonight? I am tired, and besides, I have a lot to do today."

"Of course," I said, reaching down for my bag.

"Anna," she then announced, those blue eyes opening once more, this time looking right at me, "I'm kidding. You really think I'm busy, that I have things to do? What—cook, clean, run a marathon?"

I dropped my bag and shook my head. "It's so good to see you."

"Sit down," she said. "You're hovering is making me nervous."

I sank into the vinyl armchair beside her bed. "So how are you doing?" I asked.

"I need constant, around-the-clock medical care," she said. "My children did what was best, putting me in here, did what they had to do."

"Of course," I had said, but still, I never imagined her—a mother of seven—ending up in a nursing home. It wasn't that I thought of them as bad places, just places nobody wants to be in. Then again, as a mother of three, I couldn't imagine myself intruding into my own adult children's lives, moving into a room in their house one day, burdening them.

"It's hard," she told me as her fingers fidgeted around the side of the bed, taking hold of a remote control, and pressing a few buttons. "I've lost the capacity to take care of myself. I need help now with eating, bathing, getting to the bathroom." But in less time than it had taken me to get the top down on the convertible, her bed started to rise. "Waking up is the hardest," she said, now fully upright in a sitting position, her face proud, as if she had reached a mountain summit. "But, modern technology, it makes getting up in the morning easier."

"I shouldn't have come so early."

"You're fine," she said. "Once I open my eyes, once I manage to keep them open more than a few minutes, I've made it! I know then that I've made it another day." She looked deeply into my eyes. "So what are you waiting for?" she asked me. "Aren't you going to read me that story?"

"There's no hurry," I said. "I'm here to visit with you. I've got a few days."

"I want to hear it, Anna."

"Okay," I said, "but first, I brought you something." I walked over to the bureau where I had put the bouquet of flowers and I pulled a lavender orchid out from the rest. I gently opened her fingers, placed it in her hand, and closed her fingers around the stem.

"An orchid," she declared, her lips curving into a smile. "It's been years since I've held an orchid."

"Remember what you once told me about them?"

"No," she answered, a look of strain on her face.

"You said orchids ought to remind us women how strong and resilient we are, more so than the world believed."

"I said that?"

"Yes." I nodded as I pulled the manuscript from my bag. "You learned it from your mother. You said she taught you all kinds of things about flowers, and life."

As I sank into the uncomfortable armchair facing her bed, I knew she needed to hear that from me. She needed to hear the words she once spoke to me, regurgitated and fed back to her.

"I'm glad you're here," she said, "and glad for this morning, another morning." She pulled a pillow from the side of her bed and added it to the one under her head, propping herself up as if she were ready to read a good book. She held the orchid tightly on her chest. "Now read me that story of yours."

As I pulled the rubber bands off the manuscript pages, I could feel my hands shaking. I had never read it to anyone and feared she might not like it, especially the parts about her.

"It's longer than I wanted it to be," I told her, insecure. "I could paraphrase, skim the good parts. I don't have to read the entire thing."

"Start at the beginning," she insisted. "We'll see how far we get. I may only have one foot, Anna, but don't let that fool you. I'm all ears."

How she had humor in the state she was in, I did not know, but I was overtaken with vulnerability as I started to read what I had spent nearly twenty years pouring my heart and soul into writing—a silly little story about flowers, about an overwhelmed mother and a widowed gardener, and the stages of life.

chapter four

TWENTY YEARS EARLIER

There once was a woman who lived on an island in a little house on stilts. From the outside, hidden within the forestlike branches of the banyan trees, it looked more like a birdhouse than what a family of five calls "home." On the inside the house was a disheveled mess. The floors would shake as a load of wash tumbled about in the machine, making all the pictures on the walls hang crooked, and in the days after they first moved in the woman of the house swore there were earthquakes in Florida, until she figured it out.

I was that woman. And an exhausted, overwhelmed one was I. Whether living up north, or down south, in a city or on an island, in a big house or a little house, clean house or messy house, loud house or quiet house, mornings for mothers are tough—especially mornings after having no sleep.

"It's hard being a woman, harder a wife, but hardest of all is to be a mother," I pitifully cried to myself in bed, my hand feeling its way to my daughter beside me, fumbling across her lips and nose, and then stumbling upon her forehead. It was still warmer than normal after my fierce battle to reduce a stubborn fever. All night I spent dosing in ten-minute increments, keeping watch, terrified the same thing might happen again, the muscles of her face, trunk, arms and legs contracting into a convulsion the way they had when her fever peaked in the wee hours. And the involuntary moan she had let out from the force of the muscle contractions haunted me all the hours I lay in bed facing her, crying from having gone through the most frightening tens of seconds of my life watching her seize mysteriously, while thinking I was about to lose her when the clock struck one and she stopped breathing and turned blue.

After the paramedics left and she fell asleep in the territory of the bed once occupied by my husband, only then did I let my mind wander to the fiery forest. There my thoughts scattered for hours, lost in the details of my husband's dark affair. I was frequenting this forest nightly, twisting and turning, caught up in its branches, smoldering in resentment and sacrificing sleep to go there, but my days were consumed by children and household responsibilities, and allowed me no time for thinking. And when a person isn't able to think during the day, their thoughts come out at night, darker and creepier.

With the early sun poking me in the eyes, I rolled to my side and reached for a damp cloth to put over my face, but then I heard the footsteps of a wolf entering my room. I pulled the sheet back up to my chinny chin chin, hiding a bit longer from morning and from him. He was there with us all night, picking up the fallen, damp cloths, refolding and laying them across Marjorie's forehead, and I had felt his eyes watching me as I climbed into the lukewarm water with my nightgown on so I might better comfort and hold our slippery, screaming and feverishly hot little girl. I had ignored him, refusing his help, but he hovered close through it all, kneeling on the floor beside the tub as our girl and I cried together, knowing we had lost the battle and that something worse was about to happen.

Timothy, my husband, was across my room now and I could hear him breathing, but there was nothing more I had to say to the man. I had said it all that bitterly cold morning when I confronted him, told him I knew, had seen the signs and put it all together. "You wicked animal!" I had snarled at him then. But now I held my breath, pretending to be asleep. I didn't want him leaning over me in bed like he had then, with those big red eyes, and my, what a big mouth he had, drooling out the details of how he did me wrong, drinking on a business trip, finding himself in bed with his younger coworker, and how he swore to never stray again.

Mother of three, I should have divorced him right then. But I didn't. A mother does things for her children, things that don't always make sense. "A mother's love is illogical," I said when he asked whether I was leaving him. "A natural instinct kind of love—one I don't expect you to understand."

I stayed with him for the sake of our children, and encouraged him to take the branch office promotion he had sitting on the table, the relocation offer that brought us to Florida, three hours away from where his parents were living and far, far away from his mistress, so far that he might never cross paths with her again. I would quit my job in New York City and become a stay-at-home mother in a tiny house on a barrier island in order to be farther away from her, and there we would live happily ever after, pretending, trying to believe that life was good.

When he left the bedroom and I could hear the shower, I wanted to sleep longer, but "ready or not, here I come," I heard the voice of morning—my three-year-old twins cantering down the hardwood floors toward my bedroom like ponies set loose from a stable. I would have to check outside their window for a woodpecker waking them consistently at the crack of dawn, I thought as I opened my eyes and looked around. The walls in our bedroom were yellow, and in the little yellow room there were a writing desk, red syrup on a spoon, dirty socks, an unpacked box, crumbs on my rug, and an army of bugs. It all made me close my eyes, then mutter, "good-bye, morning" and "good riddance" to writing and the sticky spoon, "adios" dirty socks and ugly box, and "bon appétit" to the bugs eating crumbs on my rug.

"Juice, juice, juice," Thomas chanted as he jumped over the black wrought-iron post of my bed, and Wil was asking for something, too, but he was grumpy and his words were more like the sounds of a dying blue-shell crab.

"Use your words, Wil. Your words are powerful. Mama can't understand you when you grunt and groan," I told him.

"Wil wants juice," his brother said for him.

"Mama will get you juice. But first she wants to cuddle," I told them, but then Marjorie awoke and I could see from her eyes that she was wondering whether the paramedics really came to see her at one o'clock this morning, or had it only been a dream. Was I really screaming over her as she vomited and jerked rhythmically in my arms?

I reached for the fever-reducing syrup I had hidden under my pillow and poured a teaspoon into her mouth, waiting for her to say something, a single word, "mama." They promised me simple febrile seizures are harmless and cause no brain damage, but until a mother sees her little one talking and playing, she remains in a worried state, for this is the way we *tend to think, tend to think, tend to think.* This is the way we tend to think on an early sleep-deprived morning.

There was nothing I craved more than to nest in my blankets forever, cuddling as we were, and not fly around like a frantic bird, but mornings couldn't care less whether a mother is rested or not, and my boys, playful as river otters, hopped down and took off out of my room—headed, I knew for the refrigerator. And Marjorie slid down too, usually following her brothers in single file wherever they went, but this time she pushed open the bathroom door and I could still hear the shower, her father leisurely lavishing himself with hot water. I didn't feel like stepping foot in the same small room as Timothy, but then I heard the toilet lid open and knew that my daughter, like a mourning dove in a birdbath, was dipping her hands in to play.

I didn't enjoy waking in the little house on stilts any more than I had the house back north: touching my feet to the cold floor, shivering like a feeble goose, taking my first throbbing steps morning after morning, laughing at the foot doctor for having told me the only way my so-called "plantar fascitis" would go away was to stretch, ice and massage my feet several times a day ("yeah, right, like who has time for that,") so, all this time after giving birth last, my feet were still aching first thing in the morning and any time I stood up, and I was a mother dancing in circles, responding to the called demands of three children, hoping the activity might warm me. It didn't matter where I lived. Mornings then and living there and now and living here, on this barrier island down south, are all the same, no longer my own. They belong to my children and household chores.

"Yuck, Marjorie," I scolded as I grabbed her by the tummy and soaped her hands in the sink. "Again, your father forgot to shut the bath-room door, you poor thing, disgusting. How many times do I have to tell him?"

"Good morning, princess," Timothy said, poking his head out from the shower, and I knew he wasn't talking to me. "Daddy is late for his trip," he continued. "I wish I didn't have to go, especially after what hap-pened to you last night, but at least your fever broke."

We both knew well how to play the silent game. Tell the children what you want your spouse to hear. That way you don't have to talk to each other. Since I found out what he did with that other woman, the two of us had become ghosts, occupying the same house but living on different planes of existence, aware when the other was present, yet mak-ing no contact. The boys had witnessed us sauntering past one another in the hallways and their eyes begged for us to communicate. But even now, as we stood with nothing but a shower curtain separating us, I hardly knew what to say to the man. I had cursed and said all there was to say in the days following his confession.

I wiped the steam off the mirror with my sleeve and took a good hard look at myself. My once brilliant eyes now looked coated in lay-ers of grime—a build-up of pain and disappointment—and my face was covered in the markings of scorn that I feared might never go away. I didn't know how one removes the resentment from their face, or renews the brilliancy in their eyes and the radiance in their skin.

Resentment does bad things to a person. It was turning me into an ugly woman.

"Who are you?" I shouted at the face in the mirror. "I'm looking for Anna Hott. What happened to her?"

"Did you say something?" Timothy asked from behind the curtain.

"I wasn't talking to you," I told him and, when the younger, happier, more beautiful me would not appear, I stared back at the exhausted, overwhelmed, joyless thirty-six-year-old telling me what I didn't want to hear, that I was no longer the fairest of them all.

Then I reached for my toothbrush, but could hear the boys bickering toward me and Marjorie was opening the drawer with the razors, pulling them out. I redirected her to the drawer with the cotton balls, and because there wasn't time for brushing my teeth, I quickly pulled my dark, shoulder-length hair into a ponytail at the nape of my neck, noticing three gray hairs growing from my head. I tugged on one until there were two gray hairs growing from my head. I pulled on another and then there was one gray hair growing from my head. That one I left exactly where it was, hoping that Timothy would spot it and know what the last several months had done to his poor wife.

By now the boys had come in, and Thomas was angry and hounding, and Wil was pathetic and whining, "Where's our juice?"

"Who do I look like, a superhero?" I asked. "Because I'm not. I'm one mommy, two hands, that's all I am. Now go into the kitchen and wait for me. I'll be right there."

I looked at my primly petite lips in the mirror, wanting to use them as weapons, wishing they had the power to tell my husband how nice it must be to be him, to be taking a ridiculously long, hot shower, and then to be going off like he was on a flight, another business trip, one more lavish hotel, and a cocktail reception, followed by a dinner, feasting on more than cereal and corn dogs like us. But he was numb to my words and would only shut me up, scold me for complaining, remind me that we live on a tropical island in Florida, and that my life isn't so bad.

"Would you hand me a towel, dear?" he asked, turning off the shower, and I rolled my eyes at the way in which he attached the word "dear" to whatever he said to me. Guilt does that. It brings out the superficial best in husbands. But he no longer held my hands, looked me in the eyes, bought me flowers, or desired date nights, so being called "dear" meant nothing at all.

I reached down and pulled a damp, smelly towel off the top of the pile of dirty clothes lying on the floor, then opened the curtain a crack and turning my head away, tossed it in.

"A clean one would be nice," he said.

"There are no clean towels," I said, letting out a wretched groan. "No clean anything. Maybe if I had someone to help me, if we hired someone to help with the laundry . . ." I stopped there, sounding more like a wicked witch than I intended.

"Well, by the time we pay the rent, car payments, insurance, and buy groceries, we've got nothing left, which reminds me. Don't spend a single penny for the next four days or things will bounce."

"You always say that."

"I'm sorry your life is miserable, dear," he said, but there were no harps playing, no trumpets blowing and I know he didn't mean it, didn't feel an *eensy weensy* bit sorry for my woes.

"You're the one who has to grow old with me, with the woman I'm becoming." I pulled a bar of soap out of Marjorie's mouth, wanting to go further, tell him I was at a crucial age, where I could either age gracefully and with an elegant look to my face—given a little help around the house—or begin to deteriorate and grow into an ugly old woman thanks to overexertion, stress and resentment.

But he wouldn't get it and, because I didn't want to stick around longer and see what the other woman saw—his naked body, thick around the middle from all those hotel happy hours—I picked Marjorie up and stormed out.

chapter five

It was a stressful stop-and-go commute toward the kitchen, with traffic, toys and my disturbing thoughts dangerously in my way, causing me to trip and swerve.

"I don't know how the house is always a mess," I told Marjorie, who was riding on my hip down the hall, "It's not like I dilly dally. Mama doesn't stop, doesn't sit. She runs from one disaster to the next all day long."

My home was gruesome enough for a wildlife documentary and if there were a narrator, she'd have said, "This is a habitat in distress, in which a bird has been trying to create a nest out of chaos." But I was no bird in distress. I was an overwhelmed mother, wondering whether one too many crazy mornings mixed with lack of sleep might have a tragic cumulative effect, like one too many huffs and puffs and the house falls down.

The refrigerator was open when I got to the kitchen, and I could see from the puddle on the floor that the boys had pulled out the gallon of juice and drunk what was left.

"I swear I'm on the verge," I muttered as I saw from the corner of my eye that Marjorie had taken her diaper off and was peeing on the couch. "On the verge of what, I don't know, but the verge."

"I'm hungry," cried Thomas, and like old Mother Hubbard I went to my cupboard to fetch that poor boy a bone, but it was bare, except for a can of beans, and I hated being that mother, always out of food, feeding her children boiled beans and butter.

"Aha! An egg," I announced, opening the carton and discovering one left. "I'll make us all an egg!" But then I noticed the sink, full with yesterday's dirty dishes, and there I spotted the frying pan sticking out from the heap. It needed a good scrubbing, but I had no soap, nor clean sponges, nor rags, and because I had nowhere to run to, nowhere to hide, I let my eyes wander to the window above my sink, and there I peeked out.

The world outside my kitchen was lighting up and I caught a glimpse of the lady who lives next door moving around like a shadow in her yard, filling her birdbath with water. This was the elderly woman I saw out there all those mornings when Timothy was out of town. I watched her then through the windows, digging holes in the soil, and later in the day taking bundles of roses from buckets and putting them into the holes. And when I was pacing the halls with whining children in my arms, she was out there spraying, pruning or tying cans in arched position to stakes. And as I sped away in my car to the pediatrician's or the store, I pretended I didn't see her watering flowers on the side of her house. What is wrong with my life, I've wondered, when I can't find it in me to wave to the cute old lady living next door?

But as I watched her now through my kitchen window, pulling weeds from the base of the birdbath, I felt a tugging from within me, a craving to write. Seeing someone passionately at play did this to me—made me wish I had an ounce of time to myself, to pursue a passion of my own! But no one had told me it could be so hard, that motherhood would give me indescribable joy in exchange for who I was as an individual, and that the accumulation of it all, of worrying, caring for my children, responding to their every whimper, oh, and all the housework and grocery shopping, the cooking and cleaning, would turn me into this woman who has no time for waving, or smiling, or getting to know neighbors, and certainly no time for writing!

I had always wanted to write, but life got in the way. The jobs I had at bookstores intimidated me, while my stint at the library overwhelmed me, and my work as a publicist for a publishing house, with all those doggone authors, exhausted me to the point of hardly being able to write a word of my own. And when I did, writing through my lunchtime, I struggled with the way an English Literature major like myself critically examines and hates every sentence she constructs, how she can hardly write a paragraph, and this results in all those unfinished stories, hauntingly occupying the drawers of her desk.

And back to life under the domestic big top, I thought as I turned from the window to find the boys climbing around the stovetop like daredevils, reaching into the candy cabinet, leaving me no time for selfish pursuits. "Boys," I shouted. "You could have been burned! Had mommy been cooking, had the stove been on, you could have been burned."

"Mama don't cook," said Wil. "She microwaves."

"True," I said, "but I was about to fry an egg."

They were hungry. I hadn't fed them a cooked meal in two days. I put Marjorie down, helped the boys off the stove, and grabbed a piece of scratch paper, then rummaged through my drawer for a pen, wondering how I might go about getting us all dressed and out the door to the pediatrician's, let alone the store, and when all I could find was a crayon, I scribbled, "to market, to market to buy a new . . . " Oh, what did I need from the store: a crispier, more colorful life; a fresher brain; a more lean body; easier-to-care-for children; a healthier husband; a larger house?

"There once lived a woman," I wrote in crayon on the scratch paper, "who lived in a little house on stilts." But then Marjorie let out a shriek and, when I looked up, she was standing on the center of the kitchen table. I flew through the air like a flying trapeze, hurrying to catch her before she fell, but once in my arms all she did was paw at my face like a hungry bear.

"No hit Mommy," I told her as I put her safely to the ground, trying not to give her kicking, screaming act the attention it wanted, and
when her tiny body came rolling my way, I hopped over it. Someone was
calling me from the bathroom, in need of a wipe, while the other had
broken the button on the water cooler, which was flooding the floor. I
spun like a top, trying to recall what I was doing in the kitchen in the
first place, tired of starting, stopping, and restarting tasks, phone conversations and thoughts, all of which lately had become like race cars taking
off, hundreds a minute, only to be sidetracked or rammed into, and none
of what I attempted was making it to the finishing line.

All I wanted was to finish an act from start to finish without interruption, so I set the egg I wanted to fry on the counter and steadily
walked to the sink, trying hard to block out the noise hitting me from
every direction. To an ordinary person, washing a pan is simple. But
for a mother, who is also like a ringmaster in a three-ring circus, doing
dishes is more hair-raisingly difficult than swallowing fire.

And then I spotted Marjorie, from the corner of my eye, dumping
something all over the floor—my jar of dried basil; red pepper, too. I
could hear Thomas screaming at the top of his lungs. I think he fell
down and bumped his crown. "No, no," I told Marjorie, who had aban-
doned the spices and was now lying on her tummy in the puddle of
spilled water, sipping it like a cat. She shook her head back at me, her
nose up in the air, and I pulled out plastic bowls with mismatched lids,
hoping they might lure her away.

"You can do it," I chanted under my breath, trying hard to be the
little engine that could. "You can make it through this day." At least *I
thought I could, thought I could, thought I could.* There was nothing I
wanted more this very moment than to become an escape artist and disappear, but then I saw from the corner of my eye the egg I was going
to make for my children's breakfast, the only egg in the house, the extra
large one sitting on the counter, roll to the edge and take a great fall. I
dropped to my knees, trying to save old Humpty, but hard as I might,
he slipped through my fingers.

It was the broken egg that made me cry, made me drop to my knees, nose to the ground, buttocks in the air. Had I been in a better state of mind I could have turned it into a yoga pose, but I was in a tizzy, breathing too fast, and when I rested my cheek on the floor, the only positive thing I could think was that at least egg whites were good for my skin—the closest thing I'd had to a facial in years!

"Why is Mama sad?" my son asked, parking himself beside me.

"Mamas can't always be smiling," I told him. "It wouldn't be natural."

"Why is Mommy stopped?" my other son asked.

Pulling my face from the floor, I looked at their little-boy faces, wondering how I should answer, whether I should tell them that a mother never stops, even when it looks like she has stopped. When it looks like she is resting, she is not. "I'm idling," I said, "simply idling."

"Why is Mama crying?" they continued, and I wanted to explain that when a mommy goes long enough without routine maintenance, or ignores all her problems, that then she begins to cry and shake. But they were too young for that, or to understand that their mother had expectations for happiness and believed marriage, career, a house and children would be her driving fuel, not her exhaust.

chapter six

Are you all right?" Timothy asked when he got to the kitchen and found me sitting on the filthy floor, my head now on my knees, the boys still beside me and Marjorie lying on her tummy nearby.

"It's what happens," I told him, "when a woman pulls too heavy a load." *Up hills and down hills!* "Without fixing her weak spots. She tries making it further." *She thinks she can, she can, she can.* "But then she stalls, then she breaks down."

"You're scaring me," he said, towering over me.

I looked up with resentful eyes at his freshly showered, damp hair, stainless starched business shirt, pressed pants, and his big, white teeth, the ones he religiously flossed morning and night, not knowing how to get my feelings across, to say that I didn't have time for any of that, for ironing my clothes, flossing my teeth, or swishing around mouthwash like him.

"Anna," he said, "I need to know, are you okay?"

"I try," I cried, wanting to tell him that all I needed was a simple "time-out"—thirty-six minutes to myself with my nose to the wall during which no one was allowed to look at or talk to me. "I try and try but I can't."

"Can't what?"

"Put it together again," I told him.

"Put what together again?"

"This house—it's a mess," I said, unable to articulate it further. My daughter was whining, the boys were bickering and the ponytail in my hair, pulled too tight, was giving me a headache. All of it mixed together made my thoughts scatter and my words run off, and I was unable to tell where to find them. "Leave them alone and they'll come home," I read from the book Marjorie put up to my face. "And bring their tails behind them."

"Anna," Timothy said, squatting down beside me, his hand touching my face. "You've got egg on your face."

"So?" I said nonchalantly.

"I'm worried about you—terrified to leave you like this, to leave the children alone with you."

"Oh, shush, I'm fine," I said, wanting to tell him that no, I wasn't fine, that I might never be fine again, that since his betrayal I hadn't been thinking clearly. It's why I walked out on my job in New York City, then sold our house in Connecticut and moved us all down south into this birdhouse. And why, since arriving here, I had been finding it harder than I imagined, and less glamorous, staying home with my children 24-7. No breaks or time to myself, no energy left at the end of the day to clean the disastrous house, let alone write, and writing was the one thing I had hoped to start as a stay-at-home mother, thinking it would be a cinch, no longer dulled from the creative pressures at work.

"Give me your hand," Timothy said. "Let's get you up."

"I don't want your hand," I told him, feeling like that person in a circus who sets up the tent, makes the costumes, trains the talent, pops the popcorn, sweeps the floor and steps out into the arena to perform an act of her own. She tries to have fun but down she goes, and only for a second do they care about the clown with the painted-on sad face lying on the floor. Then the spotlight moves to daddy—the talented, funny juggler—with the daughter dancing on his toes and the twins swinging from his hands.

As I sat on the sticky floor, listening to the laughter of my family around me, I knew I hadn't been feeling like myself. Him cheating on me, together with my new onset of tension headaches, children sick weekly, appliances breaking down one after the other—first the washing machine, then the dryer, then the garbage disposal —palmetto bugs running across my bathroom floor each night, and the pale patches of ghost ants moving about the dark wooden pantry shelves, sprinting erratically when disturbed; all these pestlike frustrations had me feeling less like the happy-go-lucky woman I once was and more like one of those Mother Goose characters, the ones I read about to my children all the while thinking to myself how certifiably "off" they seem in today's world.

"Let me help you wipe this egg mess up," Timothy said when the children deserted us and ran to the other room.

"Just go," I told him, batting away the wet rag in his hand. "Get yourself to the airport!"

"Unfortunately, I have to, or I'll lose my job and we won't be able to pay our rent," he said, glancing at his watch. "But I'm calling my mother."

"Your mother?"

"We've been here how many months now, and she hasn't seen us."

"I'm still getting settled."

"She's dying to see the kids. And starting to feel bad—every time they want to make the drive out here we tell them it's not a good time."

"This is *definitely* not a good time," I said. "Look at our house. It's a mess!"

"Our house is always a mess. And you need help. I'll have her come and stay with you."

"Stay with me?"

"She'd love to."

"I'm sure she would, but I don't want help," I said. I didn't want anyone knowing how bad our marriage was. Pride had me wanting to hide the imperfections of my life. And what would she think if she saw my house?

He looked to be in serious thought, and then said, "I'll have her and Dad come take the kids."

"Take my kids?"

"For a week."

"A week?" I gasped. "I could see a few hours, or an afternoon, but a week?"

"You need it," he said. "A week to yourself."

"That's ridiculous," I told him.

"What's ridiculous is your behavior!" he said, "And the fact that you can't get your act together."

I wanted then to tell him about the struggles I was having, tell him that when a woman becomes a mother she loses a part of herself, that the job of mothering is more encompassing than anyone could imagine and after so long with every intention, ounce of energy and action going toward my children I would no longer know how to think or what to do should my children be taken away for a week. "What would I do with a week to myself?"

"For starters, you could clean this place up."

I looked at him bitterly. "Why would I want a week to myself if all I'm going to do with it is clean, especially knowing it would only get trashed again twenty minutes after the kids come home?"

"When did you become so unhappy?" he asked.

"When you did what you did with that other woman," I said, turning my long face from him and the sulfur I smelled coming from his breath. "You are, after all, the one who turned me into the person that I am."

"You were miserable before that," he said. "I think this is a case of what came first, the chicken or the egg." But then he squatted down eye level with me and, when his eyes met mine, I knew he was thinking how lucky he was that I hadn't walked on him, taking the kids with me. "Anna," he said, softening. "I've fallen onto my knees a hundred times, begging for forgiveness."

I put my nose in the air and he saw the merciless look in my eyes that told him I could never be the same again, that the woman he had married was permanently ruined.

"I do have to go," he said, "but you've got to figure something out, decide whether you can forgive me or not. I can't go on like this. We can't go on like this. It's not good for the kids to see you like this."

"Oh stop," I said. "Let me be how I want when the kids are in the other room."

"Whatever," he said, "but you need to let me know."

"Know what?"

"Whether you can forgive me or not. I can't go on being tormented by your punishment. If my parents take the kids for a week, it'll give you time to figure it all out, determine whether you can get past this or not. And time to pull yourself together again."

Pull myself together? "What do I look like to you?" I asked, disturbed. "A rag doll—Raggedy Anna—in need of stitching, a third eye glued on?"

"You need a lot more than an eye glued on."

"What are you trying to say?"

"You need to decide, Anna, whether you can forgive me—whether we can get past this. Do you think it's possible?"

I stared at him and at the horns I saw coming from his head, and shook my head. I wanted to tell him that I didn't know how to sew a button on my own blouse, let alone gather off the floor and stuff back inside me the trust I once had for him. "I don't know," I said. "I need to think about it and I don't have time for thinking right now." But I was leaning in the direction of "*No, I can't, I can't, I can't.*"

"I've got to go," he said, picking up his duffel and suitcases. "But I feel strongly about this. I'm calling my parents. They'll come get the kids."

"Whatever," I said, not believing he would do it. "Enjoy your getaway. Must be nice."

"Actually, a comfortable dinner at home would be nicer," he said. "Something other than cereal. But look, it's not like I'm headed to the beach for a few drinks. I'm working, supporting my family."

"Poor you," I said.

"Good luck," he told me. "You need it."

"*Adios*," was all I said, and he was gone.

chapter seven

A couple of mornings later there were no tiny arms wrapping around me in the little yellow room, no fingers pulling on my hair, squeezing my neck or pinching my belly. It was me alone in our house in the forest, a forest of banyan tree limbs and hanging roots. I missed the children and their noise. I even missed them jumping on my bed and throwing their toys.

"It's good for them to get way. And it's good for you," my mother-in-law had said the night before as she helped fold and pack the children's clothes into a large duffel bag for their impromptu trip. "This time to yourself will only make you a better mother."

That *is* what I wanted, to be a better mother, more like I was before all the weedy events started tangling around my knees, yanking me to the ground. I also wanted sleep, but it would take a hundred years of deep, dark slumber to turn me back into the brilliant woman I once was, before my husband betrayed me.

Tucked within the blankets on my bed I learned that I can hide from the light of day, but haven't a clue how to hide from the contents of my mind—the worries and resentments that kept me up, returning in my sleep to the fiery forest where my smoldering thoughts had their way with me. And at last, as I was drifting into sleep—*cuk-cuk-cuk*—I heard an alarming burst, a pileated woodpecker striking its beak against my tin roof, driving me crazy as its jackhammer-like sound played with my sleep-deprived mind.

"I thought birds were smart, knew the difference between wood and tin," I mumbled as I curled like a shrimp, pulling the sheets up over my face. Alone in the king-sized bed, I stayed like a child under the haystack fast asleep, hiding from the bird, and from life and all its humdrum happenings that made me feel like I had been repeatedly slamming my own head against a tree. And because I'm not a bird designed to sustain unusual blows, I had been feeling like a woman losing her mind in recent months. It was easier having my children here. At least they kept me from thinking. And now, with them gone, I felt guilty.

"They look fine, no longer sick," I had tried reassuring myself last night as I stood in the middle of our sandy road, watching and waving, wondering if my children still loved me as their heads grew smaller in the back window of my in-law's car. It looked like they did, the way the boys blew me kisses and Marjorie cried. "She won't be crying for long," I told myself. Once she crossed those gates into the Magic Kingdom, she would be nothing but smiles, and I should be, too. I should be happy my children were spending time with grandparents whom they hardly saw when we were living up north.

Still, it's hard for a mother to turn off mothering because her children are away. I didn't know how to stop worrying about my father-in-law, and his driving too far to the left, and my mother-in-law, strict disciplinarian that she is, a firm believer in not sparing the rod. Her eyes had slapped me with judgment as the kids jumped back and forth from the love seat to the sofa, and later she shared with me her views, that my generation of mothers is letting kids get away with too much, and that our withholding of spankings is why the world is headed in the wrong direction, why children are turning into outrageous adults. I wanted then to tell her that we didn't believe in spankings, that time-outs worked well, but she had come to help me in response to a crisis, the emotional state of crisis I was in, and my husband had told me over the phone to keep my mouth shut and to not say a thing.

I don't know why I let all this negativity creep into my sleep, or why, on my first morning all to myself, I lay in bed harping over how his mother and I got into it when she told me our moving here was irresponsible, impulsive. "No one said life was going to be easy," she had said, looking me up and down as if I wore a crown on my head, her eyes declaring me an imposter, demanding from her son a castle in a tropical kingdom, a chariot, exquisite gowns and a maid. "I know your job up north was stressful, but you're only running from your problems, thinking that if you move to a beautiful place, everything will be better. You mothers today," she had said. "You think life should be all good and pleasant. And you expect it all."

I had given thought to what she said all night and come to the conclusion that, yes, I had been running from my problems for a long time now, and that it all started my freshman year of college. I felt as if I were on top of the world, knew it all, those first few days after my mother helped move me into my dorm. But then, a couple of weeks later, my mom died instantly in a car accident. The moment I heard the news my world collapsed and I no longer felt I had control over my life, or knew anything as to why things happen the way they do. And to this day it saddens me that I never had the chance to ask my mom all the things a woman-turned-mother wants to ask her own mom.

No one at college knew her. There weren't any lifelong friends there with me, so I kept my grief to myself. And I didn't feel like socially engaging. I kept everyone at bay, not joining sororities or clubs, but burying myself in my studies and in books, reading every novel I could get my hands on. I was lonely until I met Timothy. He was the life of every party and both he and our bottles of coconut rum brought me out of my shell. After graduation, we got married and together moved around the country for the fun of it, chasing his promotions. Each time we relocated to a place I had never been, it brought me back to my freshman year at college, when I moved in and knew no one and hid within my shell. And each time I started getting involved, getting to know people, I felt a sense of relief as Timothy would announce another move. It kept me far from intimacy, clinging to the loneliness that had been my state of comfort in college.

I pushed the blankets off my body. My mother-in-law was right. I was running from my problems by moving us to a barrier island in the Gulf of Mexico, but now I know that husbands and wives who fought up north are still going to fight down south. And worrywarts live everywhere, thriving in every climate. And even south of the Mason-Dixon Line bitter thoughts run wild, which explains why, well into my first morning alone, I was still strolling the fiery forest of my mind, conversing with the beasts that lived there and getting upset over all the people who have done me wrong.

"Come on Anna, get up and do something productive this first morning all to yourself!" I told myself, pushing the pillows onto the floor. Do what, I didn't know—search for my missing eye. That is what a rag doll does when wanting to feel alive. And then she shoves her stuffing back in and stitches her seams with needle and thread.

But I was no doll. I was a woman, and there were more important things demanding my attention than me falling apart at the seams. I looked around at the messy room and decided to spend the day cleaning, but then I thought of all the things a mother does in a day—things she doesn't want to do but must—and walked over to my writing desk instead. It wasn't that I did writing at the desk—I didn't have time—but it was a writing desk nonetheless, and when I cleared the clutter a desire to create flooded my mind. But I swallowed that desire back down again, sending it to the depths of my soul, where it would stick around until a time in my life when I have more time.

"But then I'd be old," I told myself, "and I don't want to wait until I am old to get started," and so I turned on my computer and sat down to write. That's when I was struck by what my husband had said about the chicken or the egg, and what came first—my misery or our rotten marriage.

As I put my fingers to the keys, I did so with the intent of making sense of it all.

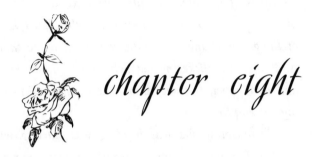

chapter eight

*O*nce upon a time there lived a woman who worked as a publicist at a major New York publishing house. There she would create and implement publicity campaigns to generate maximum book sales. It was a low-paying job and hard, promoting fifteen titles at a time while dealing with the authors, each of whom poured their heart, soul and ego into their written masterpieces. Never does a publicist meet a writer who doesn't believe that every breathing, reading creature in the universe ought to buy their book.

This publicist was also the mother of three small children and didn't know which was harder, handling their demands, or arriving at work each morning to twenty voice messages, forty faxes, and eighty e-mails in her in-box. Going to the copy machine room to make copies of press kits was often her only escape, and she spent much time in this stuffy room without fans or windows. But one day, when she lifted the lid, placed an author's photo color side down, closed it and pressed thirty-six, like her age, then hit start, all the copier did was grunt and groan. She didn't know why it was grunting and groaning, or what to do about her own discontentment. She put her hand on her head and gently pulled it to the side, hoping to release tension, but she didn't have time for this, standing around waiting for a machine to act right, and it annoyed her —as did her life, in which she no longer had time for selfish pursuits of any kind.

She watched as the machine spit out sheet after sheet, drab like the mornings of her life, one after the next, and they kept on coming, exactly the same and not to her liking, but she didn't know how to fix the color of things, or change her outlook toward a life that was bleak and fading. And when the flickering red light came on, she knew how to open the tray and add paper, but she didn't know what to do concerning her own feelings of emptiness.

The meeting she was heading was starting without her, but she was tired of hurrying, exhausted from her hectic mornings caring for her children, rushing them out the door, but the mornings kept coming, like the dull color copies, and she didn't know how to stop or alter them in either way. She could hire someone to help her with laundry, or ask the intern to make the copies for her, but she didn't know how to ask for help. She did everything herself.

She stood there dumbfounded when the copies went blank, and when the beautiful colors vanished from her life, but somewhere in the midst of pleasing everyone else, of saying one too many "yes" and not enough "nos," her identity as a person started ebbing away. She had no technical ability to fix the inkless machine, nor wisdom to change her unhappiness, and she let them both continue, disliked seconds of her life, one after the next, blank page after blank page.

"This has to stop," she declared as she pressed the "stop" button on the copier. But they kept on coming and she sank down onto the floor, wondering how we fall into routines that we hate and turn our heads from the flaws in our lives, watching year after year spew out before us while doing nothing to improve the quality.

She then pressed the "cancel" button, banging it with her fist, wondering how she might also press "cancel" with regard to the decisions she made in life. That's when she squeezed her hand between the wall and the machine and pulled the plug. The room went quiet and she felt dizzy, like *she was no longer standing in her own shoes but floating, and out she drifted, through the front doors of the publishing house, leaving her career behind. In the weeks following, she learned of her husband's disloyalty, then sold her house and urged her husband to take the job opportunity offered him, the relocation that sent them to Florida.*

"I was overwhelmed," I muttered to myself when I stopped typing. "And a woman overwhelmed for too long becomes miserable."

I got up from my desk and walked out onto my screened porch. There I stared up at the sky, tapping my foot impatiently for something beautiful to go by, like an eagle or a great white heron, but when nothing good flew by, it got me to wondering whether I had lost my ability to see beauty, for where had all the wildlife gone? And the romantic feelings for my husband, where had they gone, too? There were only ugly things roaming through my mind now, and spiders and palmetto bugs out on my lanai.

I took my slipper off and smacked a fast-moving spider hard. Then I pulled the rubber band out of my rag-doll-like hair and put my fists in the air. "Life," I cried! "It's not what I expected—all this housework that never ends, and a marriage that will not mend, and banks that won't lend. I hate my life and who I've become—this miserable woman!"

As soon as the words left my lips I felt sorry for myself. If only I had my mother to call. What woman who isn't a mother herself doesn't want to pick up the phone and call her mother, tell her how overwhelming it all is, ask her how on earth can one fold so much laundry, and say, "Help! I'm going crazy. Help! I never knew it could be so hard," for there is no one better to call when the house is falling down.

I tugged my hair at the roots and covered my face with my hands, not knowing what to do. And because there was no one that I knew of watching, I started to cry like a little girl, catching each tear with my fingertips. When there came too many tears to keep up with, I cried more like a woman disenchanted with life, and what a serious thing it is to be disenchanted with life, so when my tears ran dry, my soul—it had to be, my bitter, weeping soul—took over, releasing cries of anguish I had never heard coming from my mouth before. With this, the forest and the house on stilts were no longer silent, and the sounds were haunting and frightened me.

And then there was a knock. I stopped and heard *knock, knock, knock*. I bit my lip and listened more. *Knockety, knock, knock, knock.* It was coming from my door.

"Go away," I whined, tapping my heel, working myself into a dither. "Whoever you are, go away! Leave me alone."

But the knocking wouldn't stop.

chapter nine

I headed for my front door, sniffing and sobbing, chugging along like a train ready to derail, hoping that whoever was knocking might stop and go away. But as I peered through the peephole, smudged as it was, I saw an older lady upon my front porch. Her hair was red, her cheeks powdered white. She was wearing one of those cotton muumuu dresses—one size fits all, without buttons, elastic at the neckline. And she had on her head a flimsy, floppy hat.

I licked my forefinger and wiped the peephole, then looked through it again, catching a close-up of the woman who lived next door—Mrs. Aurelio, I heard her tell my boys the day we moved in. She had been pulling weeds and waved, but I was too busy hauling boxes and keeping track of children to give her more than a nod of my head.

"Go away," I muttered under my breath. "I will not open the door. I won't. Get back to your garden where you belong!"

Unless she was bearing lasagna or eggplant, as one might expect from a neighbor with the last name Aurelio, I was not in the mood for this, for neighbors knocking at my door, stopping by without notice. There should be rules against this sort of thing, welcoming a newcomer months after she's arrived.

But her knocking continued, and if there was anything I knew about the woman from watching her through my window it was that she had all the time in the world, and had to be lonely. Anyone who spends as much time as she out in her yard tossing seeds into dirt, waiting for them to grow, has got to be lonely.

"Goodie," I muttered when her knocking stopped. "Now, go! Hobble away, old lady." But she didn't. She stood on her side and I, holding my breath like a rabbit hiding from a farmer in a carrot patch, stood on mine. It was then that I saw the look in her eyes, a look that said, "Come out, come out, wherever you are," and it had me shaking in my slippers.

I reached for my sunglasses on the console and put them on, not wanting her to see my sleep-deprived eyes, swollen from crying. As I grasped the golden handle of the door, I quickly changed the mask I was wearing on my face from "miserable woman whose life is in disarray" to "my life is astounding." I was good at costume changing and did so daily. No one, except, now, my in-laws, knew of all the troubles in my life. I didn't want to be a burden, to be one of those women who verbally dump their overwhelmed lives on others and besides, it's simpler to pretend that all is fine. I wiped my nose on my shoulder, sniffed once more, and opened the door with a smile.

"Hi," I said.

"I was about to turn and walk away," she said. "Are you busy?"

"A little," I said, thinking of all the crying I had to do, all the harping over my husband's infidelity. "What can I do for you?"

"I don't want to keep you," she said.

"No, it's fine. What brings you over?"

"Here." She handed me a pot with a tall, slender stem, and smiled at me as if she were a fairy godmother granting me my wish. "It's yours. I'm giving it to you. I've been meaning to come by for weeks now," she said, "to bring flowers."

"Is that right?"

"I hear your children out my bedroom window in the mornings."

"We're loud, I know," I said, embarrassed.

"No, they've brought me joy. This street was too quiet before." And then she inched closer like she was going to share street gossip with me, of which I knew none. "I had seven. Can you believe it?"

"Seven kids?"

She closed her eyes and shook her head like she didn't believe it herself. "Five girls, two boys," she said. "Of course they're grown now, but I don't know how I did it back then."

"You're still smiling," I said. "What's your secret?"

She waved me off. "I don't have any secrets, and there are no remedies that make it all easier. I remember walking around in circles, like a chicken with its head cut off, thinking I had lost my mind."

"That's me," I said. "Going to the kitchen, forgetting why I went there in there in the first place."

"I do that all the time," she said. "I'm in my eighties, my children grown, and I hardly know where I'm going or what I'm doing, can you believe it? I don't know what's worse—having too much work in one's garden or not enough."

"So what is this?" I asked, holding up the potted stem she had given me.

"An orchid, a Cattleya orchid. It should flower any day—once it adapts to your home and feels no stress. Orchids dislike stressful environments."

I let out a laugh, wondering if she had a candle in her bag I might exchange it for—a more practical welcome-to-the-neighborhood gift. "If orchids dislike stress, then it won't stand a chance at flowering with me."

"You know anything about them?" she asked.

"Not a thing," I proudly replied. "Just that they're weak, delicate and die easily. You're talking to a woman who can't grow a Chia Pet."

"Then I better not forget to give you this, wherever it is," she said, rummaging through the large straw bag parked at her feet.

"What?" I asked.

"This," she said, pulling out a yellow envelope and handing it to me.

"When I give orchids to people, I like to also give tips on how to care for them properly."

I made a face but it wasn't strong enough. She put the envelope in my hand despite my not wanting to care for an orchid, or any flower. To me, flowers were something you put in a jar with a bit of water and look at every time you walk by until the day they die, and then you dump the smelly mess in the trash, wash out the jar and do it all again the following year when someone gives you flowers again.

I looked at the envelope she gave to me, with handwritten bulleted points all over it.

Cattleya orchids need fresh air but don't like drafts. You might keep a fan on for yours. I suggest low speed. You'll know it's thirsty by looking at its leaves. And keep it on a sturdy table. Orchids don't like to wobble.

I stopped reading, having no intention of catering to a finicky flower. My children were finicky enough.

"Oh, did I forget," she dared to add, "that yours—a Cattleya—prefers a view of the sunrise."

"You've got to be kidding," I said.

"I know it sounds like a lot, but we could learn a thing or two from orchids."

"What do you mean?" I asked, having no interest in learning from a flower, especially a spoiled one.

"Well, there are more varieties of orchids than any other flower in the world, and you've got to know which variety you're dealing with in order to care for it properly."

"And what is there to learn from that?"

"One must be aware of who she is before she can flourish."

"Interesting," I said, raising my eyebrow.

"It is, once you contemplate it awhile," she said. "But inside the envelope is more."

"More?"

"More tidbits about orchids, as well as a letter."

"A letter?"

"From my mother."

"Oh, really?"

"My mother was an amazing woman, who taught me everything she wanted me to know about life by way of the garden. Whenever I give flowers to someone, I include sayings my mother once wrote."

"Oh," I said curiously. I knew nothing about gardening, or life, or so I had felt lately.

"Remember," she went on, "orchids aren't weak. The world thinks they are, but they're not. In fact, I kept one on my bureau for weeks after my bunion surgery, to remind me how strong and sturdy I was despite what doctors tried telling me."

"What did they try telling you?"

She shook her head. "That my body is weak, but don't get me started."

I turned and set the pot on the console behind me, then gave the console a shake. "Too wobbly?" I asked, kidding.

"I'd say most definitely yes."

Too bad, I thought. *It'll have to do for now. I'm sure a wobble or two won't kill the thing.* But when she blew a kiss to it, I felt the burden of taking on the responsibility for a flower she loved. "Tell me," I said, "where'd you buy it?" I wanted to know so I could run to the store and replace it should it bend over and die. I did that for my sons' goldfish and they never knew.

"This particular one I started from seedlings that I bought in four-inch pots almost two years ago," she said in a proud, motherly tone. "I've nearly grown it into maturity myself."

Darn, I thought. "You're like a mother to it," I said.

"Caretaker," she corrected. "And, as much as I've grown to love it, it doesn't belong to me and I must let it go. It should flower any day."

"Let's hope," I said, conjuring how I might go about getting her to leave. "So nice of you to stop by. Did I already ask your name?"

"Fedelina," she said. "Fedelina Aurelio."

"Aurelio—I think it's the name of a place that had great pizza when I was a child. You didn't own a pizzeria, did you?"

"I married an Italian man, but no, Oscar never owned a restaurant, never made a pizza in all his life, though that is not to say he didn't love pizza. But me, I'm Irish. My father was an old-fashioned man who came from Ireland—scared to death his daughter would be taken advantage of. He told my mother the day I was born, 'Cora, you tell our girl all there is to know about the birds and the bees, the flowers and the trees! I don't want to worry about any of that.'"

She picked her straw bag up in one hand and took hold of the wooden railing with the other. It looked to me, by the way she shifted the position of her blocky orthopedic shoes, as if she were ready to make her descent down my steps, but then she turned her head and looked me in the eyes and said, "I've come for another reason, Anna."

"Oh?"

"I grew up in one of those good old neighborhoods where you knew everyone's name and could stop over to borrow an egg. Not that this isn't a good street, it is, but times have changed. People are busy . . ."

"My last egg dropped, had a great fall," I said.

"I didn't come for an egg," she said.

"You saw the ambulance out front?"

"Is everything all right?" she then asked.

"My daughter had a febrile seizure. Her fever skyrocketed within seconds."

"You must have been terrified."

"I was."

"Is she okay now? Is there anything you need help with?"

"She's fine now. She and her brothers are off with their grandparents for a week. I wish I had kept her home, told them 'no' when they came to get her. I feel guilty for having let her go."

"All mothers feel that."

"What?"

"Guilt," she said. "No mother feels she does enough. It's the hardest job in the world, isn't it?"

I looked her in the eyes, eyes that were blue and old, belonging to the era of ladies who paid for things with cash, not credit, and cooked homemade dinners. She probably dropped ten pennies a week for a year into a jar before buying a new lamp with cash. I couldn't tell her that all I do is purchase with credit and run in circles, spinning in my messy house, the house with no food. She would never understand. "It's certainly not easy," was all I said. "I hope I'm not losing my mind."

"Motherhood," she declared diagnostically, her eyes growing large and her voice intense. "You've got a full-blown case of motherhood, that's all. I know I look too old, but I remember, I do, those chaotic days when my children were small, when they had me running in circles, feeling dizzy all the time. It's a form of insanity, don't you think?"

"I've been wondering," I told her with a laugh.

"Don't worry," she said, waving me off with her hand. "It'll pass. These crazy mornings of yours will pass." She said it as if warning a princess that midnight will strike and it all will end. "It's all a big cycle. Everything is a phase. One day you'll wake and your children will be grown and gone."

"I'm in no hurry for that," I said. "I love them being small. I wish things could be easier, that's all, so I might enjoy them more."

"Mothering is hard. I don't know the secret to making it easier. You'll have to find amusement in the disorder of it all." She grasped the wooden railing again and started slowly on her descent. "I've kept you long enough. I better get on my way."

I stood there watching, hoping she wouldn't lose her balance and go tumbling down my long porch stairs, and feeling remorse for those mornings I pretended not to see her in her window watching me and my children go down our steps, dropping beach towels, falling, crying, quarreling, and me yelling as I piled them into the wagon. More than once I recognized from a distance a look of amusement, not irritation, on her face and I had suspected that we were the sounds of morning that got her out of bed, luring her to that window.

"Fedelina," I called down to her as she reached my bottom step.

She looked up at me with panting breath.

"You're more than welcome to stop over again," I told her.

"Thank you, dear, but you're the busy one. You tell me when a good time is." She bent down at the waist, putting her behind in the air, and picked a weed that was growing between two stepping stones. I waited for her to stand back up again.

"Anytime this week," I said. "It's a slow week for me."

"Enjoy the orchid—and the letter from my mother," she said, and disappeared behind the line of gumbo-limbo trees separating her yard from mine.

"I will," I called after her, then went inside and opened the yellow envelope.

chapter ten

SPRING 1907

Welcome to the world my little angel of the morning!

After hours of grueling labor, I heard through my window bands marching, people parading the streets of Portland. Daddy claims they were celebrating, cheering me on for having pushed you, Fedelina, into the world. But I knew what it was all about, that Oregon's first Rose Carnival and Festival had begun! With you in my arms, I later sat watching the children's parade from the window and, come night, the spectacular Electrical Parade, with streetcars decorated with electric lights. Life is brilliant, dear!

What a time to be born! Everything around you is blooming, and mornings are my favorite. It's morning now as I sit here in the yard with you, writing you this letter. I've always had a craving to write and can think of nothing more precious or powerful than a mother writing letters to her children. There is no novel, no poem, no literary masterpiece, nor lyrics to any song, that I'd rather write than letters to my daughter and so I will start now, and continue writing my way through various seasons of your life.

I can't promise to record the exact day you first smile, or which tooth you grow first, or whether you said "mama" or "dada," but I'll start by saying butterflies from the yard next door are fluttering over, landing on your bassinet, and hummingbirds are whizzing by, and cardinals are sitting on a nearby branch. This is the world you've entered. And it's a breathtaking one!

Every morning of your little life I've taken you out here as I sit in awe, trying to figure her magic, discover what tricks my neighbor is performing in that yard of hers to attract multitudes of magnificent beings. Maybe it's her music—Mozart, every morning. We are blessed to be living next door to one of Portland's rose enthusiasts, only I wish I knew how to grow them myself. I wish for a lot of things, darling —for a bathtub in my house, like my neighbor has, and a telephone, too. She's the only one on our street that I know of who has both a bathtub and a telephone. Her husband, by the way, is a dentist. He makes $2,500 per year. I wish your daddy was a dentist, and that our home was as big!

"What ridiculous eyes that baby has, so blue," she said moments ago, as she heard you fussing and stepped up to where my yard meets hers.

"She's got her daddy's eyes," I replied. "What a beautiful yard you have. I wish I had a yard like yours. I'd love a garden but wouldn't know where to begin. All that work."

"It is a lot of work," she said, "but I love it to where it doesn't feel like work."

"I should buy a packet of seeds and give it a try, fix up this yard of mine," I told her. "I should be productive, do more with my days."

And it was then, Fedelina, that she told me something I never want to forget. She said, "Cora, what you are doing when your children are small is working on the underground roots, the things not seen, but vital below the earth."

"Oh," I said, feeling more important than I had ever felt before. And in that moment, the hair on my arms stood up and something in my stomach fluttered, and you will find this, too, darling that your stomach flutters when you realize something you didn't know before—I call these instances butterfly sightings—and all of a sudden, in the instant that she said that to me, a metamorphosis took place within me and I will never be the same again. From now until the day you are grown, I will view my job of mothering as vital to this earth.

It was then that I heard a phone ringing and knew it was hers, for no one else on the street has a phone. She went running inside, and I thought about going in, too, to put you to bed and pamper myself—wash my hair with Borax or egg yolks, which I do once a week. A little pampering goes a long way!

But as I stared at you in your bassinet, I suddenly wondered about all the things you must know to live a vivacious life, the lessons I must teach you. For now your newborn mind is easily content, and mothering is simple—cuddling and bathing, diapering and feeding. But I'm no dummy. I know the day will come when you notice that your mommy sings off key, and forgets all the words, and knows hardly anything. I know the day will come when you no longer see me for what I am, which is perfectly in love with you, and when you no longer want to sit in my arms or hear me sing, but expect more from me.

That will be the day that I cry. But it's the other day I fear worse, the one I hear about from other mothers of daughters, the day in which you tell me you know everything and I know nothing. That will be the day I retreat into the corridors of my own insecurity, no longer daring to share with you all the things I felt were important.

And so I'll write it all down now, everything I want you to know about life, and when I'm gone someday and you reach that point—it *usually happens to women once they have babies of their own—where you wonder whether your mother might have known a thing or two, you can pick up my writings and find out.*

I'll start by saying I hope you cultivate beauty in your mornings. Mornings are important. They set the mood for your entire day. It's why I start ours sitting out here listening to Mozart and the birds. Like classical music, nature has a strengthening effect. Listen to the birds and let them sing for you. It's good for the body and the soul in ways I do not understand, but know instinctively. Ten minutes of sitting outside with you in the morning puts me in a fine mood and establishes my state of mind for the rest of the day. And if you're not a gardener yourself, living next to one is a blessing. It has me caring a little less about the small house I'm in. I like to believe that living in a small house with a good view out one's window is better than living in a mansion with no view at all.

But one more thing, Fedelina—life is short. The average life expectancy in the United States is forty-seven years. So please, baby, delight in your days. It's your life! Make it a life you relish! A life you are proud of! Live—live your life!

Being Cora, your mom, is who I want to be right now, and I am savoring it, fully engaged, aware it won't last forever, not in this way. In case I forget to say it when you're older, I will say it now, "Thank you, Fedelina," for giving me the experience of mothering you. But babies don't stay babies forever, and you are to me now like a dandelion in my hand. With each breath I take you will change, lose your baby ways, and then I must let go of who you were. When that happens, I don't want to look back, perplexed that all of a sudden a big gust of wind came and took you away, and so I try now to be aware of the subtle breezes, the things I can't see with my eyes but can feel. And I'm trying to figure out how I can make it feel like forever that I am holding you—this dandelion—in my hand.

If before having you I wanted to become a doctor, or when you're older, I feel like becoming a lawyer, all is achievable. You've been born into a world that is starting to favor women, and being a woman is the best thing to be, better than, say, an orchid. Orchids are beautiful, but cannot change their variety, whereas a woman has the liberty to constantly adjust who she is, how she thinks, behaves, reacts, what she learns, pursues, talks about, as well as who she wants to be in life. And if she finds she no longer likes parts of herself, she has the ability to change what it is she no longer likes.

Uh-oh—you're acting hungry. Time to go,

Cora, your mum

chapter eleven

O h, Anna, I miss her so much," Fedelina said when I stopped reading and looked up from my manuscript. "It doesn't matter how old a woman is, she will always miss her mother."

"Not a day goes by when I don't miss mine," I told her. "She died before I had my babies—never got to meet any of them."

"That's hard," Fedelina said, pausing before adding, "I can't believe you put that letter from my mother in your story!"

"Do you mind?" I asked. "Because I don't have to use it if you don't want me to."

She fidgeted around the side of her bed until she discovered her glasses and put them on. "I don't mind," she said. "But I don't remember seeing any ambulance in your driveway that first day I stopped over."

"I thought that's why you came by, because you were concerned."

"No, I didn't know it came to your house until you told me. I came by for another reason."

"Oh?"

"Your fire alarm—I kept hearing it go off."

"My fire alarm?"

"I'd be out in my yard chopping vines and I'd hear it—the same time every day, always around breakfast."

"I was making eggs," I told her. "And my stove top was crusted. I never found time to clean it."

"That's what I figured. I came by that day to share a trick with you, to ask if you knew about putting foil around the burners."

"Then why didn't you?"

"Oh, you looked like you were already self-conscious."

"I did?"

"Yes, that your kids weren't quieter, your house cleaner. The last thing I wanted was to make you feel embarrassed and besides, the alarm wasn't so bad. The noise of it had me chopping at my vines faster and harder."

"I know about foil on the burners now," I told her. "It's taken me twenty years to figure it out." I felt sweat forming on my forehead and wondered whether it was from all this talk of fire alarms. "Is it hot in here or is it me?" I asked, pulling off my cardigan.

"I was thinking it was rather cold."

"Then what's wrong with me?" I asked, not expecting a real answer.

"Menopause!" she said matter-of-factly, using the same diagnostic tone she had used years earlier when letting me know I was suffering a full-blown case of motherhood. "You look surprised. Am I telling you something you didn't know?"

"No, I kind of figured that's what it was," I told her, "especially after my daughter sent me a book from college, a book on menopause—how dare she?" I laughed.

"Marjorie, did she really?"

"Yes, I think she noticed all the words I was forgetting. And not sophisticated words, but basic words, words no one should forget. And I have been getting these hot flashes, I admit, but my denial has me blaming global warming. Gosh, I can't believe I'm there," I told her. "The big 'M.' How can life be going by so quickly?"

I put my cardigan back on and walked over to a blanket folded on the counter. "Of course it's menopause. I'm a dummy to think it's anything else," I said, and handed her the blanket.

"My body temperature goes up and down and I forget my words all the time," she said. "I wish it was menopause, but it's not. Anna." She picked up the orchid that had been on her stomach all this time and slowly started to caress it with her fingers.

"You remember what kind it is?" I asked her.

"A blooming cattleya," she said, her lips curving into a smile. "Some things a gal never forgets. So what happened next, after you read my mother's letter? Did you find a spot in your house suitable to the orchid?"

I picked up my manuscript and started to read where I left off last.

chapter twelve

When I closed the letter my neighbor's mother had written to her, I noticed the orchid starting to hunch, as I had for months, walking around with my neck lowered, shoulders wilting. Of all the things I dreamt of having, an orchid never made the list. But it was mine now, as was the challenge of keeping it alive and getting it to flower.

"How difficult can it be," I told the poor-postured stem, "to give you what you want, to get you to flower?"

I had to act fast. I knew it wanted a pleasant spot in my house, suitable to its needs, as much as I had for months wanted, needed, pleaded with my husband to allow me an itsy bitsy amount of time for myself —an hour, maybe two —but all he did was make me feel guilty, or give me an hour of "personal time" locked up in my room folding laundry. It took me falling apart at the seams for him to grant me this week to myself.

I carried the terra-cotta pot with me into the kitchen and placed it on the window sill above the sink. But then a red-and-green card stuck by magnet to my refrigerator caught my eye. I pulled the Christmas card, postmarked December and stamped in four different states before arriving months late and one house over, off the refrigerator. I needed to tear it to shreds, get rid of it, should my neighbor stop by, should she come in. I would cringe if she saw it, and if she saw me that day standing in the road, holding the opened poinsettia card, reading the handwritten letter inside, meant for her, the one in which her friend wrote about a lunch she had with a group of ladies, "mostly widows like us who get together every month, and how we wish we could all wake up and find the holidays over!"

You have to pretend to enjoy it, the holiday season. You have sun and warmth and none of this heavy, wet, white stuff. We got four feet yesterday. You were wise to get out. Hope your heart behaves and you feel well. Do your best to have a happy Christmas, not too easy these days.

I don't know why I opened mail that wasn't for me. Loneliness has a woman do strange things. Despite it being written from one senior to another—and I was nowhere near the age of a senior and at a completely different stage in life—I could relate. It's why I kept it all these months, I thought as I took a pair of children's scissors and started cutting it to pieces. I too, had pretended—for the sake of my children—to like the holidays. And I, too, had wanted to fall asleep and wake in the New Year. The letter, and my lack of enthusiasm for this past Christmas, was one more reminder that life does lose its magic. Once a girl grows up and becomes a woman—especially a mother—there are incalculable balls she juggles, tricks she pulls, alterations she makes behind the curtains, and it all diminishes the wow effect of the magic, making it tough for her to stay awake and enjoy the show.

And I too was lonely, as strange as it sounds for a mother of three young ones to be so, but I was in a different sort of way—hungry for adult talk and all those big, juicy, sophisticated words. But none of this justified what I did the day I stood in my street opening and reading the letter addressed to her. I should have taped it shut and put it in her mailbox where it belonged, but I didn't. I hung it on my refrigerator instead, where it had been ever since.

When I finished cutting it to shreds, I went for the orchid on the sill. "This room is too quiet," I told it as I left the kitchen on a quest to find a more suitable spot, and to find who I was as a person. After all, what my neighbor had said to me made sense, that like the orchids, we need to know our kind—who we are—before we can properly care for ourselves. *So who am I?* I asked myself as I headed into the great room like a woman sailing across the sea, with no extra arms weighing me down, or temper tantrums to navigate through. I no longer felt like the neat freak I once was, or like a beautiful woman, happy wife, or publicist extraordinaire as I had been called at work.

I am that woman who, during the holidays, hustles and bustles for the sake of her children yet never feels she does enough and, despite those seconds of glee on their faces, goes into her room and cries herself to sleep out of exhaustion. And the woman who goes six months without changing the polish on her toenails, and who, when she feels something is wrong with her body, finally makes a doctor appointment only to reschedule six times, and who hasn't read a novel in years and whose personal measure of contentment is how clean the house is and, because it is never clean, is never content. I am that discontented woman who spots herself in the mirror at the store and sees she only got around to putting mascara on one eye, and who pours herself a cup of coffee at seven and has lost it somewhere in the house by seven-fifteen and who finds it by nine and downs it cold. And that woman who drives the way I do—purposely in the middle of the road, so my tires go over the bumpy reflectors and put my baby to sleep. I am a woman who fantasizes about life as a cloistered nun—the silence and solitude of it.

"You know who you are, what you like, you cattleya," I told the orchid as I set it on a coffee table in the great room, close but not too close to the fan. "And I know who I am, too." It all depends on the morning, I thought as I plopped down on the sofa where my husband typically slept. Some days I was the little engine that thought she could. Other days Old

Mother Hubbard, and often the woman who lives in a shoe, the one with so many kids she doesn't know what to do. I could accept being all of that, but who I didn't want to be was the one my daughter would look at soon enough with eyes of justice, declaring mommy "mean" for making daddy sleep in his makeshift bed.

I got up, gathered his sheets and pillow, and threw them in a bundle on the floor, questioning which things in life a mother is supposed to tell her daughter and which she is not. Sharing with Marjorie the reasons for my wrath, that daddy is no good, would only put an end to the way in which she giggles whenever he enters the room, and how she steps on his toes, waltzing along as he steps side to side. *Dance to your daddy.* It's what I wanted for myself when I was young, and what mothers want for their daughters, to love their fathers madly. I would keep quiet about it all, but one day she would find out for herself how hard it is to be a wife, think back to those faces her mother made, and understand me better.

"It's okay. Little girls don't see it. They don't see their daddy's flaws," I would tell her on that day, a long, long time from now, the day she learned of his immorality and started sympathizing with me for grudging poor daddy—the man she felt sorry for all those years. "But it's easier for a little girl to love the man who is her daddy than it is for a wife to love the flawed man who is her husband."

"This room is too overwhelming," I declared as I took the orchid and stormed out, heading next into my bedroom. There, I set the flower on the bedside table and flicked on the overhead fan, recalling what my neighbor had said about orchids liking subtle breezes. But then I gave the nightstand a good shake. It was wobbly, and so was I, for there were moments in which I found it easier to stay with the father of my children, and others in which I knew leaving him would be best, and that the boys needed to know soon the sort of man their father was so they might never become like him.

"Should I sit my boys down one day," I asked myself, "and tell them what their father did, let them see the hurt in my eyes, so hopefully they will never do it to their own wives?" But if I were to do that, it would only raise other questions, like why didn't you leave him, Mother, and it would interfere with what I am trying to teach them—that when they do something wrong, there are consequences. Little boys need to know this. It's the only way they can grow into men who are accountable for their actions.

I didn't want to be wobbly-minded, and knew the orchid didn't like wobbly tables. I moved its pot over to my writing desk instead. "This spot is just right," I told the orchid, wishing my own contentment could be so simple. "Come morning, the sun pokes through this window and you will be a happy flower."

But what would it take to make me the happy woman I once was? I walked out my front door, got into my car and drove to Captiva Island, to the cemetery that lies next to the library, beside the Chapel by the Sea. There is no better place for a woman to go when she is grieving and missing horribly the person she used to be, back when life was simpler and more carefree. As I opened the white picket gate to the cemetery and strolled in, I was overtaken by emotion, aware that I had been stumbling in circles for too long, trapped beneath a tarp of sleep deprivation, one that suffocates a mother's spirit and smothers her ability to see both the beauty of life and her very own aliveness. And then I walked past sites belonging to babies, some with the same names as my own babies, and it was hard to see the names of my children on tombstones. Life can be short, I thought, and I wanted my children back *home again, home again, jiggety jog.* I reached up and pulled a white hibiscus off a low-hanging tree. Its petals were delicate as tissue and I could have used it to wipe my tears, but then I dropped the hibiscus and let myself be overtaken by emotion as I read the inscriptions for individuals living as far back as the late 1800s.

BELOVED WIFE, LOVING MOTHER, DEVOTED DAUGHTER

MOTHER, DAUGHTER, LOVER AND FRIEND

WE WILL SEE YOUR SMILE IN ALL THINGS BEAUTIFUL

It made me think about what Fedelina's mother had written in that letter, that a woman has the freedom to change, and left me questioning my own titles, thinking about how I had been going about my days, how I wanted to continue them, and who I wanted to be by the time I die.

I sat down on a wooden bench that was in the shade and, with lizards dancing at my feet and ants marching by, I tried conjuring what I wanted inscribed on my own tombstone one day. But other things quickly came to mind, like, why did my husband do what he did, driving that stake into my heart? I realized then a woman can go from room to room of her house trying to escape the noise and the clutter, and then go outside that house to one of the most beautiful cemeteries in the world, and the clutter and the mess that's in her mind will find her.

I closed my eyes and tried focusing on the sounds of the Gulf of Mexico, which I could hear from the other side of the trees, not far from where I was sitting. It struck me that, just as those waves hit the shore every moment of every day and night, so, too, is my mind always thinking of things it has to do, parties it has to plan, items I have to buy, people I have to call and so on three hundred and sixty-five days a year, without stopping.

I got up from the bench where I was sitting and gathered sea grape leaves off the ground and the gravesites, picking only the deeply colored ones—mahogany, red, a few deep orange—trying to conjure the titles I wanted to define my life.

WOMAN, MOTHER, WIFE

WOMAN, MOTHER

WOMAN, MOTHER, MAYBE WIFE

A LIVING BEING AWARE OF LIFE'S BEAUTY

chapter thirteen

BELVEDERE

"Y ou have a bittersweet look to your face right now," Fedelina said to
me.

I looked up from the story I had written. "Do I?"

"How are those children of yours?" she asked.

"Grown," I said, "and off living their lives."

"And you, what are you up to, other than looking around for a town-
house?"

I didn't want to admit that since Marjorie left for college all I do is
go to work and then come home and twiddle my thumbs, wondering how
I'm going to muster the energy to do anything significant with the rest of
my life. I didn't want to bore her, burden her with my woes. "Finishing
this novel is all, finding closure for it," I told her, hoping she might give
me feedback, tell me whether she liked what she had heard so far. When
she said nothing, I added, "I'm thinking of leaving my job."

"And then what?" she asked bluntly.

"It's crazy. I don't know," I said, shrugging my shoulders. "I'm nowhere near retirement and, even if I were, I have no intentions of sitting on the sidelines. I need a change. I just don't know to what or how."

"What are some things you like?"

"Coffee," I said with a laugh, "and I will admit, there's this bookstore in the city. It has a coffee shop. I think about that sometimes, but I don't know. I'm indecisive. Maybe I'll travel the world, see places I've never seen. Work with children. It's never too late, right?"

"Look at it this way, Anna, if you live to be as old as me," she started "then right now you're only a little past being halfway through adulthood, so no, it's not too late. You're ending a twenty-year cycle, that's all."

"You have a way of putting things into perspective," I told her with a laugh. "So what about you? What have you been up to?" It was a dumb question to ask a woman in a nursing home.

"I just finished training for the Boston Marathon."

"Really?" I asked, knowing she was kidding.

"Obviously, Anna, I don't lead the same life I used to. The titles that once defined me no longer consume me."

"But you're still you," I told her, "upbeat and pleasurable."

"Who were you expecting, a bored, miserable woman?" she asked. "Get me a glass of water, will you, please?"

I jumped up and looked around the counter for a glass, but the medical equipment made me nervous and I felt clumsy, knocking the glass over once, then filling it too high, then not enough.

"I'm not thirsty," she said as I put the glass in her hand.

"Didn't you just ask for water, or am I losing my mind?" I asked.

"I asked for the water because I know my body needs it," she explained. "But I've lost the sensation that makes me feel thirsty."

"Oh," I said curiously as I watched her slowly take a few sips, and then lick her lips.

"This nursing home is filled with bored and miserable women, Anna," she said as she handed the glass back to me. "When you leave, glance in the door to my right. A bored and miserable woman lives there, always yelling at the nurses, saying rude things to the volunteers, griping when children come to visit, but you know what?"

"What?"

"From what I hear, she was miserable at age thirty. Listen, Anna, a thirty-year-old grump turns into a fifty-year-old grump, and a fifty-year-old grump turns into an eighty-year-old grump. If I wasn't a grump at eighty, there's no way I'm going to become one at one hundred. Negative young wretches turn into negative old wretches if they don't do something to pull themselves out of their misery. But I'm no preacher and I don't want to lecture."

"As far as I'm concerned," I told her, "anyone your age is an expert. You can say as much as you like."

"You make me feel good. You've always been kind, listening to my rambling."

"You've never rambled," I told her. "I've always found you interesting— in-depth."

"I try," she said. "I enjoy contemplating life deeply."

"Not everyone does that, you know, lives profoundly." I checked my cell phone for the time. "Doesn't anyone come by to check on you?"

"My God," she said. "They don't leave me alone. Before you got here, they were in here, poking and prodding, hovering over me—had me believing in alien abductions! I finally told them to get out and leave me alone."

I laughed and it felt good. "And to think," I said, "when I walked in here this morning, I didn't know if you'd remember me and all those talks we once had. I didn't know what to expect."

"I remember," she said, but then yawned and I knew I had kept her awake long enough. "Most people only scratch the surface. But you and I made a point of going deeper," she went on. "I remember most of it—the things we agreed on and . . . " She stopped and I held my breath, hoping she wouldn't go there now, to the major disagreement we once had, the one that silently sent us down diverging paths, putting an end to our friendly garden chatting.

Back at the hotel I pulled the bedspread down and off the bed and did a sort of Nestea Plunge onto the mattress. At one time in my life I would have paid a hundred dollars to have an evening all to myself, and to sleep through the night in a darkened room. At this stage, personal time was beginning to feel like infinity. And too much of a good thing diminishes its value, I thought as I lay on my back, staring at the ceiling with humility, wishing I had done a few things differently in my life. It's what too much time alone does to a person, makes them think of all the things they should have done and didn't, and makes them count the hours of their life, tallying up those that mattered, were truly worthwhile, versus those that were meaningless.

I wondered, too, whether the hours I put into the writing of my story were worthwhile, or if were they wasted hours of my life. There was a vulnerability to me, having flown to Indiana like I did to share my story with Fedelina. I had never read it to anyone before and, to me, she represented the world. It was hard sharing my creativity with the world.

I finally fell asleep, but as a result of my vulnerability dreams of being naked started and I spent the hours of the night running in the buff down Periwinkle Way, the birds gawking at me, flowers whispering, and raccoons chasing at my heels. Even the alligators had parked themselves in my path, forcing me to leap over them, and the sight of a menopausal woman hurdling naked over the back of a gator had the island's wildlife roaring loudly.

"To this day," I said to Fedelina when I arrived at the nursing home the next morning and pulled a rose from the bouquet of flowers I had brought, "whenever I smell one of these, I think of what you told me."

"I've forgotten most of what I've said in life," she said with a dumbfounded look on her face. "What did I tell you?"

"Don't worry," I told her as I placed the flower in her hand, and then pulled my manuscript from my bag. "I've got it all right here, all that you said about roses."

"Hope I didn't bore you."

"No. You inspired me," I told her, "You said roses aren't always in bloom, nor can I be."

"I'm remembering now," she said, "but it wasn't me who came up with that."

"I know," I told her. "It was your mother. I wish I could have met Cora. I feel like I knew her—all those letters you shared with me. Would you like to hear what happened next, after I left the cemetery on Captiva?"

"I was hoping you'd read more," she said.

chapter fourteen

I took the sea grape leaves with me as I walked out the white picket gate of the cemetery, wanting never to forget that one day those leaves would be falling on me. The leaves inspired me, made me want to go home and do something spectacular with my time. And because my children were gone, all I wanted to do was write—turn the story I had started into a novel, and finish it by the time my children returned.

"How hard can it be?" I asked myself as I drove down a long stretch of road with a view of the Gulf of Mexico on my right. "A woman can build an empire—she can do anything she puts her mind to—in a distraction-free week to herself."

As I turned onto the sandy road to where I lived, I felt my creativity lifting me off the ground as if I had the wings of an osprey. In a private frenzy I tiptoed quietly past my neighbor, who was working in her garden. Small talk of any kind, even big talk, would ground my mood for writing.

"Hello, Anna," I heard as I started up my steps.

This is your week in which to do what you want, I reminded myself, acting as if I didn't hear her. *And no one is getting in your way!*

I heard a couple of more "hello Anna's," and wanted to tell her of the profound impact her mother's letter had on me, but fully in the mood to write, I pretended I didn't hear her and hurried into my house—the rental house that would further inspire me. I knew the first time we toured it, walked its wooden floors and looked at the banyan trees out the windows—their branches and aerial roots hanging in lieu of curtains, creating a canopy of shade, making me feel like a creature ready to take flight, stirring creative forces within me—that it was too small for a family of five, but that it was wooing me, playing with my mind, telling me, "This is the house in which you will do it, the bird house in which you will write something good!" There is no way one could live tucked within a banyan forest and not write a short story, a poem at least, or, like Cora, emotional, heartfelt letters to her children—even if they weren't a writer and had never written before, I thought as I went to my bedroom and turned on my computer.

While waiting for it to warm up, I took the letter my neighbor had given me from my pocket and set it on my desk for inspiration, then pulled my clothes off and rummaged through drawers in search of anything comfortable to wear. There was not a single clean garment to be found in my house, so I stood on my tiptoes and reached high in my closet, pulling down the box in which, long ago, after the birth of the twins, I had stashed my sexy items. The long, red, silk nightgown I wore on our honeymoon was no longer my style, but oh, well, it was clean, and Timothy wasn't home to see me looking ridiculous in it, I thought as I sat down at my desk and put my fingers to the keys.

I sprinted past the conference room and out the front doors of Anchorage Publishing Inc. like a woman whose feet were freshly unshackled and set free. As I ran into the parking lot, I pulled the happy, competent, confident mask off—the one with the smile and the expression that said that I loved my job and that I was fine, my life was fine. And as I put my key in the ignition, I felt shame for having let things bother me to this point without voicing it, without changing the things I did not like and for letting the stress of my job root its way under my skin. I had been operating for too long like a vehicle in perfect working condition, but there had been lights flashing in my head, strange noises in my mind, indicating a problem for months and cautioning me to slow down. But I hadn't. I kept going.

"I can't go on like this—running on empty," is all I said as I sped out of the parking lot, fleeing my career.

Like the orchid, I no longer wanted a stressful environment. It's why I quit. I did it for myself and must never forget the story of why I left my job behind. There won't be room on my stone someday for the whole story, but there won't be room for a phrase as big as "publicist extraordinaire," either. I don't think it would be hard to fit "mother," and I could shorten it if I have a smaller stone. I could just have "mom" or, if really pressed for space, "ma."

I wrote until the wee hours and, after dropping into bed, let my subconscious think about what to write next. And the next morning in the little yellow room, there was an orchid sitting in the early sun, and a woodpecker having fun hammering its beak into my tin roof, drilling my nerves. I went to my window, wondering how I might steer the bird toward my neighbor's roof instead. People her age go to bed at dusk. They don't mind birds waking them at the crack of dawn.

And there she was out my window, this older woman watering roses and loving her life, and the sight of it got me to thinking about the story I was writing. I no longer believed that a story about a young woman bemoaning her life was anything the world would want to read, nor was it the life I wanted to live. "Fedelina, Fedelina, quite contrary, how does your garden grow?" I thought as I stared out at the colorful varieties of flowers that had newly opened. Then, with the letter my neighbor shared with me lingering in my mind, I sat down and began to write again.

A cattleya will always be a cattleya whereas a woman has the ability to change, constantly adjust who she is, how she thinks, behaves, reacts and so forth. This freedom and ability to change is why I quit my job and moved my family down south. The problem is, moving to an island didn't fix my problems. It didn't repair my glitches.

After a few paragraphs, I got up and walked over to the stack of books I kept in the corner of my room—books I once promoted. I picked one up and stared eye to eye with the author on the back cover.

"Anna Hott—best damn publicist in the country," the author had said to me. "I see now why a book can live or die in your hands, and it's you I thank for turning me into a best seller, so what the Hell were you thinking quitting as you did?"

From the bedroom of my stilted house in Florida, I questioned myself for having left behind the job I was good at—all that professional praise. But then I heard the voice of another one of the authors I had promoted—the demanding, egotistical, publicity-obsessed type.

"Get me on this show, that show, and every show in America! My book is perfect for them all, Anna!" she would call me five, six, seven times a day for months, stalking me. I took hold of the spine of her book, pulling it from the stack.

"You looked like a fool," I said as I flicked her glossy photo, "and nearly damaged my credibility by going behind my back, stalking the producers on your own like that. You wrote a book on baking muffins! I'm sorry, but a book on muffins is not controversial news."

My room was turning warm and stuffy, and I feared the orchid might wilt, so I opened the window, the one without a screen, and I tossed the book out much the way I had my career, tossing it out too. Then I walked over to the stack of books and picked another up. "I know you thought every living, reading creature in the universe ought to buy your book," I said to the four-color author photo as I carried it to the window, "but you put unrealistic expectations on me and couldn't care less that an in-house publicity department is a hectic place, that I was swamped, that I had fifteen books at a time to promote!"

I threw his book out my window and walked back for more. I couldn't stop. "Bad publicity is still publicity, Terry," I said waving to another book as it landed in Fedelina's hydrangea bush below. "I told you a thousand times to stop calling me up, moaning over the negative review in the *New York Times.*

I turned from the window—and from the should haves and could haves in my mind—wishing that instead of exhausting my energy all those years in a non-lucrative, anxiety-producing, adrenaline-rushing, coffee-addictive career as a book publicist, promoting twenty egocentric authors at a time while running on fumes, that I might have instead written something myself. With this in mind, I sat back down at my computer and started to write again.

Time gone by makes it easy to forget the details surrounding why a woman once did what she did, said what she said, and reacted in the ways in which she reacted. It's why she's hard on herself looking back. But if she were thrown back in time, given a second chance, she'd do it all the same. Everything is harder when going through it, and I never wanted to start living in a constant state of judgmental hindsight, critical of myself for having walked out on my career, a career I was good at. A woman should forgive, but never forget the details leading up to where she is now. And I knew "best damn publicist in the world" wasn't something I wanted on my tombstone someday. I wanted: MOTHER—WOMAN WHO LIVED—CULTIVATOR OF BEAUTY.

I got up from my computer and walked back over to that stack of books, the ones I promoted, this time picking up a highly publicity-driven title, one dealing with sticking by your man after he cheats. I returned to my window and held it tightly in my hand, but Fedelina was down there, holding her hands to her eyes like a visor shielding them from the sun and looking at the sky over my house as if she had spotted a flying object. I didn't want anyone her age to start believing in UFOs, but I found the activity of throwing books out my window therapeutic and couldn't stop.

I waited for her to turn her back and, when she did, pulling shears from her apron pocket and using them to snip roses off a bush, I pitched a fast one out my window. "Yeah, right, you so-called relationship guru," I said, hanging my head out to watch it hit the ground below. "How dare I find out, after scheduling you that ten-city tour that you were divorced four times?"

My yard, as it filled with the books I once promoted, looked as colorful as Fedelina's yard next door, but I feared this act of throwing reading material from one's windows might be sacrilegious, against literary law or unpatriotic, and that my neighbor might be the type to report me. I should go down there and pick up all those books littering my yard, and bag up and toss the regrets that were filling my mind, wondering again whether I had done the right thing, quitting my job as I had. I stood there, trancelike, watching Fedelina with her handful of fresh-cut roses as I had the fading copies that last day of work. I was thinking of all the dull conversations with my husband, for they kept coming too, along with my mornings, and I didn't know how to stop or alter them.

I moved the orchid pot over four inches, making sure the subtle breeze coming through my bedroom window wouldn't upset it. I felt envious of it, a flower, for it knew what it liked—sturdy tables, sunrises, and environments without stress, how simple! It was a cattleya, but who was I?

"A woman," I said. "A disgruntled wife, an overwhelmed mother, no longer a publicist extraordinaire."

"And who are you without all those titles?" I think the orchid stem asked me.

"A woman wanting to delight in her days, relish her life," I answered, just as I had read in Cora's letter. "And a mother—a beloved mother."

I ducked from the window, not wanting Fedelina to see me standing there, watching her. And there were no more books left in my room, which was good. Throwing things out had to stop.

"This has to stop," I had declared that day at the publishing house as I pressed the "stop" button on the copier. It's why I squeezed my hand between the wall and the machine and pulled the plug, and why the room went quiet and I felt dizzy, like I was no longer standing in my own two shoes, but floating above them. There had been something wrong with me that day. And there was something wrong with Fedelina, too. I worried as I looked again out my window and saw her wobbling around, wiping her forehead and then bending at the hips, bracing her hands on her knees as if to hold herself up.

I should walk over, ask her if she is okay—tell her to consider hiring a landscaper. She had been out there toiling long enough, and how much time should one old lady spend working in a garden?

She dropped the snips from her hand, and the roses, too, and I watched as she fell down in the grass like an overheated person. She needed help and I had to go. I took off running in my nightgown, racing across my yard and over the books that were scattered like stepping stones under my feet, hurrying toward my neighbor who was down in the grass.

chapter fifteen

"Fedelina," I said when I reached her sitting on the ground, sweat raining from her forehead. "Are you okay?"

"Fine," she said, but I knew from personal experience not to believe a person who says they're fine. I got down on my knees and looked her in the eyes.

"What's wrong? What's happening?" I asked, wondering if she had been drinking.

"I'm dizzy, that's all."

"How can I help? Do you need me to call someone?"

"No, don't call anyone," she said with a slur, her eyes gazing past me.

"But your hands are shaking. Your feet, too," I said. "I need to do something. I'll call an ambulance."

"No," she blurted. "Candy!"

"You mean sugar? Do you have any?"

"In my bag, get me my bag," she said, her voice trailing off.

"Where is your bag?" I jumped up from the grass and spun in circles, scanning the yard with my eyes. I was ready to rush back to my house, get some of the boys' candy when she mumbled, "upstairs."

I hurried around to the front of the house and up the old, tilting-to-one-side wooden steps, tripping and bruising my shin. When I spotted the straw bag, I wanted to go inside and phone for help, but it was easier in the moment of emergency to do what she told me to do rather than what I thought I should, and I returned to where she was, dumping the contents of her bag into the grass. Out came a meter, a syringe, insulin, alcohol, wipes, and a piece of paper with handwritten emergency names and phone numbers.

"Can . . . dy," she mumbled, her voice deteriorating in tone.

"I know," I said, spotting a roll of hard candies. I tore the wrapper off and, when I saw her hands trembling worse than mine, I pressed a piece to her lips, but they remained closed and her eyes were suspiciously confused.

"Here's the candy," I said. "Open your mouth."

She parted her lips and, one by one, I fed the candies into her mouth and she chewed. I glanced at the handwritten names and phone numbers, fearing that if the sugar didn't soon stop her slurring and shaking, I would be held responsible, having to explain to Liam, the first name on her list—maybe her son—why I didn't call him or an ambulance when I first saw his mother collapse in the grass. "One more piece. Come on, Fedelina, keep chewing."

It was this last piece that started to settle her. I took hold of her hand and held it softly. I would sit in the grass holding her hand as long as was needed, until she stopped shaking. I had nothing better to do with my day.

"Oh, I needed that. Thank you. I'm feeling much better now," she finally said without slurring, her voice clear again. "See that shrub?"

"That one over there?" I asked, shifting in the grass to see where she was looking.

"Yeah, with the long pointed rose buds in clear pink—the Prairie Princess. I don't know if you know anything about roses."

"I don't," I told her.

"It's excellent as a cut flower." Her voice was turning calm and conversational, as if nothing had happened.

"Aren't all flowers good cut?" I asked, feeling ignorant. But I didn't care. I was still trying to breathe normally after what we had gone through together.

"That one blooms in great mass, and then rests awhile to put on growth before blooming profusely again."

"Oh," I said.

"It does this over and over."

"Does what?"

"Blooms and rests, blooms and rests, speaking of which, it's my turn now."

I looked at her like I didn't understand. "Your turn for what?"

"To rest," she said. "It's a good thing."

"Rest?" I asked, catching on.

"Women," she said, nodding, "like those Prairie Princesses, need restful periods, too—non-productive times in their lives in order to prepare for their next bloom."

"That reminds me," I said. "I enjoyed that letter, the one your mother wrote."

"I'm glad," she said. "My mother had a certain wisdom to her. She was always teaching us things."

"How nice," I said. "I hardly have time to teach my children anything other than, 'Don't jump on the sofa with grapes in your mouth—you can jump on the furniture, just not with grapes!'"

"You're in that 'get them through alive' stage," she said with a grin, "but the time will come when you want them knowing more about life, things you've learned yourself."

"I don't know," I said, and let out a laugh. "I don't think I'll have anything good to teach my kids. I hardly know who I am anymore."

"I had a friend," Fedelina said. "She spent decades of her life searching for, of all things, herself. And one day she woke up and knew exactly who she was."

"Who?" I asked.

"An old lady on her deathbed," said Fedelina, and we both laughed.

"I never had time to go searching for myself. But my children, I taught them the basics. They could all cook at least one meal and press slacks by the time they left the house. I threw my son Liam out when he turned eighteen, but told him first, 'I'm going to teach you how to make beef stew, and then you're out.' He's a vegetarian now, so it never helped him any."

I shifted on my knees, relaxing in the grass, crawling a bit to gather the items I had dumped out of her bag. She stretched far enough to reach the syringe. "In case you were wondering, I have diabetes," she said, tossing it into the bag.

"Type one?"

"No, the other," she said. "Had it for years and didn't know. But now it's obvious. My body produces insulin but no longer responds to it, or there's not enough insulin. My doctor tells me to stay active, keep moving. I try not to sit around all day. I work in the yard every morning."

"You think you overdid it today?"

"Hypoglycemic attack," she said. "I usually eat breakfast and lunch at the same time, but this morning the roses were calling. I couldn't resist. It happens to me in the garden. I lose track of time. My blood sugar dropped."

"Are you going to be okay?"

"Yeah, but I could use a little rest."

I got up from the grass and offered her my hand but she got onto all fours, like a cat, and from there stood on her own.

"I hope I haven't kept you," she said.

"Not at all," I told her. "I wasn't doing anything. That's bad, I know. I'm unproductive lately. I don't know why, but I dislike it. I feel ashamed when I'm unproductive."

"Then I should give you some roses to remind you that they aren't always in bloom, nor can you be."

"Nothing in my life is blooming at the moment," I said.

"Such is life," she said. "Not everything can be blooming at once and sometimes it feels as if nothing is blooming at all. Why don't you gather up those Prairie Princesses that I dropped in the grass over there? Take them home with you, will you? See this one here?" she said, tilting her head toward an open flesh pink flower growing on another shrub alongside her house. "The definition of a rose, always my favorite." She held its branch until I hurried over and touched my nose to it. "We'd see it near the beach when I was young. It's why I like to grow it now." She reached into her pocket, pulled shears out and snipped it off. "Take this one home, too," she said, handing it to me. "It's a Susan Louise Rose, 1929, and it's truly recurrent, giving happily and constantly," she stated, and then paused and added, "like mothers."

As we meandered further alongside a fence in her yard, I didn't want to tell her that I disagreed, that as a mother I was constantly giving, yes, but happily? No. It's hard to give happily when tired, or when there's never a break from giving, when no one is there to give to you for a change.

"See this one?" she asked. "Iceberg, Climbing, 1968, it blooms so prolifically you can cut large bouquets for the house, yet seldom see where you have cut. I cut tons of them yesterday. If you have time to come in a minute, I'll give you a few of them to take home, too."

I followed her around the house and up the steep wooden steps. "If a mother takes care of herself," she said as she held the screen door open for me to go in, "she can give much of herself and no one will see what has been taken from her." She put her finger to her lips. "We have to be quiet. I don't want to wake my son," she whispered.

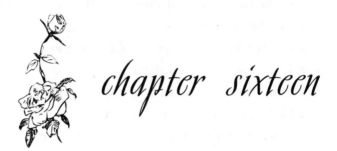

chapter sixteen

Your son?" I asked, confused, and upset that she hadn't sent me running straight into that house to get her son when she was down in the grass.

"He's visiting for the week."

"But why didn't you . . . "

"I don't want him to worry," she whispered. "Now wait here. I'll be right back. I need to get something in the kitchen." When she returned she was eating a protein bar. "Now come with me," she said, "so I can get you those Iceberg, Climbing." I followed her down a long hallway, my arms already full of the roses she had me gather from her grass. "Remember," she said more loudly as we went. "The roses should remind you to rest. One needs rest in order to bloom again. I know it sounds hard, but mothers must take care of themselves. They more than anyone need sufficient rest."

"You're not writing a book, are you?" I asked. "A book on gardening?"

"No, why? Are you?"

"Oh, everyone, I think, has a novel in their drawer, don't they?" I said, hesitating, "but yes, I am. I guess I am writing one myself." I stopped talking when a door in the hallway opened and a man stepped out. He wore boxer shorts, a gray T-shirt and black-rimmed glasses and all I could think was that somewhere in my life, a dream, maybe, I had seen him before. His hair was the color of northern sand and looked windblown and wild, as if he had been pounding a few waves on the beach the night before, but standing nose-to-nose in the uncomfortably narrow hallway, there was a look on his face—that of a raccoon caught in a headlight—and I felt embarrassed by it, and the silk nightgown I was wearing, and the way I felt my face flushing. Like a self-conscious schoolgirl, I held the roses up to my chest—trying to cover up the laciest part of my gown—then looked at his mother and gave her a raise of my eyebrows, the kind that says, "Okay, escort my nearly naked body away from your strikingly handsome son now."

"Anna, meet my son, Liam, art history professor. After visiting me, he's off to England—a sabbatical—so he can get to know better, experience on a deeper level, the places he talks about."

"Wow," was all I said, glancing at him and quickly back to his mother. I could only assume he wanted us out of his way and was hoping for a strong cup of coffee, not a conversation with his mother and her neighbor.

"He's an artist, too," she went on, squeezing my arm. "Give him a pencil and a piece of paper and my son will draw you a masterpiece. But Oscar and I, we always told our kids artistic endeavors don't put food on the table. And he listened. It's why he got into teaching. You can never go wrong with teaching. And Liam, he's always been a good boy, nothing but a joy."

"You pretty much summed up my life story in record time, Mom," he said, clearing his throat and looking at me. "Well, there goes any mystery surrounding me, Anna. It was a pleasure meeting you."

I wanted to tell him, "No, there is still mystery around you," but I was finding it hard to touch my teeth to my tongue and talk. I don't know why he had this effect on me. We had never met before, I don't think, yet I felt a familiarity toward him, as if he were the blue sky, white clouds and fresh air I had known and loved all my life.

"England," I managed to say.

"Stonehenge," he told me. "I'm starting at Stonehenge, and from there taking a year, visiting the world's most famous sacred places—ending, hopefully, at Delphi in Greece. As an assistant professor, I need to write a book so I can work toward tenure."

I could think of nothing more fascinating, and for the first time in my life I felt aware of space, as if all the particles in the space separating us were dancing, making me want to dance, too, and I wondered in that moment whether Fedelina's hallway where we were standing was sacred in and of itself.

"Anna's a writer, too," Fedelina said.

"What do you write?"

"Chaos," I said, and then wondered why I had said that.

"Is your chaos published?"

"No," I laughed. "Not yet."

"Anna's also the mother of three kids," my neighbor chimed in.

"Where did you learn to write?" her son asked me.

"I'm an English Literature major," I told him, noticing he was studying my eyes as if he was interested in what I had to say. Timothy never looked at me this way, never heard anything I had to say. "Where did you learn to draw?" I asked, feeling safer with the attention off me and my writing.

"I don't know," he said, gazing at me through his dark-rimmed glasses. "Just drawing, I guess."

"Liam's hardly taken any art classes," his mother said.

I looked back at her son, my eyes asking how that could be true, how a person can create a so-called masterpiece having taken few or no relevant classes.

"I don't know whether I could sit through a class that tells me how to draw, or how not to draw," he said. "A class like that would put the fear of artistic gods in me, and make drawing a form of homework, a task I have to do and dread."

"I hear you," I said, not wanting to tell him I was one of those writers who work in fear of breaking rules, who feels the grammar patrols at her heels, waiting to pull her over every time she writes a word. "But drawing, how interesting," I said. "What do you draw?"

"Anything related to the outdoors. Trees, mostly."

"As far back as I remember," his mother said, "ever since he was a small boy, Liam has always loved the outdoors. He'd pace back and forth in front of the window until I'd open the door and, whoosh, out he ran. It was like I had a puppy that I was always chasing."

"Okay, Mom," he said with a grin. "I do need coffee. If I don't make it to the kitchen by noon, I might get a withdrawal headache."

"You might have to reheat it," she said. "I made it at five."

I didn't expect him to hold his hand out to me, but he did, and I shook it, feeling once more embarrassed by the way I was dressed. Then again, he wasn't wearing much more than me. In fact, with him in his boxers and me in my gown, the two of us matched. We were both underdressed for the occasion of first meeting. But when he smiled at me with big brown eyes and then kissed his mother good morning on the top of her head, I made a mental note to ask her later how she had done that, how she raised a boy into a man so kind to his mother.

Fedelina motioned me to follow her. "I want to give you more roses," she said.

"It looks like she's got enough roses, Ma," he said, turning back to look at us.

"No such thing," Fedelina told him. "No such thing as a woman with too many roses."

When we reached her bedroom, I noticed a long, dark, wooden bureau full of roses, some in jars, others lying in piles. But then I saw several framed photographs sitting on the bureau and, because it might take hours to look at all the pictures belonging to a woman with seven children, I honed in on only one, picking up a decorative gold-framed snapshot of her son, the one I had just met.

"What's he doing in a cave?" I asked, holding his picture close to my face for a better look.

"That's Lourdes."

"Lourdes?" I asked.

"With the healing spring—Bernadette—the Virgin Mary."

"*That* Lourdes," I said. "Of course."

"Liam has summers off. He's always traveled, loves to see all these famous places. But I think he's trying to find himself, trying to find meaning after his divorce."

"Divorce?" I asked.

"It breaks my heart," she said, "People always told me when my children were small—'Litte kids, little problems. Big kids, big problems.' It's true, Anna. Keep the temper tantrums in perspective, because they grow up and you'll wish you were dealing with a temper tantrum you could walk over. But I try not to worry about Liam. He's too much of a free spirit for me to worry about anymore. He's around your age, thirty-nine."

"Thirty-nine?" I gasped. "I'm only thirty-six. Come to think of it, a whopping thirty-seven the day after tomorrow, but not thirty-nine, not me, not yet! Thirty-nine is practically forty, so, no, your son is definitely older!"

I was afraid she was starting to count, notice all the times I brought up her son in conversation, and that she saw it on my face, the look a woman gives when she sees the diamond ring she really wants but cannot have. She cannot have it because there's already a diamond ring on her hand—one she no longer likes, but it is hers nonetheless.

But then she walked over to a recliner. With her back to the chair, eyes focused out her window, she strategically positioned her feet on the floor, bending her knees, putting her arms straight ahead and dropping her buttocks down into the cushiony seat.

"Yeah, your son is older than me by two years," I continued helplessly. "Whew—I'm not ready to leave my thirties behind just yet."

"This will make you laugh," Fedelina said. "He said to me the other day, 'You know, Mom, I used to think you were so much older than me, but the older I get, I realize you're not that much older than me.' He's witty like that, a deep thinker, too." I knew then she wasn't counting how many times I had brought up her son, and that she liked talking about him, too. But then she stopped talking and sat upright in her recliner, staring straight ahead with a focused look on her face, like an astronaut preparing a rocket for takeoff.

"Are you all right?" I asked.

"Oh yes, I've been doing this for years. I sleep in this thing." She shifted her buttocks, reached down and tightened her fingers around the lever on one side. When she pulled the lever, off she went—feet up, upper body down. One deserves a close-up view of the moon after all of that, but there she sat, looking out her window at my noisy house. I wanted to tell her the truth about my life and what things were like inside that house then, but I didn't want to ruin her view of it.

"Did I mention Liam is working toward tenure?" she started back up again, gravitating toward the topic of her son as professor.

"Good for him," I said.

"Yeah, but he was married to this—pardon my language," she said in a whisper, "but a pampered witch. It's sad, Anna. A guy can have the greatest mother on earth, but it's the wife that destroys him."

"So he's single now?" I asked, still standing in her doorway, trying not to drool over the roses lined up in jars along her bureau, the roses that I could smell, the ones she promised to give me.

"I don't know that my son will ever get married again. He dates." She rolled her eyes and smiled. "Women, they fall all over that boy, but a mother knows not to ask too many questions of her grown sons. I don't think he takes any of the girls too seriously. Teaching and traveling—I think it's enough for him. So is your husband buying you a cake?"

"No," I said. "He's away on business. It's okay. I don't really like cake."

"Then I should bring you a pie."

"No, no, no," I said with a blush, never the type to tell the world and get people revved up for my big day in advance.

"Oscar loved his cherry pies. He didn't care much for cakes either, so I always made him a cherry pie on his birthday. This was our dream—my husband and I—it was our dream to move to Sanibel. The man worked hard his whole life—worked so much I felt at times like I was raising these kids myself. But he did provide. I will say, Oscar always provided for his family. And he never took a sick day—worked for the same company since he was twenty-two. He didn't take vacations, but saved his money—always made sure we'd be set for retirement—then suffered a stroke and died shortly after we moved to Florida. Oh, how I miss him. I could have done more when I had the chance, could have loved Oscar more. The pain never goes away. It changes with time, but never goes away."

"I'm so sorry."

"I think of all the annoying things he used to do, like leave the kitchen cabinet doors open after he took his vitamins, and how he snored, and how he'd take his shoes off in the middle of the room and leave them there on the floor, you know, typical things husbands do that get under our skins. But now, Anna," she continued, "to have him back again, I'd put up with most anything. But I should let you go now, dear," she said. "And I should rest. I've been up since four-thirty."

I looked at her like she was crazy. "Four-thirty in the morning?" I asked.

"It happens," she said.

"What?"

"Around age sixty-two, people start waking fifteen minutes earlier for each year they live thereafter."

"Then I should go now, let you rest," I said, hoping she hadn't forgotten that the reason I followed her in was to get more roses. I put my nose in the air and sniffed the room. "It smells good in here," I said. "Must be all the roses."

"Anna," she called after me.

"Yes?"

"I call out to him still. I know I sound crazy, but I do. 'Oscar, Oscar,' I say, and if anyone heard me, they'd think I was nuts. I swear the other day I saw him standing in the doorway, right where you are now. He had on his old flannel shirt, the one the kids bought him for Christmas years ago. He wore that thing for over fifteen years and we all begged him to get rid of it . . . but I've kept you long enough. You must have a million things to do."

"Changing out of this nightgown is all."

"Oh, you're being polite. I've disrupted your day."

"No, you haven't."

"Well, you saved my life today."

"It was nothing."

"I don't know what I would have done, had you not noticed me," she said, and then matter-of-factly added, "Go to that bureau there." She pointed. "Open the top drawer."

I gave her a curious look but did what she told me to do, opening a drawer full of old photos, a heart-shaped box of chocolates and envelopes.

"There should be a little red book," she said. "You see it?"

"Yes," I said, picking it up. It had a faded red cover with a black title and a rose imprinted on its cover. "How to Grow Roses," I read the title out loud.

"Inside are all the other things my mother once wrote to me."

"Your mother wrote this book? Your mother was an author?"

"No," she said with a laugh. "Members of the American Rose Society wrote the book. My mother wrote me letters and tucked them throughout its pages. And she jotted down notes in the margins of the book, most of it blips of inspiration she tapped into while sitting outdoors."

"So this is where you learned about roses," I said, sniffing the oldness of its cover.

"No, it's where I learned about life, and my relation to nature," she said. "My mother, she taught me a fresh way of looking at things, that's all, a beautiful way of perceiving the world. Why don't you take it with you, keep it for awhile."

"I couldn't."

"Go ahead, I'll lend it to you. I do owe you for your help."

"No you don't."

"Take it, read it when you find the time. See if something in it, anything my mother wrote, inspires you with your writing."

As I fingered through its pages, I discovered it was published in the early thirties. It contained culture and care of flowers, and there were the most beautiful full-color pictures of roses, as well as black-and-white illustrations. But most astonishing were the added scribbles in ink on every page, and the handwritten letter to Fedelina on the front pages, which the publisher had left blank. I also saw stationery folded and tucked throughout.

"Are you sure you want to share this with me?" I asked her.

"I wouldn't have offered it if I didn't. Oh, and take some of those roses, too, whichever ones you like."

As I walked out her front door and down the steps, roses in my arms, her mother's gardening notebook clutched in my hands, and all the things Fedelina had said to me fluttering through my mind, I felt a tingling in my gut, the kind one gets when strongly compelled, and I could see in my mind more regarding the story I was writing—plots, themes, characters, emerging like a plane from the clouds overhead. I knew as suddenly as a hummingbird appears that it would be more than a story about flowers, but that I would have to write it down quickly, before it disappeared, and that it should be about a younger woman and an older woman, and the stages of life.

I went to my bedroom and set the roses on my desk next to the orchid, hoping they would all get along, and then I sat down with the intention to write. But instead I opened the book, *How to Grow Roses*, and pulled out worn and faded pieces of paper on which Fedelina's mother had written her a letter.

chapter seventeen

1920

My precious thirteen-year-old,

You've been sulking around with a pout on your face for a long time now. I keep telling you that if you don't take that look off your face, it's going to stay that way forever and no one will want to marry you. But you tell me you don't like boys, nor do you believe a word I say. You don't believe a lot of what I have to say anymore. And I don't believe you, either. I also don't blame you. It's been a hard year.

I know you miss your father and your friends and Portland with all its parades. The year 1918 was dreadful, the first year since you were born that Oregon cancelled its Rose Festival. You were mad at the war then, for raining on your parade, and soon after for taking your father. I'm mad, too. I miss my husband.

As we reached the final stages of the war, I thought you might be turning back into the happy little girl I once knew, but then the influenza pandemic erupted, killing more people than the Great War and before we knew it, one-quarter of our country and one-fifth of the world was infected. I think your pout returned, but I couldn't tell for sure since the public health departments had us all walking around with gauze masks on our faces.

A few of my friends were playing bridge late into the night. Come morning, three of them had died, as did the lady next door. I saw her watering her flowers in the morning and she must have developed the flu thereafter, for three hours later she died.

We left Oregon around the time her roses suffered an outbreak of black spot or mildew. I tried telling you they would bloom again, and people would find new reasons to parade, but you didn't believe me. The war, combined with the devastating disease, stole the optimism of most, and even the birds stopped chirping in the mornings. Or we didn't hear them anymore. I know I look too old to understand, but it feels like yesterday that I was your age. And I know how you're feeling—like nothing is blooming. That's where you're at right now. All I can say is that not everything in our lives can be constantly blooming at once, and sometimes it appears as if nothing is blooming at all. You need to find some buds, Fedelina. There have got to be some buds!

But what do I know? I'm just your mother. And all I can do is pray that my daughter, the one who used to wrap her arms around my neck and squeeze with all her might, the happy-go-lucky girl who talked a mile a minute and asked me questions as infinite and brilliant as the stars above, might reveal herself to me again. It's as if I left that girl behind when I moved from the place she loved to this farm in the Midwest where we live and work with the relatives who took us in. I see it in your eyes, that sometimes you despise me for moving us here, but sometimes a mother does things that don't make sense at the time. She does them for the well-being of her children. And change—is okay. Be careful, Fedelina of planting yourself too deeply. Remain flexible, movable. The major cause of plant death after planting, by the way, is planting too deep.

We're surviving. Our relocation, and living on this farm are keeping us alive. But I fear I can't be the mother I wanted to be—one who gives her daughter the lavish house, a cultural life in the city, ballet, voice and piano lessons, and, basically, the world. And as I go about without passion, toiling under the sun, I worry that you're detecting in my eyes that your mother no longer knows who she is. When faced with survival, life is no longer about passion and frolicking in self-thought as to who we are or who we might become. It's then that our survival mechanisms kick in, turning us into who we need to be. And the Lord has stepped in, too, reminding me through it all who I am—always with Him, and why I am here—to love the Lord, my God with all my heart, soul and mind. People travel the world over and search their lifetimes for the meaning to it all. I don't want to search. I've already found.

Still, life is hard. And I must say, neither I nor your father when he was living dreamed things would turn out like this. I never thought I would be working so hard, growing rice, while you roam about the field, lost and lonely, with nothing but daydreams to keep you company. I feel bad that you miss your friends and pray that your time all alone will enhance your imagination. I tell you daily that, when alone, some people feel loneliness. Others feel inspired. And a girl walking through a field full of the Spirit, full of ideas, is never truly alone.

But ideas will remain ideas if you never pursue them. They'll be like seeds in a packet that never gets opened. Times are tough but that doesn't mean we should forget our hopes and dreams. The other day your father's second cousin returned from town with cotton sacks of cattle feed, and it was you who noticed it first—rosebuds, daisies and lilies printed all over those sacks of feed. My heart wept because the flowers reminded me of the goals I once had for you, the goals of any mother, that her daughter have a beautiful existence. I stayed up all that night turning those feed sacks into clothes for your dolls and, by morning, I had thought up one more thing that I wanted to share with you about life.

That nations could rise up against one another in war, and that a single strain of the influenza virus can, within two years, wipe out hundreds of thousands of people, was proof enough to me that bad things happen. That one moment you're sitting around admiring a bouquet of flowers on your kitchen table, and the next they have wilted, with their petals fallen to the floor. Houses burn and automobiles break down, jewels get stolen, hobbies grow old and loved ones disappoint. Everything in life will dry up and crumble to the ground, but a soul in love with the Lord remains intact for eternity.

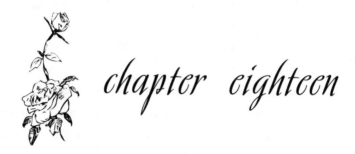

chapter eighteen

By late afternoon I was fully in the mood, enjoying the process, and whenever I paused in my typing I could hear birds out my window, like a chorus of angels, their singing growing louder than the voice of my own internal self-doubt. I liked what I wrote as much as I liked the quiet, and the mood I was in for writing, but with only a few chapters down I would never have the novel written by the time my children returned. The vision I had in my mind would take longer to complete. It would take me well into fall, and possibly winter, if I wanted to write it beautifully.

Two hours later I looked up from my computer and my urge to write was gone. I wandered through the quiet rooms of my house with tissues in one hand and roses in the other. The tissues I used to kill the legions of sugar ants that had been feasting in my kitchen cabinets, while the roses helped me ponder over all that Fedelina had said about women needing periods of rest in order to bloom again. That idea worked nicely with my own gusts of inspiration, and I jotted ideas down on colored construction paper as I went.

There's always that one type of flower, the one that everyone wants when it's in and seldom do nurseries have enough plants to supply its demand. It's the same with mothers—everyone wants them at once, and there's hardly enough to go around, to get everything done. That's okay. It's not always about being productive. Sometimes it's simply about being there. That's what everyone wants of a mother—for her to be there.

When I had filled ten sheets of construction paper with ideas, I decided to rest. I carried the roses with me into the bathroom and set them on the counter as I removed grimy pirate toys from the tub, then filled it with water as I thought about all that I had read in that letter from Cora. Suddenly I no longer felt justified in moaning over the challenges of motherhood and decided instead to put all my energy into the story I was writing. I didn't want it to be an everyday, ordinary story, but rather, something life-altering, and I didn't care whether it would alter the lives of others. I only wanted it to alter my own, and it wasn't the story itself that I hoped might instigate change within me, but the process of writing it.

I lit a candle and dimmed the lights, trying not to care about the toothpaste smeared across the counter, or my body, a glimpse of which I caught in the mirror with all its imperfections, the body that long ago was so in shape. Instead I thought about what Fedelina had said, that if a mother takes care of herself, she is more happily able to give. I stepped foot into the bath, the first such that I had taken in years.

I stared at the roses beside the tub and saw plainly what Fedelina had been talking about when she said that aspects of our lives go through cycles of blooming and non-blooming. There were times when I had nothing better to do than soak in a tub all night, times when Timothy and I were getting along, laughing, loving, and times when we were not. There were weeks of making homemade dinners nightly, followed by periods of visiting Chinese buffets. It was the same with the house. Some months I kept up with it and other months I let it go. Early morning power walks felt great, but then the kids would get sick, or work took over, and walking was pushed aside, like coffee with friends, an activity I savored years ago. Then I started to find myself too busy to return a call, and how sad, for friends put on hold are friends no more.

It all made me wonder when these aspects of my life might bloom again, and whether my relationship with Timothy could re-flower. I turned the bathtub water off, as I had long ago turned off my attempts to make him understand how overwhelmed I was with work, home and our kids. It was why I had let the nonverbal cues take over, the glares, the sarcasm, the coming to bed later than him and rolling onto my side silently, without saying "good night" when the sun went down or "good morning" when it came up. And to think, we once loved mornings together, sipping coffee on the mattress on the floor, sharing our dreams. Not anymore.

I held my breath and slid under the water, hoping to drown my melancholy. When I surfaced, I heard a man's voice outside my window.

"This, right here, is a good spot for it," he said.

"A few feet closer to the house would have been nice," said a woman.

"Too close to your house, and the branches won't have enough space to fully develop. Keep in mind" —the man said, and I recognized the voice; it was Fedelina's son— "it's small now, but one day this thing could grow upward of sixty feet, Mom."

"I didn't know Southern magnolias get that big," his mother said. "How many years are we talking?"

"According to the girl I bought it from," Liam told her, and I was hardly breathing so as not to miss a word, "an average tree will grow from sapling to the top of your roof by the time a kindergartner heads off to college."

"Good, I'll be alive to see it," declared my neighbor.

"That's twenty years from now," he said.

"I know," she said matter-of-factly. "That'll make me around one hundred. Oh, stop looking at me like that."

"Like what?"

"Like my doctor when I told him I was going to live that long."

"You told your doctor you were going to live to be one hundred?"

"I did, the day he told me the disease had already wreaked havoc on my body," she said. "The day he told me in so many words that my life span wasn't going to be all that long, so yes, of course I told him that."

"Good for you, Mom."

"Never let anyone put a timeline on your life, Liam."

"Don't worry about me, I won't," he said. "So where do you want this tree?"

I could stand it no longer. I had to see the tree they were planting. And I had to see her son! I stepped out of the tub and tiptoed over to the window, and there I stood, naked and dripping wet, watching that grown-up boy of hers carefully steady a tree down into a hole. His mother then held it firmly in place as he went for a shovel.

It was a small tree, handsome, with dark, lustrous green leaves, and he was handsome too. I could hardly take my eyes off him. Standing in a puddle of water, I felt rooted. My feet wouldn't budge but I was content to stand, forever gazing down at the beautiful evergreen tree and at him, breaking apart clods and removing stones and other debris, then backfilling the hole with soil.

"Done," he said when the hole was filled, but I didn't want him to be done. I wanted to stay perched in my window all spring, admiring from afar the small magnolia tree with its one and only waxy white flower. It was a beautiful flower, with a splash of bright purple in its center, and he was beautiful, too, Fedelina's son, the man who planted a tree for his mother and who was now gathering up shovels from her yard.

"You know, Mom, Southern magnolia suffers transplant shock."

"So?"

"So you can't take it with you when you move. It would die for sure."

"Who says I'm moving?" his mother asked. "Because I'm not—there's no reason for me to move. The girls, they say they've found me a condo, but I don't want a condo. And Suzie, can you believe, had the gall to tell me she toured an assisted living community on my behalf."

"They love you."

"Then tell them to leave me alone and let me live where I want to live. It's my life."

"We know that, but you're all alone here."

"Yes I am! For the first time in my life! And has anyone heard me crabbing?"

He laughed and so did I, alone in my bathroom, standing in a puddle of water with goose bumps forming on my arms, legs and stomach.

"I have no intention of leaving here," my neighbor went on. "Tell that to your sisters, will you? Or better yet, I'll call them myself."

"What if something happens and you need help. What if you fall?"

"Lord," she said, "what if a papaya falls from a tree and hits me in the head? Let me assure you, Liam, if I fall, I wouldn't call any of you."

"You wouldn't?"

"No, you're not paramedics. I'd call my neighbor, and then I'd call 911."

I put my hand to my mouth. I would have to set her straight, tell her not to call me, because I didn't know anything about the physical care of senior citizens or saving one's life, but then her son took care of it for me.

"No offense, Mom, but a woman coming over to your house like she did, in that nightgown, and then all those books in her yard . . ." He looked over in the direction of my house, forcing me to duck. "What's going on with that?"

"I don't ask," said Fedelina. "She was throwing them out her window this morning. She's a lovely woman, truly lovely—the kind I always imagined you with—but when it comes to certain things in life, Liam, I mind my own business. I don't ask too many questions. I know better."

I gasped, covering my mouth with my hand, while trying to hear what they said next—something about him going kayaking in the morning and that he craved a good rowing experience, time alone, with nothing but nature to regenerate his cells. I didn't hear it all because they went into the house.

I went to my bedroom, sat down at my computer and started to write.

I once loved baths, and taking them with my husband—loved them as much as I did working out. I once loved all sorts of activities, even clean-ing. I was a neat freak—the slightest piece of lint had me sprinting toward my vacuum. Not anymore. And getting roses from my husband—I once loved that, too. The hardest thing about turning thirty-seven is missing all the things I once loved but haven't time for anymore.

I was fully involved, in the creative zone, when one, two, buckle my shoe, three, four, there was a knock at my door.

"I know it's late," Mrs. Aurelio said, "but I saw your lights on. I hope I'm not interrupting. You're not busy, are you?"

"No," I told her, "just resting." *Resting so I might bloom again,* I thought. "Why, is everything okay?"

"Well, I told my son I was coming over to borrow an egg."

"Would you believe I still don't have any? I haven't gone shopping."

"I don't need an egg," she said, lowering her voice. "I'm here to ask a favor of you. If you see my son, swear you won't breathe a word to him about my attack in the garden."

"I won't say a thing," I promised. "But if I hadn't found you, and you didn't get that candy, how serious could it have been? What would have happened to you?"

"Possibly convulsions," she said.

"Oh."

"Then unconsciousness," she added, "but at that point there's an injec-tion that could have helped me. It's important that you know—I keep it in my bag at all times. It stimulates the release of sugar into my blood. You could give it to me in the arm, buttock or thigh."

"Me? Give you a shot in the buttock?" I made a face.

"Yes, if necessary, but I prefer the arm. It starts to work in five minutes."

"Why don't you want your son to know?"

"Anna, I've spent years of my life handling their needs and worrying about them, and lately it feels like roles are reversing. I don't like it this way—all seven of them calling constantly, questioning me. Mother, you're all alone, are you eating right? Sleeping enough? Carrying your candy with you?" She put her hands in the air. "If I tell them what happened to me, they're going to insist I sell this place and move closer to them."

"And you don't want to do that?"

"It's hard to know," she said, "Change—it's hard for young people to understand this, but it becomes harder the older you get. And up north isn't the same anymore. The old neighborhood has deteriorated. It's not safe, and my friends have died, or moved away, and to tell you the truth, I hate the cold. Up north makes me feel old, keeps me sedentary. I like the seasons on Sanibel. Things here bloom year round and there's always gardening to be done."

"What do you tell your family?"

"Some roses are tough and hardy and have a natural ability to withstand severe cold, but I'm not that kind of rose. Walking out to the mailbox would be one errand too many for me in below-zero weather. No, really, what I tell them is that if they want to see me, they can come here. That's what I tell them," she said. "I do feel guilty. My daughters keep telling me, 'Mom, why don't you move back closer to us?' They say they'll get me a condo, or we'll shop around for one of those communities." She shook her head, and then looked me seriously in the eyes. "I remember looking into colleges with them like it was yesterday, and now they're researching assisted living communities for me. It goes by fast, Anna."

"That's what everyone says. It's why I want to make the most of it now. By the way, your mother's letter put things into perspective. I no longer want to waste time moaning about my life, grumbling over every detail. And after what she went through, I don't feel I have reason to grumble."

"Lamenting," she corrected. "My mother used to always tell me that as long as you crab to the Lord, it's called 'lamenting' and it's okay, productive."

"Whatever you want to call it," I told her. "The daily woe-is-me complaining that I do. I've wasted too much precious time fooling my mind into believing I'm a prisoner in a dungeon, without pleasure and tortured, without freedom to change the things I dislike." I stopped there, not wanting to tell her I had spent all afternoon figuring out how to articulate it that way, turning my bitching into literary art.

"Should-haves, could-haves, Anna," she said. "I tossed mine in bags and tied them up years ago. Unless you feel like driving yourself into a state of depression, they're not worth a swarm of bees in May."

chapter nineteen

D^o you still feel that way today—that regrets aren't worth having?" I asked her when I stopped reading and dropped the manuscript into my bag.

"I didn't do everything the way I could have, but I did the best I could at that time. However, I was a worrywart, and I see now that most of my worrying was over nothing. Life happens whether you worry or not. It does no good, other than rob you of the moment. And I was busy all the time—overwhelmed. I look back and can hardly think of a time in my life when I wasn't busy with something. I wish I had spent more time doing nothing," she said with a laugh. "Then again, look at me now. I have all the time in the world for doing nothing. So maybe I should have done more! What about you, Anna?"

"Me?" I asked. "I wish I hadn't gone on living miserably for so long—all that wasted time of my life," I finally said. "I do regret that."

"I don't see it as wasted time," she said.

"You don't?" I asked.

"No. There's no such thing. To me, your garden was in disarray, that's all. No one's garden is perfect all the time." She was holding the roses I had given her tightly in her hands. I pulled a pen from my bag and began writing all she had said as quickly as I could, knowing her words were the sort of material necessary to turn my dark story into an uplifting one. I stopped writing when I noticed her voice cracking.

"I don't know why roses do this to me," she said, looking ready to cry.

"What have they done?" I asked.

"Make me emotional," she said. "About my life. I do wished I could have certain times back again."

"You're tired," I told her. "You'll feel better after a nap."

"No, Anna, this is where I'm at in the cycle. Look at me! My days of full bloom are over, my petals no more. There's not a whole lot more I can do at this age, no dreams to chase, fairy tales to believe in. You asked me about regrets."

"Yes, and I regret that I asked you about regrets in the first place." She was crying now and I felt responsible. I hadn't meant to upset her. I was nervous about her health, her blood pressure going higher, so I leaned onto her bed and awkwardly cradled her in my arms, wiping her tears the best I could, thinking hard for comforting words of wisdom I might share with her. "I feel bad I've upset you," was all I could think of.

"It's not your fault," she told me. "Regrets set in when all a person does is look back—when they're no longer moving forward. But this is life, right? And we are constantly moving from one phase to the next, redefining ourselves as we go." She stopped when there was a tap at the door and a nurse walked in.

"Blood pressure time," the nurse said with a smile. "Then the doctor will be in."

I stood up and went to kiss her good-bye for the day, but she took hold of my hand like she wasn't ready for me to go. "I don't let myself soak in them, but if you truly want to know my regrets," she whispered, pulling me close, "I'll tell you I regret the things I didn't do in life more than the things I did. I wish I had pursued more of the ideas I had. It's like my mother said—ideas not pursued are like seeds in a packet that never gets opened."

I watched as the nurse wrapped the cuff around her arm. "I'll come back," I said. "I'll come back after the doctor."

"I need to know that I made the most of it," she went on.

"Made the most of what?" I asked, bending down closer to her.

"My life, Anna," she said. "Did I live a beautiful life?"

I looked at the nurse, at the curious look to her eyes. "I'm sure you did," I told her, "but only you can answer that. Do you think you did?"

"I don't know," she said. "These are the thoughts that keep me up at night, if you really want to know. When this whole place is sleeping and no volunteer visitors sit in that chair, I cling to the random memories of my life, wondering the same darnn thing. Did I cultivate beauty each and every day?"

"I'm sure you did," I said again, feeling self-conscious, not knowing how to articulate anything profound with the nurse listening.

"Oh, you're just saying that."

"How about I come back in a little bit? Would you like that?"

"Yes, but I don't want to keep you," she said. "You probably have plans."

"I've come to Indiana for no other reason than to see you."

"Are you sure?"

"I promise. I have nothing else to do."

I left the room and went to get a cup of coffee, feeling glad to be here. My friend was like an overflowing fountain and needed to talk, to let it all out. I was thirsty and felt like listening, taking it all in. I wanted to hear more about the stages of life, especially the stage she was in now that I would be in, too, one day if I lived as long.

I watched her door and, when the doctor left, I returned to her room, only to find her fast asleep. Pen in hand, critic hat on, I sank into the chair and started editing my novel, crossing things out and making notes in the margins. I spent the next hour doing this, adding a layer of embellishment to the part I would read next, as if I were an artist painting a tree, and now I was adding flowers to that tree. Fedelina needed this. She needed to hear, to see in her mind this layer of beauty.

Some roses have one annual flowering that is astounding, while others have lovely clusters of blooms. And then there are those roses that do not bloom, but explode, only to drop their spent petals afterward. Such are the cycles of life.

"Working on your story, Anna?" she asked an hour into my editing.

"I'm always working on my story," I told her and then laughed. "Even in my sleep it seems my subconscious is working on it for me." I was hoping then that she might compliment it, tell me she liked what she had heard so far.

"Anna," she said, "I was thinking, just an idea—you don't have to do it."

"What?" I asked.

"What if you were to include a section on me now, here in this nursing home?"

"Oh," I said. "I hadn't thought of that."

"I know it sounds boring," she said, "but it's not about me. I was thinking more of this entire population to which I belong—twilighters, I'll call us. All the men and women, like me, who are sitting out here on the beach after the sun has set. The younger ones have left, gone on their way, but we stay put, trying to distinguish stars from planets and memories that are no longer visible to our mind."

"I could add all that," I told her, putting my pen to the paper.

"Good, because I've experienced it, Anna," she said. "I've watched the horizon fade before my eyes and I'm still here. The sun no longer illuminates the sky, but I'm still here. And you want to know what the best part of it is for me?"

"What?"

"That I'm not here alone."

"That's good," I said, writing fast and furiously, trying to capture it as she had said it.

"I'm blessed to have a big family, to have had lots of children, and now, visitors, coming to visit me at dusk, but I know women who never have anyone stop by. They're sitting here in the near dark, all by themselves."

When I finished writing, I looked up at her and asked, "Is there anything else you want the world to know about you?" And by "you" I was referring to this population of people living out the dusk of their lives in nursing homes.

"I'd want them to know that we do still have regrets," she said.

"I don't think a person your age ought to have any."

"You mean I should be excused from everything I did or didn't do?" she asked.

"You're too old for regrets," I said. "You're nearly a hundred!"

"I'm curious," she said. "What do you think I should be focusing on?"

"I don't know. You should be happy to be alive, that's it."

"But I'm still a thinking woman, more so now with all this time on my hands, and I see now that life didn't always go the way I planned. I'm okay with that, but I wonder at times whether I saw enough sunsets, if I appreciated things the way I could have, and you know what I regret the most?"

"No. What?" I put my pen back to the paper, ready to write.

"Why didn't I plant a Royal Poinciana?"

"I don't know," I told her. "What's a Royal Poinciana?"

"Oh, Anna, it's one of the most spectacular trees in the world," she said, "with orange or red flowers."

"You planted a magnolia tree. That's good, isn't it?"

"Yes, but why didn't I plant a Royal Poinciana?"

"There had to have been a good reason for you not to have planted one. Why do you *think* you didn't?"

"The tree is messy," she said. "Its flowers make the ground slippery, and its droppings and seeds, they're unattractive. It gets so big that you need a tremendous amount of space."

"See? There were good reasons why you didn't."

"You're right," she said. "I guess I'm okay with that, but sometimes—on those days when no one comes by—what I wonder the most, Anna, is did my life matter?"

I started writing again. "Of course it mattered," I said, scribbling as fast as I could, trying hard not to skip a single word she had said.

"But was it significant?"

"Yes!" I said, desperate to say something good, to comfort the woman who once comforted me. I put my pen down. "The impact you had on me was significant. It's why I wrote the book that I did, why I've flown all this way to see you."

"That's nice, Anna, I'm glad, but there were people in the world in need of help, real help, people who needed more than a beautiful bouquet of flowers. They needed food and clothes and roofs over their heads. I read about them in the paper, watched it on television. I'd cry. But did I do anything? I don't believe I did. I never inconvenienced myself, went out on a limb to clothe or feed a starving child. It's a major regret of mine. Why didn't I go out into the world more and try to help?" she asked, her eyes tearing up again.

"You're not Mother Teresa. Not everyone is able to be Mother Teresa," I said. "But you're Fedelina Aurelio, mother of seven and a wife who did the best she could in her own yard. Look what you've done—you added seven productive adults to this world. Without you they wouldn't be here. And they've produced, too. Your family tree is bigger than any Royal Poinciana! And all the things you once said to me, well, they had a profound influence on my life."

"Thank you," she said. "I needed to hear that."

I realized then that I had helped her. It was the first time I had helped her. "You were the one who told me," I said then, "that when a rosebush isn't in bloom it still makes a lovely backdrop for those that are. I hope you see that now. Your son, who I talked to on the phone, your other children, your friends and the nurses, they all love coming to see you, not because you're blooming, but because you're still beautiful. You're as beautiful as ever."

"That's nice of you, Anna," she said.

"I'm only using your own words."

"I do appreciate that, how nice you are."

"Want to know what I did next, after you gave me all those roses, and your flowers influenced me?" I asked her.

"Tell me you didn't pursue my son," she said.

"You really want to know?"

She nodded and I began to read from where I left off last.

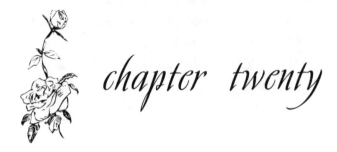

chapter twenty

They say kayaks rarely tip in calm water, and that unless someone is horsing around, there's no reason one should flip. But if I happened upon an alligator, if I tapped one accidentally on its head, my jumping, screaming, would be all the coaxing necessary for tipping a kayak upside down and trapping myself beneath.

So I decided against kayaking and rented a canoe instead. As I climbed into the center cockpit, steadying myself with a hand on each side, I knew it was foolish for a woman who had never set foot in any form of craft with a paddle to now be embarking on a solo expedition. I took my seat on the bench and picked up my paddle, making a mental note to teach my daughter never to do the irrational things I've done, especially going out of her way, taking up activities she otherwise wouldn't, with the intention of bumping into a man.

"But hard as she tries, hard as she might," I said to myself as I paddled gently away from the shore, keeping one eye out for gators and the other for him, "a woman can't always do the sensible thing."

And as Cora had written in her letter, the day is going to come when Marjorie no longer views me as the omnipotent, omnipresent all, and no longer wants to hear mommy's knowledge of life. "It's why I must tell her everything I want her to know by the time she is five," I said out loud to no one but the birds. "I will say to her before she turns six, 'When you are married, Marjorie, never go canoeing in search of a man. Go canoeing in search of yourself, darling, but never a man.'"

I was going at a good pace now, looking over my shoulder as I do in my minivan when I hear strange noises coming from my children, but there was nothing in the water behind me—no gators, no other rowers as far as I could see, and no children in the backseat feasting off stale crumbs unearthed from the crevices of their car seats. Oh, how I gagged recently when I pulled to the side of the road to pull a blue piece of hard cheese—the type I hadn't bought in months, since before our move—out of my daughter's mouth.

The quietness of my ride was haunting, making me miss the sounds of my children and feel guilty for what a lacking mother I was. I was not programmed like all the other mothers of the world, the ones with shiny, showered hair, sitting on the benches at parks, unwrapping perfectly well-balanced picnic lunches for their kids, their boys with groomed hair, clean faces and stainless shirts. All I could picture of my three now were their noses pushed to grandma's window. Where was mama, they were wondering. Where oh where did she go?

There was frustration in me as I rowed, and I started to cry at the thought of Timothy asking me to forgive him. I cried harder, knowing I couldn't. But staying with a man I would grudge the rest of my life, until "death due us part," was what had me crying hardest of all. By staying with him, I was making him believe that one day I might come around, forgive and forget. It was easy to lie to Timothy. He had done so to me, and his was the big, bad, hurtful lie, whereas mine was a dreary gray lie, bordering between a little white and a great, big, bad lie.

A woman, I told myself as I reached a wide-open area of Tarpon Bay, is allowed so many gray lies throughout her life. But then I stopped rowing, put my paddle down and leaned to the side, noticing in the reflection of the water how big my nose looked. It had to be an illusion. Water

does that, distorts one's features, I told myself, but knew the truth, that
my nose had grown. Not from all the white lies every woman tells, but
from parading around like a cheerful soul, pretending my marriage was
good and that the only love I needed was the mommy kind coming from
my children, when in reality I longed for the romantic kind, too, the
kind of love that lets a mommy feel like a woman. The truths a woman
refuses to acknowledge about her own life are the worst kind of lies.

When I looked up from my reflection in the pristine water, there
he was across the bay, near the edge of the mangroves—the man I had
watched plant that magnolia tree. But then he disappeared into the Com-
modore Creek Water Trail. I picked up my paddle and followed after
him as though I knew him—everything there was to know about the
man—and how ridiculous, I thought, for he was a stranger, a beautiful
man playing tricks on my mind, confusing me as to that which is or
isn't possible.

I only knew that I no longer wanted to be a miserable person caught
up in lies. I row, row, rowed my boat merrily toward him with ridiculous purpose, all the while feeling blind, unable to see the meaning of
life. Despite my thirty-six years of experience in the world, I felt lost
and poor, regardless of material possessions, wobbly, for one day wanting to stay with my husband and the next wanting to leave him, and
lonesome—for what? I did not know, but as my canoe glided across the
water, not moved by wind or engine but by my own strength and will, I
felt free from my wearisome captivity and all the chronic stress that for
so long had been settling within me, attaching to my organs, my cells,
and eating away at my essence.

As I entered the mangrove tunnel I should have slowed, stopped
paddling, but I was too deep in thoughtful confusion, and I was used
to driving a minivan with excellent breaks, not a canoe. He heard my
paddle hitting the water and looked over his shoulder, and saw me coming straight at him. I wanted to slow, to stop, but didn't know how. I
was glad when he reached his paddle out to defend his ship from the
fender bender headed his way. It worked. His paddle stopped me from

ramming into him, but the impact sent me rocking wildly in another direction.

He looked at me with deciphering eyes and I felt my face turn red as a woodpecker's crest. "You must think I'm crazy," I said, looking over my shoulder at him, my canoe drifting back in his direction. "I don't know where my mind was—lost in its own thoughts."

I expected him to laugh, to ask me if I was okay, but instead he looked at me as if I were a freak, like he didn't know me at all. "I live next door to your mother," I told him.

He paused and said, "Yes, it took me a second to recognize you."

I wanted then to tell him that of course it did. His mother's hallway was dark when we met, and my hair is down, and I'm not wearing the goofy nightgown that I wore the day I found his mother collapsed in the garden, the day I saved his mother's life. I wanted to tell him all of that, but I didn't. "It took me a second to recognize you, too."

"Where are you going in such a hurry?" he asked. "Trying to beat rush hour traffic?"

"No," I said with a laugh. "I thought I heard a gator behind me."

"You mean that stick in the water? From the right angle it might look like a gator, or just a big stick."

"Oh, that's funny," I said. "So what brings you out here today?"

"Taking time for myself, enjoying the moment."

It was then that I noticed a small pad of paper and a pencil in his lap. "Are you drawing?"

"I was."

"What were you drawing?"

"I was working on a Great White Heron until you scared it away."

"Oh no, did I really?"

He shook his head and gave me a smirk. "No, I'm doodling, still looking for something that inspires me."

"You like to joke, don't you?"

"Only when the moment calls for it. So what brings you out here—in search of your own inspiration?"

"Sort of," I said. "I guess you could say that."

"So what's your novel about?"

"It's really just a silly little story," I said.

"A silly little story about what?"

"Flowers."

"So is this story about flowers also going to be about a man in a kayak that you almost knocked over?"

"I don't know," I said. "I'm just getting started. I'll see where it takes me, see what kind of inspiration I find."

He looked at me oddly. "I guess we're both looking for something, aren't we?"

"Everyone is, don't you think?"

He nodded. "I've never met a person not looking for something." He was holding onto the side of my canoe now, keeping our boats locked. "So you come out here often?" he asked.

"My kids are too young."

"How old are they?"

"My girl is almost two and my boys are three."

"You've got your hands full."

"Crazy full," I said.

"You look good for having that many children."

"Do I?" I asked, flattered for the first time in years.

"So where are they, babysitter?"

"No. They're with grandparents," I declared. "Gone for the week, and I'm trying to make the most of it, get reacquainted with myself. My husband's gone, too," I added.

"It must be hard when he's away, with the three little ones."

"It is, but I'm getting used to it."

"Is he gone often?"

"Most of the time, yes," I said, aware of my own melancholy. I changed the look on my face and perked myself up, asking him, "So, do you kayak often?"

"Kayak, hike, bike—I do it all."

"You're a real outdoorsman," I said.

"I feel most alive, at peace, when I'm outside. Now put me in a mall," he said with a laugh, "a crowded amusement park, or confine me to a house for too long and I'm a walking dead person, I kid you not."

"Oh come on, everyone loves a good mall once in awhile," I said. "I'm sure you appreciate a few modern luxuries."

"A good hot shower and a beer mostly, but I can't tell you how many times I'll return from a trip and walk into my house feeling like one of those persons you hear about that has a near-death experience. You know, they get a glimpse of the other side, the side in which they are free from the burdensome weight of their lives, their bodies, their aches and pains, and then they come back to physical life and it feels cumbersome. My ex could never understand this, and I don't blame her. We never should have gotten married. We were mismatched souls from the start."

"I do understand," I said. "I'm thinking of leaving my husband. In fact, I'm almost sure of it. We're mismatched souls, too."

He let go of my canoe and I feared he thought I was one of those loony chicks who chatter, blab about everything upon a second encounter, and I wanted to tell him that I wasn't loony, even though I know there are a lot of loony chicks out there and I had been friends with many, but that I myself wasn't loony. I was normal. I wanted to tell him all of that, but instead I tightened my lips and refrained from saying anything else.

"It's none of my business," he then said, "and they say every person's experience is unique—but you will come out of it a whole person. You can at least. I did."

"That's good to hear," I said formally.

"You might be more hardened than before," he added, his face growing serious, "and shy, too, shy of getting involved in certain things. At least I was. It wasn't easy at the time, but it's a good thing now. We're better off without each other."

"It's nice that you can see the good in it."

"There's still the whole 'failure' thing, you know, feeling like I couldn't make something so important work. But we try. That's all we can do is try, right?"

The look in his eyes told me he was still suffering. I wanted to tell him I was too—suffering—but the distance between his kayak and my canoe was getting wider. "Are you friendly?" I asked, wanting to keep us going, for our conversation to never end.

"Depends who you ask," he said, his back facing me. "The guy at the four-way stop who almost hit my car might say I'm not."

"No," I said with a laugh. "I mean you and your ex-wife."

"I don't know," he said, facing me again. "We never had children so there's no reason to keep in touch. I have no ill will toward her, or anyone in life, really. It was mutual. We both march to a different beat. And when I marched home one day I didn't expect to find her in the arms of another man. I walked out of the house and left it all. To this day, the thought of buying another house sounds like confinement to me. Neighborhoods make me claustrophobic. And women who want to marry right away make me nervous."

"So where do you live?"

"I rent a place near campus, and travel summers. I go light when I travel. I'm happiest that way. There's something carefree about roaming the world with nothing but the shirt on your back and a pair of jeans, and I can sleep most anywhere. Just give me a big old oak tree and I'm dreaming in seconds."

"So you're migratory by nature," I said.

"Funny you should say that. I've got a lady friend who calls me, 'free bird,'" he said with a chuckle, "but no, I guess the divorce did this to me."

"Sounds to me like you're not meant to be living in modern America. Maybe you should have been born a couple of centuries earlier, maybe as an Indian, or an eagle."

He laughed. "You're probably right."

"You ought to move here, to this island. It's busy during the season, but slow the rest of the year. It's a wildlife sanctuary, not your typical place to live."

"I'll bet it must be nice living here. Do you like it?"

"I do," I said, "but life is life. I used to think there was a utopia, and if I moved and moved and moved I would eventually find the perfect place. But now I know it doesn't matter that you're living on a subtropical island if your marriage is bad. If you've got problems, escapism only goes so far. You must be glad not to be married to her anymore. Sounds like you're better off on your own."

"Without a doubt," he said.

"Good for you. It sounds like you have things all figured out," I said in a final tone, as if letting him know we should both say good-bye.

"I can't believe I said all that," he said then.

"What?"

"All that stuff about me. You must think I'm a total sociopath talking so much about myself like that."

"Not at all," I reassured him, and put my hands in the water on both sides of my canoe like a beginner, hand-paddling my way closer to his kayak. "It sounds like you know who you are and what you want. That's good."

"I don't think anyone truly knows who they are," he said. "Do you know who you are?"

"I haven't a clue," I said.

"That's okay. Why do you have to know who you are? Why limit yourself?" This time he was using his paddle to move closer to me. Our boats were touching again, our eyes locked. It was easy for our eyes to lock. The water trail was shady from the mangrove branches. If we were still on the bay, with the direct sun coming down on us, our eyes would have a hard time locking.

"I feel like I know you from somewhere. Did you ever live on the East Coast, New York, or Connecticut—maybe when you were a kid, or in college?"

"Nope," he said. "I'm a Midwesterner."

"Then no, I don't know you," I said, shaking my head, trying to figure out why I felt like I knew him, like we had met before, grown up in the same home town, gone to school together, been side by side like we were now since the beginning of time—there and together at the creation of the world. How ridiculous, I quickly told my right brain, my left brain and all the vibrating cells of my body—we didn't know one another at all! I had been with Timothy since college and still didn't know him!

"You weren't in the Peace Corp, were you?" he asked.

"No, were you?"

"No," he answered. "I just thought it would be a cool question to ask." And it was after we stopped laughing that I knew he felt it too and was searching for an answer as to why we felt the way we did, as if we had met before.

"I should get going," I told him.

"Me, too," he said, looking at his watch.

"Well, it was nice bumping into you."

"I'm glad you did. Bye."

"Bye," I said back and closed my eyes, listening to the sound of his paddle slapping the water, while thinking about what I wanted to write, that once upon a time there lived a woman who believed a big rock on her left hand would bring her happiness. Now, I thought as I pulled and tugged at my wedding ring until it made its way over my knuckle, that woman would trade the rock for a pebble if the pebble promised happiness.

When I could no longer hear the sounds of Liam's kayak moving through the tunnel ahead, I opened my eyes and saw I was headed right into a mangrove. I ducked, but one of the branches scratched across my forehead. Crouching as low as I could on the floor of the canoe, I was struck with inspiration and wanted to write it all down, but instead I got back on my seat and used my paddle and hands to push my way out, the canoe rocking and tipping. Once dislodged, I paddled and maneuvered my boat backward. Then I grabbed a pen from my bag and started to write.

A woman stuck in a mangrove might look like a mangrove, taste like it, smell like it, but that doesn't make her a part of the mangrove. Once she gets herself out and washes off, she no longer looks, tastes, or feels like the mangrove, and it's the same with misery.

I put my notes back into my bag and started paddling away from the mangrove I had been caught up in. "I was stuck in it, but I was not it," I said out loud as I started to paddle harder and faster than I had before, knowing I could never forgive my husband for what he had done to me and declaring with all my might that I would leave him once he returned, move on with my life, taking the children with me!

And I would write! I would write to comfort me, write to counsel me, write to make sense of it all, and write to create for myself a better life, a life where dreams come true and people live happily ever after. Then again, it wasn't as easy as it sounded when there was always someone or something getting in my way. It wasn't the act of writing I found hard, but my finding an uninterrupted chunk of time in which to do it.

When I entered the wide-open bay I put the paddle down, letting the canoe slowly drift about under the morning sun while questioning how a mother knows when to give up certain selfish passions and fold laundry instead. I struggled with this, and needed to know whether I should hang my cravings to write out to dry until a different stage in life, or when I am old as Mrs. Aurelio and there is no one to answer to but the flowers in my yard.

I reached for the book my neighbor lent me, the one containing a mother's inspirations, sealed in a ziplock bag. I pulled out a folded piece of stationery, opened it up and began to read.

chapter twenty-one

1933

My Dear Daughter,

With one in four Americans wanting to work but not finding it, the world is once again a difficult place to be. No mother wants to see her children hungry and coveting things they cannot have, but worse is when she sees them no longer dreaming, pursuing, seeing in their minds the things they believe in.

I'm fearful, Fede, that this depression America is going through, and all the labor you are doing out in the fields, is limiting your mind's capacity to believe—to believe in a beautiful world. And believe me, of all the things I've wanted to grow, rice never made my list. It's why after hours in the field I gathered the coins I had been collecting, the ones saved for an emergency, and walked to town and bought the book I am now writing in, the book that cost more than a week's worth of potatoes! Guilt-stricken, I have been hiding it under my bed, pulling it out after everyone is sleeping. The men of the house, they couldn't possibly understand my longing for beauty, the kind that flowers bring, and so I'm keeping it my secret, flipping through its pages, crying over the colorful pictures while wishing for flowers in our life.

I don't want you to think I spent all that money on a simple book on roses when it was actually a reminder of the possibility of a splendid future, the preparation I needed to take to move toward a destiny of my own choosing, of optimism, of hope and what lies ahead, a reminder that, as roses bloom prolifically, then don't bloom at all, only to bloom yet again, so it is that life is as short as it is long. Despite these depressed times that seem to never end, we will all look back on them as only a season of drought in our lives.

There are an infinite number of things a woman must do in her life-time, more things she doesn't want to do but has to than there are things she wants to do and can. And whether she is doing what she wants to be doing or doing what she must, there is never sufficient time in a day to get it all done. All I can say is, cut out that which isn't needed in your garden, in your life, once or twice a year. Trim away that which serves no purpose and benefits neither you nor others. Trim it all away. And space your plants appropriately. Overplanting, crowding your days with too many commitments, activities and involvements, may lead to disease and fungus, and the things you want to do won't stand a chance of surviving.

I want a rose garden, darling. I can't help it—I do! As I flip through the pages of this book, I want, imagine and believe I already have an amazing garden, abundant with roses. I also educate myself, read all there is to know about the growing of roses and, the more I read and learn of them, the more I believe in things I don't have and in my power and ability to reap what I sew. A couple of mornings ago I took you aside and closed my bedroom door, telling you I had a secret and pulling the book out from under my bed. Fedelina, your eyes grew big like when you were a little girl, and you burst into tears when I flipped it open to the colorful pictures of roses. It was then that I told you, no matter what your situation, Fedelina, never look at a rose as a luxury item. It is not. It is a necessity in a woman's life!

On those mornings, dear, when I awake and feel overwhelmed, defeated, exhausted with regard to what has become my life, when all I want to do is turn over in bed and crawl under my pillow to hide, I force myself to open this book of roses, to look at the colorful pictures. I read from the Bible, too, and then pray, begging that the dull and boring routine which is my life will blossom into more. After doing this, I find my mind unfurling. Even as I'm picking rice all day in the field, I see my dreams and work on them in my mind. I've done this so many times that my dreams have become far greater than I originally imagined, and it's because I'm seeing instead the dreams that the Lord has for my life. The creator of the shells on the shore and the fish in the sea has adjusted my small way of thinking to dreaming bigger for my life.

And now, I'll let you know what your mother has been up to. Early to bed, early to rise is what I've been doing, waking one hour earlier than my norm. Sometimes it's the only way I can get an hour to myself. With my morning hour I've been sneaking outside for a walk, to a patch of dirt that no one is using, and there I've been selfishly playing, at least that is how others might see it. You see, darling, when you pursue what you are passionate about, to others it might look like you are only playing in the dirt. But you will know the difference between playing and toiling in that toiling brings forth changes in your life—even if that change is in your state of mind.

A wife and a mother sometimes feels a certain guilt when she plays frivolously, which is why sometimes she must keep quiet about what she is doing. In case you're wondering, I'm out here secretly trying to grow a few things of my own. I don't feel right telling any of the men what I'm up to. Even if your daddy was alive, I might keep it from him, or he might call me selfish for growing flowers in a time of depression, when each of us is only getting a mouthful of food per meal. Or he'd at least persuade me to grow the practical, edible kinds.

But I'm not growing anything edible. I'm growing roses, or trying. I'm sitting out here on a tree stump now—alone and inspired—overlooking my disturbed patch of soil and hoping I can do this right, grow roses not to eat, nor to wear, nor to live in, but to look at in and of themselves for no other reason than pure loveliness and delight. It's something I feel compelled to do. It is my wish that one day soon I will hand you a dozen roses, and they will make you smile and have you believing again that you are stunning, life is lovely and that you deserve abundance in your life.

As I write this to you now, my hands are the hands of a woman who has been toiling in dirt, going to extremes for her daughter. It's okay. Mothers do that. They cannot help it. You'll do it yourself one day. And besides, I've always believed a woman should get down in the dirt on her hands and knees, and immerse herself into life.

Sincerely,

Mums

P. S. So far, nothing has sprouted and winter is growing near, but it's okay. I will not cry when the hummingbirds are gone because I feel all the time the spirit of the Lord hovering above me, and there is no greater thing on Earth—no breeze coming from the north, south, east or west, or raindrops from above—than experiencing that, than feeling the hair on your arms standing because you know, not because you've seen, or touched or heard about it from someone else, but because you know firsthand that it is true, that the good Lord does exist and that he is here and there and everywhere, through winter and through spring.

chapter twenty-two

You know," I said to Fedelina when I looked up from the manuscript. "After reading that letter I closed my eyes in the canoe and said a prayer, the first I had said in a long time."

"I hope it was a prayer of confession—over how you felt for my son."

"You knew about us, didn't you?"

"Had no idea," she said.

"I thought a little bird would have told you by now."

"No little bird told me anything," she said adamantly. "I must have had my head in a hydrangea bush."

"I don't mean to stun you," I said, "but I was lonely, not that loneliness justifies it."

"You were a married woman, mother of three!"

"I was a lot of things back then," I told her, "and a little bit of everything, especially lonely. It isn't only for old people. Even with three small children depending on her for their every whim, a woman can feel the loneliness that comes from not having another adult to talk with."

"I agree, Anna, and let me tell you from my own personal experience that it doesn't matter where you live—a bustling city or a small-town island—a person can get lonely anywhere. Back then, I was lonely, too, and until I met you, I was going about my days not making a whole lot of personal contact with anyone, other than cashiers, waitresses and boys bagging my groceries. But guess what!"

"What?" I asked.

"I realized it's a choice. Loneliness is a choice!"

"Why do you make so much sense?" I asked her. "You should have been a counselor."

"Anna," she replied. "I was a counselor! All mothers are, whether they see it or not. We listen for years to our children's problems, starting in preschool when they come home telling us there's a bully hitting them over the head with a toy train. And it's then that we start giving advice, teaching them how to survive in the world, how to handle difficult people."

"That's true," I said.

"Yes, but at a certain point," Fedelina said, "they want us staying out of things, that is, until you get old like me. Then they'll make pilgrimages to come see you, as if you were an old sage full of historical secrets. And then you'll learn of all their secrets, too, things you never knew about your own children, which reminds me—what happened next between my son and you? Did the two of you meet up again?"

"Oh, I've read enough for one day," I said with a smile and a raise of my brow. "How about you get some rest and I'll come back in the morning."

"Okay," she said. "But did he feel the same about you?"

I gave her a soft kiss on the cheek. "Are you in the mood for daisies?" I asked her.

"I'm always in the mood for daisies, but I forget what there is to know about them."

I crossed the room to the bouquet of flowers, pulled out several black-eyed Susans and put them in her hands. "Come morning, I'll remind you," I told her. "I'll tell you what you once told me about daisies."

 *chapter twenty-three*

The next morning, I opened my eyes and looked around. The orchid, still closed, inspired me to get up, stand tall, and start my day as a strong, sturdy woman on a quest to get to know herself. The roses instilled in me a desire to better care for myself so that when my children returned I might give more happily as a mother.

I touched my toes to the ground like a ballerina ready to leap through her day, when suddenly I heard a noise— Oh no, not again, not a knock at my door. Whoever it was, they had switched from using their knuckles to the old rusty knocker and it sounded like they were knocking to the tune of "Happy Birthday."

But who knew that this was the day, the day I turned thirty-seven, other than my in-laws—who probably forgot, as I forget birthdays, too, when consumed with my three children—and my husband, who was far, far away, and my biological father, the man I never knew, a married man who never intended to get my mother pregnant and who went away upon hearing the news, and who probably to this day cringes around the time of my birthday, regretting what he did with that woman, my mother thirty-seven years ago. I thought about the question as I pulled my unruly hair into a ponytail.

I wanted to ignore the knocking at my door. I wasn't in the mood for anyone fussing over my birthday, and all I could think of was my children and how they would feel if they knew today was mama's special day. Children expect hoopla and believe in celebrations. I didn't feel at all sorry for myself. I only felt bad for them as I headed for the front door.

"Oh," I said when I opened the door to find Fedelina Aurelio with a small, round pie, and the large straw bag parked at her feet.

"It's today, right?"

"I'm afraid so."

"I was trying to recall, you're thirty-nine?"

"Thirty-seven," I corrected. "And trying to get used to it—this new age."

"You think thirty-seven is hard? I put my underwear on backward three times this morning," she said.

I gave her a fake laugh. I had told her to stop by again this week, but I wasn't in the mood and wanted for her to leave my front porch quickly so I could take the pie inside and dump all those fat calories into the trash. "This was nice of you, but your son is visiting," I said. "I don't want to keep you, take you away from him."

"He's fixing my stairs," she said. "So what have you got planned for yourself today?"

"Not much, just rest," I said, and thought *So that I might bloom again.*

She handed me the pie and said, "Here, this is my way of saying 'thank you.'"

"For what?"

"Helping me like you did," she whispered, looking back toward her yard. "It was either a pie," she said, her voice picking up again, "or more flowers."

"The pie, it's nice of you," I said, although a woman can never have enough flowers—those were her words.

"I do know what it's like to be alone on your birthday. Why don't I have a piece with you, if you'd like?"

I tried thinking of an excuse as to why I couldn't, not today. It wasn't that I didn't want a piece of the pie, but that she was showing strong signs of being a lonely old woman and I didn't know whether I wanted to assume the responsibility for alleviating another person's loneliness when I myself was a lonely woman and hardly knew what to do for myself. I could invite her inside my house, but the mess would spook her, and anyone as old as she might trip on the kids' toys and fall down, holding me accountable, and then I would be on the news and the whole world would know I was the woman with the messy house—the messy house that killed someone.

"I know," I suggested. "Why don't we sit right here on the porch steps and have a quick piece of this together?"

"Don't you have a table in your yard?"

"A small one, come to think of it, but it's rusty, and my yard is a mess, full of toys. And my grass, what little grass I have, hasn't been cut in weeks—it scratches the ankles, you know—and there's fire ants, but we could go down there if you like."

"It sounds lovely, Anna."

"Silverware," I said. "Let me run inside and wash some."

"No need," she said. "I've got everything under the sun in my bag."

I followed her down, barefoot and kicking broken seashells off my steps as we went. "I should get out here and clean this yard—get it done before they return," I told her. "I don't know how it gets like this. All I do is clean. I don't stop, never watch television, or read."

"I used to keep my house so clean you could lick butter off the floor," she said. "But you know what, Anna? My children, if you ask them, don't remember a spotless house. If I could do it over, I'd spend less time cleaning and more time enjoying them."

"Everyone says that," I told her with a smile that said, "Thanks, but it didn't help." "I'm sure I'll say it myself one day, but it's hard to play ring-around-the-rosy and fall down onto an ant-infested floor."

By now we were in the backyard and I was using my sleeve to wipe dirt and small bugs off the cast-iron table before steadying it the best I could on its unsteady legs. I then looked around the yard with my hands on my hips, the way I stand when I see a major project but have no time to embark on it, only time to think about it.

"My house is so messy that I dread the delivery guy showing up," I said, and when she let out a loud laugh I went on, feeling like a stand-up comedian full of hilarious one-liners, "and my yard is such a mess that I fear someone on this street might report me to the Center for Disease Control. My car is so bad that when I open its doors in the parking lot of the grocery store, things fall out. I don't feel good when everything is a mess. It makes me feel mentally chaotic, but the problem is, as often as I clean it, an hour later it's a mess again," I said, and finally laughed myself.

"I know," she said, nodding her head as if ready to applaud. "You clean one disaster, another is made. I do remember. It's like chasing the wind, but one morning, Anna . . . " She tapped my arm and looked me in the eyes. "It was a long time ago, but I'll never forget the morning I woke to a perfect house—immaculate, no speck of dust, no dirty dish, no pillow cushion on the floor, no toothpaste in the sink, and I went to bed that night and woke the second morning, and guess what?"

"It was all trashed again?"

"Nope." She shook her head. "It was immaculate the second morning, too, and the third, and the fourth, and I couldn't figure out why the mess was no longer an issue and all of a sudden, on the fifth morning, I woke and it struck me hard. I knew why the house was staying clean."

"You hired someone to help?"

"No, my children were grown and they were gone. It was me and Oscar in our perfectly clean house, with hours upon hours of calm, quiet stillness in which I had nothing to do but dust and mop. I would have paid a million bucks at the time to have my children small again and my house a mess. Oh, how I missed the chaos of it all that morning I woke and my children were gone."

I wasn't ready for that, and didn't want to contemplate it now. I grasped the back of one of the wobbling iron chairs, steadying it as she sat down, hoping it would hold her weight. Then I looked around. The yard, with all its weeds, looked more like a field, and the birdbath, overflowing with yellowish-green water and soggy leaves, had to be harboring disease. The table Fedelina set her pie on was full of rust. But if the children were here, they would not care about the weeds or the dirty water or the rust. They'd only see the candles Mrs. Aurelio was sticking in my pie.

"There's only thirty-four to a box. Mind if I'm short by two?" she asked.

"Stop," I said, pacing. "One candle is enough for me."

But she kept going, one after the next until most had a place. "Why don't you sit down?" she finally said. "You're making me nervous."

"I'm not in a hurry for my babies to grow up," I started. "I want things easier, that's all. I want more time for the basics—baking pies, like you."

"It's store-bought, dear," she said. "They do a fine job nowadays."

I sat down with my elbows on the table, my face resting on my fist. "Then I wish I had time for other things, for beautiful things, like gluing seashells to my mailbox as I saw you do, or planting all those flowers, but I don't. I can hardly get a load of laundry in without interruption. Look at me," I said. "Would you believe I used to be a neat freak? Not anymore. All I am now is a mess, an unhygienic mess of a woman."

She stopped putting candles on the pie, which was too small to fit all the years of my life, and then she tossed the box with the remaining candles into her bag.

"There's absolutely nothing easy about being a mother, Anna," she said, shaking her head. "If someone claims it's a cinch then they're either lying or they're not doing it right, that's for certain."

"You had seven," I stated suspiciously, "and I've heard all about your generation of ladies, how you had homemade suppers on the table three hundred and sixty-five days a year, and kept your homes immaculate. Tell me the truth, how?"

"We never slept," she started. "I stayed up until the wee hours. Nothing was easy. There's no secret to making it all easy. You have to say 'no' to certain things, say 'yes' to others, recognize the beautiful moments when they're in front of you and take hold, which gives me an idea."

"What?"

"Why don't you go pick flowers for our table?"

"Pick flowers? From where?"

"Your yard," she said.

"There are no flowers in my yard; only weeds."

"Anna," she said. "You're talking to a woman with poor eyesight. I see dark spots, flashing lights, rings around the lights—all thanks to high blood sugar—but I can still see those daisies in your yard. They're over there," she said, pointing.

I stood up, my eyes squinting. "Daisies?" I asked.

"Yes, go pick a few."

 *chapter twenty-four*

I walked over to where the daisies were growing and, with the long grass making my ankles itch, I squatted down and started to pick. But then I heard a car door slam out front and, seconds later, a familiar and friendly but loud voice from back north briskly rounded the corner into my yard.

"You're kidding me, oh no," I said, my hands over my mouth. I had forgotten that she had called and told me she was coming to Florida, that we had made plans to meet for coffee, today.

"Anna Hott," said Gwendolyn Sprigs-Burton, an editor I used to work with. "Tell me you didn't forget. We talked a few days ago, remember? I said I was in southwest Florida with my husband and that I'd stop by for a cup of coffee the morning of your birthday. Then you gave me directions." She put her black-rimmed glasses on, the ones that were hanging from a chain around her neck, and looked at me down in the grass. "You forgot."

"My mind," I said, rolling my eyes.

"Anna," she said again, giving Fedelina a quick nod of her nose. "They're talking about you at work."

"There are so many better things to talk about, don't you think?"

"I told them," she started. "I said Anna turned four books into best-sellers last year alone, and I think she felt she was doing all this significant work for very little pay and that's why she quit—she's got three kids and needs more money."

"That's not why I quit," I said, feeling the same frustration that I did every time I heard Gwendolyn talk *to* me and *about* me in story form, as if I were a third person. "I wish you didn't tell them that—that I quit because of money."

I made a mental note that if there was anything I wanted to teach my daughter, pass on to her as my own Cora-like wisdom, it would be to look for and don't become one of those big-mouthed hawks flying through the sky with other people's words twisting like fish, falling from their mouths. "Never feed women like this a morsel of personal information," I would tell Marjorie when the time came for her to know.

But Gwendolyn had come to this island and it was a long way for her to travel, to be standing in my very own yard telling me untrue things about me. So, instead of getting irate and telling her off, I gave her my "I feel sorry for you" look because I knew that being the expert on everyone else's business was her confidence.

I thought she would then switch to talking about the weather. A normal woman would do that, would read the look on my face and talk about the humidity instead.

"Then if it wasn't money, what was it?" she asked with bulging eyes. "What had you booking out of work that day? I've never seen anyone run so fast through a parking lot."

"N.O.Y.B.," I told her.

"N.O.Y.B.?" she asked. "What on Earth does N.O.Y.B. mean?" She gave me her look of utter confusion, the one she gives when she reads a manuscript that doesn't make sense.

I didn't want to shatter her to pieces by telling her it meant "none of your business," and was an acronym I used in jest with my sons whenever I was talking on the phone and they would follow me from room to room, asking me what I was talking about.

"Gwen, I'd like you to meet my neighbor, Fedelina," I said. "Fedelina Aurelio."

Gwendolyn walked over to the table where Fedelina was sitting. "The pleasure is mine," she said, giving her an elegant handshake, but then quickly turned her attention to the pie. "They spelled your name wrong, Anna. Did you notice?" she said, looking as if she was going to pull out a red pen. " . . . spelled it with one 'n.' There's two 'n's' in Anna, am I right?"

"Yes, but it's a pie, not a book, and it's only going to be eaten, not reviewed," I said from where I was in the grass.

She walked back over to me. "So what do you think of Florida? Are you glad you left New York?" she asked, giving me her deciphering look, the one she gives to prospective authors when she doesn't understand the objectives of their books. "And what's with all the books on the ground out front? It's odd. You've gone from being the best damn publicist I've worked with, to . . . I don't know . . . stay-at-home mother playing in the dirt. Where are your children?" And before I could answer she bent down to be at eye level with me. "It's wasn't the big 'M' that made you go awry, was it?" she whispered.

"I already told you it wasn't. It had nothing to do with money."

"I mean the other 'm,' the big 'M,' because if it was, I should give you a pen so you can write it all down. Others might relate. I've been playing with the idea of doing a book on the big 'M,' but I need to find an author. I've been roaming all the corners of the Earth for one."

"It's already been done," I said, not knowing what she was referring to—motherhood, midlife crisis, menopause, misery or momentary mental malfunction. They all started with the letter "M" as did money, madness, misery, Mrs. Aurelio, and mingling with the daisies. "Go to the bookstore and see," I told her. "There are countless books on the big 'M' and besides, it's not what you think."

"From publicist extraordinaire to Victorian maid living in a birdhouse, picking daisies out back? You didn't burn all your bras, I hope. C'mon, Anna Hott, what else is it?"

I looked her in the eyes, and then glanced over at the black cast-iron table with Fedelina and my pie. Marriage—if only she knew it all had to do with marriage, the other word starting with the letter "M." When that "M" goes bad, it's a hard one to admit at first, especially to a woman like her, who takes my words and flies off with them for everyone to see, like fish, dangling from her beak.

"My fellow editors in the acquisition department, Anna, we all miss you. And your authors do, too. It's baffling. When I tell them you're living amidst swamps and with gators on a sanctuary island—isn't that what they call this? And now, what are they going to say when I tell them I found you out playing in the dirt? Sand is one thing, but dirt?"

"Mud therapy," I corrected.

"Oh, Anna, that isn't funny," she said, scanning me with editorial eyes. "Maybe work will take you back. What do I tell them? They know I'm here. They know we're having coffee."

I shrugged my shoulders. "Tell them we had pie instead," I said. *And when the pie was open, the birds began to sing.* "Tell them it's hard to articulate, but Anna said she needed a break from her mundane routine, that's all."

She walked back over to the table and sighed heavily. "I brought you this bottle of Australian wine. Promise me you'll curl up in bed with a cozy blanket and read its label."

"I prefer reading books."

"Funny you should say that. I'm contacting the family, to see if they want to write a book, a true rags-to-riches story," she said, looking at her watch. "For which, by the way, I've got to get going. I'm calling Ben this morning about the idea."

"Would you like a piece of pie before you go?" Fedelina asked.

"I don't know," she said. "Can I go inside and use your phone, Anna?"

"It's a mess in there." I cringed.

"Like I care," Gwendolyn said. "I recently acquired a book on messy homes, and you know what they say about keeping a house clean with children?"

"No, what?" I asked.

"You teach your kids—early on—to pick up after themselves, and whatever they leave around, you bag it up temporarily."

From the corner of my eye I saw Fedelina's head turn quickly toward me, and I looked at her, and the two of us cracked up. "I hope they only devote one chapter to that concept," I told Gwendolyn.

"Oh come on," she said, shrugging her shoulders. "How hard can it be?

"Harder than it looks," I told her from where I was, still squatting in the dirt. "Way harder!"

"You're staying for a piece of pie?" Fedelina asked her again.

"Why not," she said, looking over at me as if she were determining how she might incorporate me, if not as author of the book, at least as an example of a woman in the midst of the big letter "M," whichever "M" it was. Once she had a book idea in mind, there was no thinking beyond it.

"The act of picking daisies," I heard Fedelina say to her. "Once you start, it's hard to stop."

"I suppose, if you're a daisy sort of a person," Gwendolyn said. "My husband sent me a vigorous bouquet of Dutch tulips and ranunculus with lime hyacinths for our anniversary. I've always preferred a more sophisticated flower, an amaryllis over a daisy anytime, or faux dogwood blooms are exquisite."

"I'm not trying to belittle the daisy," she went on, and I rolled my eyes at Fedelina, wanting to tell her about Gwendolyn's bullish side and how she loves a debate. "In all fairness, it has played a role in history— embraced by different generations as the symbol of freedom, power, and life. But daisies are . . . oh, I don't know. They're weeds, aren't they?"

"Asteraceae," Fedelina corrected. " . . . wildflowers belonging to the Asteraceae family—a family at least fifty million years old in its full for-mation."

"I guess it doesn't matter what family they belong to," Gwendolyn said, "unless you're writing a book, a book on flowers. You're not writing a book, are you?"

"Is everything a book to you?" I called out to her.

"Yes—potentially. Why?" she asked, arching in her chair to better see me.

"What more can one write about flowers that hasn't already been written?" I asked, keeping secret the story I had started to write about flowers, and about motherhood, marriage, messy homes and Mrs. Aurelio. "Looks like I picked more than I had to," I said when I joined them at the table, giving the daisies a good shake.

"One can never pick enough daisies," Fedelina said. "We never had money when I was little, and there were times when my parents couldn't afford to buy me presents for my birthday. My mother would say, 'Fedelina, go pick daisies!' I'd do as I was told and, when I returned, she told me the most beautiful gifts in life are the simplest, the things that don't cost money."

"Profound," Gwendolyn said, and then added, "however my Porsche is beautiful and it cost a fortune."

I sat down at the table and said to my neighbor, "I didn't know I had daisies in my yard. I never saw them before, until you pointed them out."

"It's always children who spot them first," said Fedelina. "Adults get sidetracked, setting their eyes on more expensive, complicated forms of beauty."

"Are you sure you're not writing a book?" Gwendolyn asked again.

"No," I said firmly on Fedelina's behalf. Gwedolyn needed to hear a firm "no." She was a strong personality and it was only strong "no"s that got through to her. And besides, I didn't want Fedelina to slip and tell her about her mother, and all those letters and the gardening notebooks. Gwendolyn would eat it all up, take it back to New York, digest it and, within a year, Cora's intimate letters would be sitting on bookshelves nationwide. As wonderful as it sounded, I didn't want Gwendolyn to be the one when it was me privately reading them and inspiring ideas of my own.

"So Anna," Gwendolyn said next. "What is Timothy getting you for your birthday?"

"I don't know," I said, not wanting to reveal anything about my marriage. "It's a surprise." I plucked a petal from a daisy I was holding beneath the table. *He loves me.* I wanted to believe. But I couldn't. *He loves me not.* I knew that as I plucked another.

"My Oscar, he never told me he loved me," Fedelina said, "in all our years of marriage. 'I'm still here, aren't I?' he'd say when I asked him. He was a hard man to figure. It's why, from time to time, I had to stop and ask him what he was thinking."

I plucked another petal. *He loves me.* Nope. *He loves me not.*

"Why don't we sing to Anna now," Gwendolyn announced. "I do have to get going."

"Skip it," I insisted. "Cut the pie."

"Don't be ridiculous," Gwendolyn said, looking at her watch. "Like it or not, we're going to sing."

chapter twenty-five

BELVEDERE

A few more mouthfuls and I'll be done," Fedelina told me early the next morning, when I stopped my reading and looked up. She had a tray propped over her and was slowly eating what smelled and looked like pancakes.

"Take your time," I said, setting my manuscript on the floor and sinking more comfortably into the armchair beside her bed. "So how was your night? Did you sleep okay?"

"Yes, other than wondering whether this is going to be the night," she said.

"What do you mean?"

"The night that I die," she told me.

"Fedelina!" I said in a scolding tone.

"It's okay, Anna. When you're my age, that's how you think— You think about how you want to exit the world. And if you really want to know, I hope I pass in my sleep. It's what I wish for now."

I didn't know what to say. I had wished for all kinds of things throughout my life, but never gave thought as to how I wanted to exit the world.

"I don't want to die in the morning," she went on. "I like mornings. I never know who might show up for a visit. But sometimes when my family, and now you, come and sit in that chair, I feel pressure, like I better have something good to say, and not talk about the pancakes that I'm eating for breakfast."

"I don't mind hearing about pancakes," I said. "Are they good?"

"They're soggy and I'd rather be eating pie," she said. "I told my children when they started looking, searching for a nursing home, that my number two criterion was good food. Would you believe they sampled the breakfast at each facility, and this place was the best? Would you like some?"

"No thank you," I said. "I had a coffee and biscotti at the hotel."

"I know it sounds bad, Anna, but I'm not always in the mood for talking or entertaining," she went on, "or saying anything good. Sometimes I want to listen. It's why I enjoy it when all my children come at once. I can then passively lie in my bed and listen to them all talking, not to me, but to each other. It's my favorite form of entertainment."

I didn't want her feeling like she had to say anything good or maintain a conversation with me, so I sat there, not saying a word, watching as she spooned pancakes into her mouth. It was the first time I had seen anyone eating pancakes with a spoon. Then again, they didn't look like pancakes are supposed to look. They looked more like mush.

"You're quiet today," she finally said, after wiping her mouth with a napkin. "What's wrong, are caterpillars eating your herbs?"

"I was letting you eat," I said with a laugh.

"Well, I'm done. Help me slide this tray away, will you?"

I did, and then sat back down, watching her fingers fidget at the sides of her bed as they had the day before, and I knew she was looking for the remote control. I also knew where it was, wedged between the bed rail and the mattress the way her glasses had been the day before. I handed the remote to her, and it felt good being helpful. Helping her wasn't hard. I was learning her routine, and a simple routine it was.

"I'm glad you're back," she said. "I woke up looking forward to you showing up. Just don't ask me any of life's big questions."

"Why would I do that?" I smiled.

"It happens when you're as old as me—people look at you like you're an exhibit in a museum. I just hope, if they stare at me long enough, something I say might make sense or sound wise so they can go home and feel content, like they got their money's worth coming to see me in the first place."

I didn't want to tell her that, while sitting here, I too was expecting to catch from her mouth a falling morsel or two of life's precious insight. It's what people hope for when talking to a woman of her age.

"To tell you the truth, Anna, the older I get the more I realize how little I know."

"You might think you know very little," I told her, "but I think you know a lot."

"I may *know* a lot," she said, "but there's very little I am *certain* of. There's a difference between the two."

"What are you certain of?"

"I don't want to bore you."

"You couldn't bore me," I insisted. "No one is bored by what a nearly one-hundred-year-old woman has to say."

"Jobs, Anna, they end. People disappoint, and children grow up, but there's this song—this simple childhood song that I can't get out of my head. I find myself humming it all the time now, especially at night, when it feels like everyone in this place is sleeping but me."

"What song?"

She took a big breath in and let it all out. "It goes like this, Anna, if you really want to know." And in a cracking voice she sang the words, "Jesus loves me, this I know, for the Bible tells me so."

I wanted to join in, for I knew the lyrics as well, but I didn't. I listened and, when she finished, I told her how beautiful it was.

"Nothing too scholarly or profound," she said. "Nothing I had to search the world over to discover. It's just an old childhood song and, as old as I am, I cling to it. You can add that to your book if you like," she said.

I took hold of her hand, not knowing what to say.

"Read me more of your story," she said, and so I did.

 *chapter twenty-six*

Funny how the "Happy Birthday" song—one sung to me thirty-seven years in a row, one of the happiest songs there is—could suddenly sound different, sad. I didn't want tears dripping down my face in front of Fedelina and Gwendolyn as they festively gave it their out-of-tune all.

"Make a wish," Fedelina said when it ended.

I closed my eyes and tried, but what is a woman to wish for when none of her ridiculous little impractical dreams have come true?

"She's giving this serious attention," said Gwendolyn.

If only they knew that for years I had been longing for the same thing, and how, when I turned thirty-one, I gave myself one more year for it to come true, and when I turned thirty-two I put an extension on the wish, and when I turned thirty-three, I did it again, and how I gave up on it for a few years. Now that I was turning thirty-seven, time was up.

"We'd love to know what you're thinking of, Anna," Gwendolyn said.

But I would never tell. I could never tell anyone of my wish to write, my longing to add a simple piece of literary art to the world, and about how many times, while blowing out candles, I had said, "This is the year." Rather than planning, brainstorming, outlining or talking about what I might write, I wished for nothing more than to write, to find the time in my crazy, hectic life to write!

"The look on your face, dear, has us wondering," my neighbor said.

I could never tell them I was wallowing, not wishing, and grieving the realization that many wishes a woman has for her life never do come true. And despite the story I had started this week, at thirty-seven, if it hasn't happened yet, if I haven't penned a slightly good novel or written a pleasant short story, well— I didn't want my candles burning out, so I started hoping instead for more attainable things, like a more adult-oriented, spalike bathroom, with a scumless round tub and no pirate toys. Oh, and love, the romantic kind I hear about in songs—the ones that make me cry.

I opened my eyes and, to my astonishment, felt my latter wish coming true, for there he was—the kayaker I bumped into in the water, Fedelina's son, Cora's grandson. Now I believed—believed that somehow the two of us were meant to meet, that there was a reason, unbeknownst to me, but a reason. And he was looking at me oddly, in a way that Timothy never did, like he could see through me and was reading my mind, and had heard what I was wishing for. I wondered whether he could detect the liking I had for him, the liking I could feel on every level of my existence.

"It only comes around once a year," he said, "Don't let me stop you."

"Stop me from what?"

"Blowing out your candles."

"Oh," I said. I could feel my mind getting away from me, floating to the top of a nearby Brazilian pepper, and Brazilian peppers are bad, non-native and intrusive, and should be pulled from the island, and my feelings for him were bad, too. They didn't belong in the mind of a married woman, a mother of three! And I wondered whether he was feeling it, too. I think he was. The laws of science don't allow a powerful reaction on one end without an equal or opposite reaction on the other, and if it wasn't scientific—the effect he had on me—I don't know what it was, only that a connection so strong doesn't exist on one end only. But as I blew out the flickering flames representing the years of my life, he looked away like he didn't care at all.

"I'm heading to the hardware store," he told his mother as she pulled the candles from my pie. "I'll be working on your stairs today."

"The stairs aren't so bad, Liam," his mother said. "Why don't you relax?"

"They lean to the left. It's dangerous," he told her, casting me a glance.

I quickly nodded, like I agreed with his assessment of her stairs, and with anything else he might have to say—his views on politics and religion, too. I think I would have nodded and smiled had he told me there was a bobcat about to jump into my lap.

"You need anything from the store?" he asked her.

"No," she told him, and I felt like blurting out, "nails." Suddenly there was nothing more I wanted on my thirty-seventh birthday than general household nails, and to run off with Liam to the hardware store. I don't know why, but there are things in life no one will ever understand, things that are beyond our comprehension, defy logic and make no rational sense, like why did the cat run away with the spoon?

"Then again, I could use a bag of potting soil," his mother told him.

"You got it," he said, "One bag of potting soil."

She rolled her eyes, and then smiled at us. "My son," she said. "I do appreciate him."

I could hardly talk, could hardly remember my words. One would think I had just washed ashore in a boat from another country and could hardly speak a word of English. But it was a good thing. Anything I uttered would give away how enamored I was, and why? I do not know. Why are bulls and hummingbirds drawn to the color red? And sharks attracted to silver at dusk?

If there was a class I could take that might teach me the reasons behind these things, and why women feel the way they do, I would enroll, but I don't think chemistry, biology, or quantum physics would have the answers for me. My attraction to Fedelina's son surpassed any textbook explanations. It was more like magic. And, a*bracadabra*, he might disappear. Then I could feel my lips again, my tongue would reappear and I'd be able to talk.

"Would you like some pie?" I finally said in a tone that was way too properly formal, and I saw Gwendolyn reading my face. When she looked full—full of theories—I could tell she was ready to leave, and that she would return to work spitting out mouthfuls of information about me, which made me want to say, "By the way, *me* starts with the letter 'm' and is the real reason I quit my job—I did it for me!"

"I do love cherry pie, but I'd better get going," Liam said, and I was glad when he kissed his mother on the cheek and walked out of my yard, glad he had said nothing about our seeing one another in the boats. Glad for so many things, for having met him, and for knowing that, deep within me, I still have it—that mechanism that makes my heart leap over the moon. I was especially glad, after he left, to have my mind back. And more glad when Gwendolyn left.

My neighbor and I sat there savoring our pie a long time, long enough for the northern cardinal that had been in the tree in my yard to move to the bird feeder filled with sunflower seeds in her yard, and then fly off. She told me that the male northern cardinals are territorial, and will attack their own reflections in mirrors, and it got her to talking of Oscar and how possessive he used to be of her when they were dating. We chatted about everything, from garden pests and how to handle difficult people, to water shortages and living on a budget. When she finally got up to leave, she told me to bring the daisies into my house and put them in water. I gave her a look.

"My mother always told me, 'Fedelina, when life gets ugly, look for daisies.' They're all over—in fields littered with trash, behind dumpsters, along highways. They might be mingling with the weeds, but you'll spot them if you look."

"I can't tell you how much I'm enjoying your mother's letters," I told her.

"I'm glad," she said. "I may as well share them with someone. I don't think she would have minded."

I credit the daisies. As I brought handfuls of them into my house and filled a pail with water, dropping them in, they and what Cora had said about them got me to thinking about some aspects of my life, and how ugly they had become. My house was a cluttered mess and, as I stood staring down at the floating members of the Asteraceae family, the walls of the tree house that was my home closed in on me, as did my problems, and I knew something drastic had to be done.

"This is the day," I announced. "The day in which I will clean."

But as soon as those words left my lips, I was struck with an urge to write instead, and there was a battle going on in my mind as to whether cleaning was more important than writing. I knew that if a woman lives in a cluttered mess for too long, her mind becomes like a junk drawer, with dusty thoughts and too much in it she doesn't need. I didn't want that happening to me, and feared it already had.

I knew I should put my rubber gloves on and clean, but instead I grabbed the book, *How to Grow Roses*, and took it outside with me, sitting at the top of my porch steps, eager to read more of what Cora had written to her daughter. This time, a letter I found tucked and folded within the pages.

chapter twenty-seven

1934

Dear Fedelina,

We're still living with relatives, packed like sardines into their small house, but I'm starting to feel more like a hermit crab than a sardine. I've said "no" to several social gatherings, and at times feel self-conscious, but after my mornings trying to grow roses, and then a long day out in the field, all I want to do is to get into bed and read a good book, better yet, write something myself—these letters to you! The women in this house tell me I am hard to get to know, and I say they're right. Both gardeners and writers are difficult people to know because flowers and writing will be their best friends.

I'm better off hiding in my shell. One of your aunts likes drama. She likes it as much as chocolate. I like chocolate. I do not like drama, and they wonder why I don't join in, why I don't react. The truth is I don't care about conversations from yesterday, or feelings from the past. All I care about is what I'm currently planting in my garden, for what I plant today is what I will reap tomorrow. But these silly women I live with accuse me of not caring, and I'm ready to tell them it's not that I don't care, but that I don't feel a part of it, that I feel more a part of the birds I hear out my window and the crickets as I lie in bed. It is this form of simplicity that makes me feel alive.

But these gals are unhappy. Everyone I know is unhappy and I can't name a single person who is truly happy. And, to be honest, I think they are so comfortable being unhappy that happiness might be uncomfortable for them. Quite frankly, they are crabs, and I fear that being with them too much might turn me into one, too. I say this because when I'm with them too much, I find myself "crabbing" just to fit in. It's a way of bonding with the clan but it does me no good other than keep me a part of the tribe. And everywhere we go, when we go to town together, we attract, meet and talk with others just like us—crabs bemoaning financial stress, lacking husbands, messy houses and field work we dislike. I'd rather cry out to the Lord than to the women of this house.

It's not that I think friends sharing problems with friends is a bad thing, but I fear too much of it will turn us into one big cluster of crabs, stagnantly stuck in our swamplike circumstances and which no one will dare crawl out of or walk sideways away from because then they would no longer be a part of the "crab cluster." They say when two or more people gather in the name of crabbing, it's considered, "commiserating," and that commiserating brings comfort, but there should be rules amongst friends that, if you crab for more than a month about the same situation, then the recipient of your crabbing is allowed to stir up ideas or solutions.

I wonder sometimes whether numerous grown women are meant to be living in one small house together, but it only has me missing your father. He and I got along well. We complemented one another. Here, there is a second cousin who is always getting hurt by the things I say to her. You have witnessed this yourself and I hope you learn two things from this person. First, avoid unnecessary drama. Just as high winds are disturbing to roses because the flowers cannot easily stand being whipped about, the gusts and gales that go along with gossip and drama can damage you.

And second, don't let another person's perceptions of you change your perspective of the person that you are. She tells the others that I'm always out to hurt her. If your father was still alive, he'd tell me it's ridiculous. "Cora, you have a sweet tongue and a passive heart. Don't start thinking you're a mean person. Instead, beware! Beware of insecure people. It's not your job to fill them with worth." Your father was solid like that— practical, and he talked sense into me. There will always be people who accuse you of not liking or loving them enough. But you do not have to prove your love to anyone. Love is not measured by deeds or mannerisms or words. Love is! It just is!

One more thing I've learned living amidst all these women. Don't for a minute think that, by pointing out the weeds in another's garden, it will make your garden look better. Au contraire! It'll only make your weeds stand out that much more, dear. I guess what I'm saying is, there are people who like to critique. Criticism has become a sport of the soul. Some hardy climbing roses resent pruning and will not bloom freely if they are rigorously pruned, whereas other varieties demand it. Choose your variety, dear, and stay true.

There are too many larger things for us to all be thinking about than who hurt who with their words every day. The Depression, as well as our own daily routine, long and dull, goes on without change. You told me the other day that you feel like a caterpillar stuck in a cocoon, desperately wanting to claw your way out, to become a butterfly. Still, I have to believe, Fede, that the circumstances of our lives might not always make sense at the time, but the meaning behind events will unfurl later, one petal at a time.

But I myself have started wondering, what happened to the brilliancy of dreams, and where are all the hummingbirds and butterflies when we need them the most? We are all doing strenuous labor for which we have no passion or desire. I can't pull America out from its depression, or find you the love of your life, but I wonder whether it's true what they say, that we have the power to change our circumstances by changing our internal thoughts, and then by taking action. A few weeks ago I got down on my hands and knees and begged the Lord to give us something beautiful. My wants are not elaborate. I do not wish for a million-dollar mansion or a fancy wardrobe, but that my daughter will see a speck of pure and natural beauty in this depressed, poverty-stricken world.

The moment I said that prayer I felt a smile form on my face. And the very next morning we were out in the pasture with the cows when a few wandered too far, and it was our responsibility to bring them back. Little did I know as we begrudgingly chased those animals that the mighty forces of Heaven were reacting to my request for beauty, working in my favor. Suddenly we were standing, not in roses, but in a field abundant with an infinite number of daisies. I knew it to be our time for receiving as we spent the morning tying together flower necklaces and crowns to place upon our heads. We felt like children.

I guess what I'm trying to tell you, Fedelina, no matter how desolate life becomes, always search for beauty. Do whatever you must to find it. Do away with the foolish clutter—in your house and in your mind—and you will find it. I promise.

Love,

Mums

 *chapter twenty-eight*

That's it! It's time to pull weeds, time to clear away all the physical clutter that has become me, so I may see and smell and touch that basic, nonmaterialistic beauty that Cora describes," I decided as I folded the letter and stood up.

But how much easier life would be if I didn't have a creative compulsion. I could mop floors, fold laundry and feel content, I thought, taking the bucket of daisies and the things Fedelina had said with me throughout the house, as I scraped bubble gum off the floor, dumped cups of rotten milk hidden beneath the sofa, and swept beachloads of sand into mounds near the door. It was there, coming from the front hall closet, that I heard a gang of boxes hollering out for me to unpack them—boxes marked with my own black graffiti, identifying to which room they belonged, boxes I had stashed away, having no space to put them, or time to unpack, or adult company with which to use elegant glassware. I picked up a black marker and pulled a faint idea from my head—something I wanted to include in the story I was writing—and I jotted it down on a cardboard box.

There's no need for toxic chemicals. Keep your plants properly fertilized, mulched and watered, and you won't see many bugs. Set your boundaries, caring for and strengthening that which lies within, and you won't find many pests entering your space.

I then moved to the kitchen. cleansing, not cleaning—there is a difference between the two. I opened cabinets, pulling out mismatched mugs, eleven-year-old kitchen towels, burnt-black hot pads, extra tablespoons we never used, and I bagged dragged them all down the steps and under the house, where they joined the books I had tossed out there the day before, and then I went back for more.

A thousand plastic food storage containers came tumbling out as I opened a door, and I didn't need a thousand plastic food storage containers. No one does, so out they went, onto my lawn. All the junk Timothy crabbed about. "Crab no more," I muttered as I cleared away place mats with stains, centerpieces with dead, dried flowers, and half-burned candles.

It was late afternoon when I moved to my bedroom, putting the pail of floating daisies on my desk, introducing them to the orchid in its pot and the roses in their spot before continuing with my in-house "weeding." Flat sheets, fitted sheets, red sheets, blue sheets, sheets of every color, sheets of every fabric, wrinkled sheets, ironed sheets—all sloppily shoved into the linen closet. I didn't need ten comforters to make me happy. It only made me dizzy, so out they went with the other clutter that had become me, the socks without a match and the dresses without a sash. I would dump, donate, no, sell it all. It would bring me a year's salary minimum, which I needed now that I no longer worked and we were in debt, and the credit cards that once were my friends had become my enemies. I dropped it all under my house, making several trips, and it felt good, as if I were removing mold and mildew from my mind.

I continued the activity of cleansing, not cleaning, and moved to the bathroom. There, in my makeup drawer, I found enough lipsticks to paint the lips of every woman in the world, and nail polish to coat all the walls of my house, and perfumes stinking back to my college years. I didn't need ten different bottles of shampoo in the shower, or fifty bath towels, all of which were dirty. It overwhelmed me to have to decide what to wash my hair with, and to fold all those towels . . . It all had to go, I decided, and by early evening I had carried outside years' worth of physical accumulation—dusty things I once thought made my life beautiful, when in reality they only entangled me into pretending I had it all when I didn't.

Around dusk, I felt unwell as I stood underneath my house on stilts, which no longer looked like a house on stilts but a department store. I feared I had gone too far, ridding myself of all these things. But when I walked back into the house, it was calm and uncluttered, as was my mind, and I heard that familiar something ringing out like a church bell in the distance. I stood still as a statue and listened, praying I might hear it more clearly, and then I did—that inner call to write serenading me more closely. I grabbed a pen and scribbled down a quick thought.

All this stuff was hindering my view of true beauty. It'll be easier now to see the daisies.

I went to the kitchen, opened the bottle of wine Gwendolyn had given me for my birthday and, without reading the label, I poured myself a glass. Then I went to my bedroom and turned on my laptop. As I waited for it to warm up, my habit of self-doubt crept like garden pests into my mind, gnawing at my self-confidence. I read what I had written so far and disliked it immensely. It was nothing the world would want to read, and I was disappointed with it and myself, for getting this old, for reaching this point in life and still not having a good piece of written art to show for it.

Granted, there were still a few days left, time to myself in which I might create something good—but with the return of my family and household responsibilities I knew my writing would only sink back down into the depths of the earth, buried beneath adulthood and all its layers of obligations.

Self-doubt and fear do bad things to a person—freeze them creatively and age them mentally—and my hands as they slapped down on the keyboard felt heavy. My fingers—no rings or polish, just knuckles knobby from bearing children three times—were like the bare branches of an old tree on a wintry day without snow. I knew that a writer who studies her hands like I was mine was a writer whose mind has gone blank, but as I looked out my window instead, I could see no flowers or fruits or birds sitting in the tree, nor good ideas perched on my mind.

I opened the book, *How to Grow Roses*, and flipped through its pages, looking at the blurbs that Fedelina's mother had written with ink in the margins and white space. I read a few:

> *How should you be talking to yourself when you're feel-ing down and out? The same as you would to a flower when wanting it to bloom.*
>
> *Self-doubts are like weeds, a constant part of life, but you must inhibit the weed seeds from germinating. I've learned to control them with the least amount of time and energy, but strong weeds, I've found, have a way of emerging through con-crete.*
>
> *When you try something over and over to the point of insanity and it still doesn't work, keep in mind that pinching off spent blossoms and leaves encourages other blossoms to open and makes their flowers last longer.*
>
> *When you know with certainty that your leaves are spent, let go and move on. It's okay.*
>
> *Any time you put effort into something the world declares a failure, it only makes the future things you do more prolifi-cally successful.*

Holding onto your disappointments will result in loss of energy. Holding onto spent blossoms takes from the flower the energy it needs to stay alive. Trimming these away helps the flower to channel its energy to healthy parts.

chapter twenty-nine

When I got done reading the blurbs of inspiration from Cora, my hands no longer looked to me like the barren branches of an old tree in winter. Rather, I saw them for what they were capable of producing, and my story for what it could become.

As I began to write—my mind coming to life with everything one imagines in a springtime tree—I knew that people garden for reasons similar to those for why they write; they enjoy the process, while hoping to produce something useful or beautiful. I wanted to create something beautiful. Like Cora, I would put forth time and effort, enjoying the activity, but expecting and believing that one day it might sprout forth every bit as beautifully as a rose.

I had caught hold of several good ideas, churning them into sentences that I liked, when all of a sudden there was knock at my door—and there was no person in the world I could like at the moment as much as my writing. I grabbed my glass of wine, taking it with me. A woman opening her door with a glass of wine in hand looks socially engaged, I told myself, in the midst of something important.

"Oh, hi," I said—spilling pinot noir on my toes—expecting to see Mrs. Aurelio, not her son, standing at my door.

"Sorry to bother," he said, eyeing the glass in my hand and the wine on my toes.

"It's no bother," I said, formally, too formally for having bumped boats and for talking as we had. "What brings you over?"

"My mother," he said.

"Your mother's a wonderful person."

"I guess she never mentioned how she used to chase after us with a frying pan."

"What?" I asked, and when he grinned I said, "I don't believe you."

"No one does, but it's true. The seven of us—we were a handful."

"The most I know of your mother is what I've seen through my windows, all that time she puts into her garden."

"Yeah, she's always had a real passion for it, but let me ask you a question," he said, lowering his voice. "She's getting older and having some issues. You don't think she's working too hard, do you?"

"Why do you ask?"

"She's not in the best of health."

"Oh?" I said, biting my lip. If only he knew of her collapse in the yard, and how I saved her.

"It's hard," he went on, "tough knowing she's here alone. It's why I've come to visit—to check up on her situation, see how she's doing, whether she's getting by on her own. My sisters put me up to it. They're trying to make arrangements for her."

"Arrangements," I said, making a face. "What sort of arrangements?"

"Move her back north, closer to them."

"You think that's a good idea?" I asked in a tone reflecting my neighbor's desires. "I see her out there all the time, and she looks fine to me, fully capable of living her own life. I should mind my own business, but I think it's vital to her health that a woman lives where she wants to live." I thought about what his mother had told me of orchids, that even *they* will wilt if they don't like their spot.

"Just covering my bases," he said, "making sure I'm not overlooking anything."

"Not to my knowledge," I said, telling a white lie and fearing it would turn into a big, bad lie if something worse happened to his mother. "Anything else I can do for you?"

"Actually yes," he said, looking back out over the porch railing. "You've got a lot of stuff outside. I thought maybe you might need help moving it back inside."

"That's not necessary," I told him, embarrassed he had seen the years' worth of accumulated junk associated with my life. "I'm having a yard sale on Saturday." I made a mental note then and there to call the paper in the morning and place an ad for my sale.

"If the raccoons don't throw a party before then," he said.

"They better not. I'm hoping to make a lot of money."

"You should," he said. "I stepped on a couple of ties on my way over here—good ones."

"Oops," I said, and it wasn't the most caring-sounding "oops" a wife should voice when her husband's seventy-five-dollar ties are lying in the dirt, getting stepped on. But that is what Fedelina's son, a glass of wine, and a productive writing session had done to me—turned me into a merry old soul, and a merry old soul was I. "There is one thing I need help with," I said.

"There is?"

"If you don't mind, I've got this love seat inside that I hate—the world's ugliest love seat. It's terrible-looking. I could use help getting it downstairs."

"Why don't you show me?" he said, and in my mind I said, "so long" to my mood for writing—there was always tomorrow. And so long to loneliness.

He followed me down the hall and into the great room. "Nice clock," he said when we passed the cuckoo that Timothy and I got as a wedding gift from his parents.

"You like it? It's yours for twenty bucks."

"No thank you. I don't really like clocks that tick constantly, reminders that I have to hurry—have to be somewhere. Your house smells good. Are you baking?"

"No, it's a sugar cookie candle."

"Oh."

I stopped in front of the love seat. "Here it is," I announced. "It's horrid, isn't it?"

"It's not bad."

"You're being kind. My husband insisted we buy it, and did I mention he's gone?"

"As a matter of fact, you did," he said. "Why don't you take that end and I'll take this end. Are you okay walking backward a moment, until we turn it?"

"Oh, fine," I said, putting my wineglass down, then arching my back for a quick stretch before grasping the love seat. "I'm sore from canoeing."

"That goes away the more you do it," he said. "If you want to feel sore, you should try rock climbing!"

"Do you do that?" I asked, "Rock climb?"

He laughed. "Not as much these days. I'm more of a hiker now. Last summer I trekked through the Amazon rainforest—a four-day guided tour starting in Lima."

"Did you go to Machu Picchu?"

"I sure did," he said. "It was amazing."

As we maneuvered the seat down the hall and through the front door, I no longer noticed the pain in my muscles but felt a tingling in my gut instead. Maybe my gut was tingling because my eyes were on him, and liking what they saw—his biceps were strong and his face was rugged, with the sun-carved lines of a man who likes to hike and I could picture him trekking through the Lost City of the Incas, climbing the Andes Mountains without a care in the world. His nose, cheeks and chin were chiseled handsomely, like a statue. At least that is how I saw him.

"Why don't we set it down a minute and rest before going down the stairs with it?" he suggested, and then asked, "Did you have a good birthday?"

"Yeah," I said.

His eyes stayed on mine. "Just yeah?" he asked.

"Yeah, it was fine," I told him, looking away. "Birthdays aren't a big deal anymore—not at my age. So it was fine—not great, nor grand, just fine."

He stared at me like he didn't believe me—like he knew that I was lying, but how could he know I was lying when he hardly knew me at all? "Can I ask you a personal question?" he said then.

"It depends," I said. "What kind of question?"

"What were you wishing for?"

"What do you mean?"

"When you blew out your candles."

"I'd love to tell you," I told him, flattered that he wanted to know. It was something Timothy would never bother to ask, nor care to know. "But wishes don't come true when you tell them."

"It's just interesting, that's all."

"What?"

"Oh, nothing," he said.

"Tell me," I said, my eyes urging him on.

"Pick up your end," he said, "and maybe I'll tell you."

As we slowly carried the love seat down my stairs, I thought about how easy he was to talk to. It was as if he was hearing every word I had to say. Timothy never listened to all my words. At best, he heard every other word, or more accurately, every other sentence, and even then he never made me feel as if anything I had to say was important anymore.

"You had this look to your face," Liam then said. "When your eyes were closed—when you were wishing."

"I did? I'm so embarrassed."

"It was sweet."

"It was?"

"Like you really wanted to believe in something," he said as we reached the bottom. "I'm only telling you the truth." We dragged the love seat under my house. I didn't want to tell him he had been wrong, that what my face showed on my birthday was more the look of a woman *not* getting the things she had wished for.

Suddenly there was a silence between us, and I was glad for the sounds of the island critters croaking, for it gave us something to laugh about, but then we stopped laughing and stared awkwardly at each other until I asked, "Would you like to sit down a minute?"

"On the world's ugliest love seat?" he said. Then, with a shrug of his shoulders, he decided, "Sure, maybe for a minute. If I nudge this thing over a foot we won't be sitting under your house."

"That's right," I said, knowing that then we'd be sitting under the stars. When I sat down beside him, I didn't mean for the side of my leg to be touching his as it was, but those things happen when two people sit together on a love seat. I think it's what the furniture designers had in mind when they named it a love seat in the first place. I tried nudging my thigh over an inch, but Florida's nights are humid and I felt stuck to him. "You know," I said then, "I'll never tell anyone what I was wishing for."

"I don't blame you," he said, raising his eyebrow at me. "I normally wouldn't have asked, but I was thinking how you asked me on the water yesterday whether I ever lived on the East Coast, that maybe we knew each other from somewhere. I don't think we do, but I have to say, I feel it, too. I feel like we do. I guess that's why I find it easy to talk with you. I just hope I haven't talked too much."

"Not at all," I told him, and it was then that our eyes met and I could hardly look away. But I did, and happened to spot a brown glass bottle, round and squat, sticking out of a box of glassware. "Would you like a drink?" I asked him and all I could think was, my, what a bad girl am I!

"What do you have in mind?" he said.

"Grand Marnier," I told him, getting up and pulling it from the debris. "It's all I have. It was a gift."

"It serves its occasions—Grand Marnier. What's it doing outside?"

"It's sweet for me. I was going to sell it."

"I don't think you can sell that at a yard sale, darling. You need a liquor license."

"Then maybe we should open it now and enjoy it. Would you like some? Otherwise I'll probably dump it."

"All right," he said. "I'll have a little. I'd hate to see you pour it out your window. It would kill my mother's flowers."

I handed him the bottle and, as he tore its foil off, I rummaged through a box, pulling out two glasses and using the bottom of my blouse to rub them clean. As I held them out for him to fill, I thought quickly of the next morning and whether I might come to my senses, regretting what I was doing—talking the way I was, and having a drink with another man. As I swirled the liqueur in my glass, my thoughts were swirling, too, and I didn't know which I dreaded more—the morrow and my own disappointment with myself, or the day my daughter might discover my mistakes and throw stones at me as daughters do when they learn, not from their mother's words, but by seeing all the flaws in their mother's life.

The first sip made my eyes tear, but the second sip went down smoothly. By my third sip I was drinking, not the way a mother is supposed to drink, but like a woman who has had a bad year. I was hoping the cognac with tropical orange might put things into perspective for me, like why being with this man made me feel the way I did—as if I were riding through the air on a very fine gander.

"Do you have a coaster or something I could set my glass on?" he asked.

"Don't worry," I said. "You can rest your feet on this old table if you like. It's a replica of a much bigger one my husband and I saw a long time ago, on a trip to California, while touring Hearst Castle, but I don't care the least bit about it." I wondered instantly whether it showed that I no longer cared the least bit about him, either—my husband.

"If you say so, but I wouldn't set my glass down if it was still in your house and you cared about it. I hope you mean what you say."

"Oh, I do. I don't care about any of this stuff anymore. In fact, this cleansing frenzy of mine was the result of an epiphany I had," I told him, my eyes tearing from the liqueur. "If I rid myself of excess, I may start seeing real beauty again, and start fresh." I didn't tell him it was his mother, his grandmother, and the daisies that sparked me.

"I wish my ex-wife had you as a friend," he said with a grin. "She could have learned a thing or two. I probably shouldn't say this. I don't want to bore you, but I was married to a woman who could talk for hours about designer comforters and decorative pillows. She kept at least twenty of them on our bed, and each night she had me remove them—carefully set them on the trunk at the foot of our bed. And if one slipped, and she found it on the floor, look out! Going to bed should be the most relaxing part of one's day. For me, it was the most stressful. It sounds funny now, but at the time, when I was going through it, I was a tiger in a cage."

"You really were mismatched."

"My ex could shop daily. It's all she wanted to do, and we were complete opposites like that. All she thought about was the clothes she could buy. Call me an extremist, but all I kept thinking was how much easier life would be if we didn't have our bodies, if there wasn't the whole physical realm, so then we could focus instead on our souls and who we are on that level. Some people have different notions of what insanity is. Little decorative pillows are mine. But enough about me— I have no desire to talk of her, and I hardly think of her anymore." He looked at me oddly. "So what about you?"

"I don't know. What about me?"

"You're a deep thinker. I can tell."

"It's a curse, don't you think—being a deep thinker?"

He smiled and nodded. "How are your ideas coming for your story?"

I laughed. I laughed and laughed and couldn't stop.

"What's so funny?"

"I don't know. I have no idea why I'm laughing."

"Must be your story. What are you currently writing?"

"A scene about this woman," I said. "I'm always writing about this woman—an overwhelmed woman."

"Why is she overwhelmed?"

"She has three kids and a messy house."

"Sounds interesting—strangely original, sounds like a real *New York Times* bestseller, Anna. Thinking about making a movie out of it?"

I shook my head, thinking to myself how ridiculous my own story sounded. "I'm not that far along. It's just a novel in my drawer, like every other person has. Only I care about it, I really do."

"Let's toast," he said. "We've already started to drink, but let's toast to the novel in your drawer, the one you care about, and to the overwhelmed woman." We touched glasses and I downed the rest of my drink.

"So how do you like the Grand Marnier?" I asked as I set my empty glass down on the ground.

"It's good."

"Would you like a little more?"

"In a minute," he said, and then poured *me* more.

I felt self-conscious for having drunk mine first, so this time I sipped more slowly, feeling the drink settling in my toes.

"I hope you don't mind my asking—tell me if you do," he stated in a serious tone, "but you mentioned in the canoe the other day that you are going to leave your husband. Is that something you really plan to do?"

I felt myself sober immediately. "I don't know," I told him honestly. And then I told him more, all about my freshman year of college—how my mother had died and I escaped into the pages of books—and, until I met Timothy, how lonely I was. And even after we married, the comfort I found moving from state to state, knowing no one, but finding refuge in editing, or jobs at libraries, and eventually the publishing house—anything related to books, for books and the characters living within them had become my closest friends.

"But are you planning to leave him?" he asked again, firmly, but with a respectful look on his face so that I didn't mind his asking.

"I don't know," I said again. "I'm a mother. And as a mother, a part of me is deprived. Going back to what you asked me before, what I wished for, well, I don't know if this is going to make sense to you or not, and stop me if it doesn't," I said as I looked up at the dark sky. "But I remember how it felt when I was young, when there were as many options for me to choose from as there are stars up in the sky tonight— infinite choices—with countless possibilities. And even after I married," I went on, looking at him now, "I still believed I could become who- ever it was in life I wanted to become. But then I became a mother— once, twice, three times—and don't get me wrong, I discovered for the first time in my life things like abundant joy and unconditional love, but when I looked up at the sky one night, I no longer saw any stars with my name on them. I don't wish all that many things in my life anymore, and most of the ones I do wish for are no longer about me."

"They're about your children, now," he said.

"Yes. And it's daunting sometimes, that my life and love belong first to my kids, and that at this stage in the game, the ages that they are, every waking hour, thought and action goes to them. But they're the brightest stars I see up there now, the reasons I look up when everything feels down. They're the only brilliancy I see to life lately, but gosh, I don't mean to sound poetic. I'm horrible at poetry."

As I held out my glass for him to pour more, I wanted to go on and on, tell him everything about me—a woman trying to reunite with her true self, a woman who for so long has been covered partially by clouds, like the moon that Liam, with his head resting on the love seat, was staring up at.

"Expert, oh, expert, oh, what would you say?" I wondered in my mind until I knew what they'd say, "I'd tell you it's a rebound and run far away!"

But I could care less what any experts had to say, and I knew there were no words in the English language to describe it, to truly articu- late how Liam made me feel. When looking at him, I knew who I was, could see my core, and liked it. And I felt like I knew him, too, and what I didn't know, I wanted to know. Ours was the sort of thing that only comes around once in a lifetime, and no one or nothing could do anything to deny it.

chapter thirty

BELVEDERE

I can't believe what I'm hearing," Fedelina said, interrupting my reading.

"To this day, I can't believe it either," I told her. "I cringe as I read it. But I did the right thing, getting rid of all that junk of mine, don't you think?"

"Oh yes, it's meaningless," she said. "I see clearly now how meaningless all the belongings in our lives are. When they moved me into this place, I had to decide what to take. The rest I gave to my children and told them to pick through, get rid of whatever they didn't want. I felt like I had already passed, deciding who got what, boxing things up, storing it all. My first week here, I questioned why I had put the music box Oscar got me when we were newly married, or the glass platter belonging to my grandmother, into storage boxes. What was I storing for? That's when it hit me, that we store and collect, and all of a sudden the process reverses and we have to start shedding it all." Her eyes were starting to close.

"Are you tired?"

"Yes," she said. "But I'm waiting. Do I dare ask what happened next—between my son and you?"

I continued to read from where I had left off.

chapter thirty-one

So tell me," I said to the man sitting next to me. "Do you ever get lonely?"

"I'm not the type to get lonely," Liam told me then. "I enjoy my own company. I'm content."

"You're one of those," I said.

"What?" he asked.

"A lone soul."

"I'm no monk, don't get me wrong."

"No, I can't see you as a monk," I said, imagining women from around the world, including his own students, falling for him as I was. Asking him a question after class, but, because he was easy to talk to, pouring out their innermost thoughts on life instead. "A good-looking professor like yourself, do you date your students?"

"I try to keep the scandals down at the university."

"Oh, come on," I said.

"I dated a student once. We didn't go out until after the semester ended, and she was fifteen years older than me."

I did the calculations in my mind. "Do you like older women?"

"It's not about age," he said. "I like women who are wise, not ignorant, nor innocent, but who have experience in life and have walked away
from their experiences a better person, if you know what I mean. I'd do
well," he went on, "with a woman who lives more contemplatively, on a
deeper level, but for now, I'm not looking."

"You're not?"

"No. I don't think I would make a good husband. I'm not saying I
was rotten or unfaithful when I was married. I wasn't. But I'm too much
of a free spirit to belong to another person, to be another person's abso-
lute everything. And I learned too late the kind of woman I like, one
who isn't afraid to let her toes touch the ground, to get her feet dirty.
But enough about me," he said. "I've told you more than you wanted to
know."

"I wasn't thinking that at all," I said.

"Then what were you thinking?"

"Oh," I said with a shameful smile, "I'm just curious, that's all."

"Curious about what?"

"Things I shouldn't be curious about. I have no right."

"If you really want to know," he said. "If you're going to keep asking, then let's see, there's a professor in the art department, and another
who runs the overseas program and another in the academics department, who I sort of see when I'm in a midlife mood and need career
counseling. But, mostly, I'm focusing on other things at this point in my
life, and they know that. I've told them, so enough about me."

"We haven't talked that much about you," I told him.

"We have!" he insisted, "and I'm boring myself."

"What would you rather talk about?"

"I don't know. How about we count shooting stars?"

"I don't feel like counting shooting stars."

"Then we can look for UFOs."

"I don't believe in UFOs," I told him.

"Then let's talk about you. I want to know more about you."

"You keep saying that, but I don't know," I said, wanting to tell him more about myself, who I was, my variety, and all my particulars. But I wasn't an orchid and it wasn't that simple. "What do you want to know about me?"

"What makes you tick?"

I looked at my feet, which were filthy from having gone barefoot all day, and then I laughed good and hard, deciding that a woman drinking with a man beneath the stars is able to answer whatever questions she wants about herself. "I'd like to focus more deeply on things that matter, but there are countless things demanding my attention and my energy daily—namely housework. It never gets done and, even after I spend a good four hours at it, five minutes after my children wake it's an embarrassing mess again. There's nothing I'd love more than to sit and read to them, or sing songs, or hold them in my arms all day long, but they have so many needs, crises and emergencies that, one-by-one, make up my day."

"So the overwhelmed woman you're writing about—is it you?"

I took a big breath in, let it all out, and tried shifting gears. "So what's your mother doing tonight?" I asked.

"She went to bed," he said.

I looked at my wrist and remembered I had decided to sell my old watch, and that it was ticking away somewhere in the piles of stuff. "It's early," I said.

"She's in bed by dusk. And coffee's ready by four."

"Oh," I said, but suddenly, all I could think about was my children and what they were doing tonight. "It's a good thing," I told him then, "how all of a sudden a mother cares more about the choices her children will make in their lives than the ones she made in hers, and that if her own life doesn't measure up to her expectations—the dreams she set for herself—then it's okay as long as her children's lives are good. But listen to me rambling. Why are you so easy to talk to? Do all your lady friends talk to you like this?"

"No," he said, "They don't, and I don't think for an instant that it's easy juggling what you do."

"Well," I said then. "I know they'll grow up and go off, and when they do, I want at that stage in my life to be more than a woman going for weekly pedicures—not that there's anything wrong with pedicures. I do like them, but I also want to be doing more, if you know what I mean. What exactly do I want, and who do I want to become? I don't know," I told him. By now the liquor in our glasses was gone. I could have gone on like we were, sitting close, as two people are forced to sit when sharing a love seat, but it was getting late and nothing good comes from a woman telling a man everything there is to know about her in a single night, and so we said good night.

chapter thirty-two

BELVEDERE

When I stopped reading and looked up from the manuscript, I was ready to hear feedback from Fedelina, find out whether she liked the story I was reading and if she minded all the parts about her son.

"I'm still in shock over the two of you," was all she said. "I'd like to hear more, but I'm tired."

"I read too much," I told her, "too much for one day. I'll be back in the morning."

The next morning I knocked lightly on her door and went in. She was done eating her breakfast but, by the look and smell of the unidentifiable mush left on her plate, she couldn't have enjoyed it. I waited for the girl to take it away and then handed her the fudge I had bought on the side of the road.

"It's sugar-free," I told her.

"Put it over there, on the counter, would you?"

"You don't want some now?" I asked.

"It's too early for fudge," she said. "I usually wait until one-thirty for things like that. When you get to be my age, routines are everything, they keep you going—give you something to look forward to. By the way—I'm looking forward to hearing more of your story."

"You are?" I asked as I sank into the armchair beside her bed.

"Waking up this morning wasn't so hard. It's your reading," she said. "It's given me something to look forward to. But tell me, after that night on the love seat, did anything else happen between you two?"

# chapter thirty-three

I stayed awake all night, regretting my intimate talk with another man. I was aware that it's a woman's right to live and love, but those rights are altered when she must first consider the best interest of her children. And I felt their fingers at all hours, tugging at my heart, and their voices reached my soul and their curiosities raced through my mind. They never asked the simple stuff. It was always complex, like, "Mommy, why did my balloon pop, and goldfish die and Daddy leave on a trip again? And why aren't bald eagles bald, and why don't hummingbirds hum? And why do the ospreys return to the same nest year after year, and when will Daddy return?"

I got up from bed, turned my computer on, and spent the rest of the night and into the wee hours of the morning researching the answers to everything my children might want to know. By the time I turned it off again and slipped back into bed, I felt like I knew it all, why the big, yellow, fuzzy bees don't sting and the other ones do. I had learned how to cut the top off of a pineapple, so when my children came home we could plant it in the dirt and grow our own. I had spent hours looking up the answers to things they've already asked, and those they might yet ask, and I found there are answers to everything, except "Why are their starving children in the world when you can toss a seed into the dirt and produce a fruit-bearing plant?" I would look further into that when I wasn't so tired, I decided as I turned out my light and pulled the blanket up to my chin.

I hardly felt like I had slept when there was a knock at my door. I could see through the peephole that it was Fedelina, and I feared she had come to tell me that a married woman has no right entertaining her son, like I did in my yard until way past midnight.

"Hi," I declared when I opened the door.

"Are you sick?" she asked.

"Why? Do I look sick?"

"Tired. You look tired."

"Missing my children is all," I said. "I was up all night. It's been too long. I'm ready for them to come home. An afternoon would have been fine, a couple of hours to myself—a day at most—but it's getting long, them being away like this."

"Are you bored?"

"A little," I told her. "I don't want to waste my precious time, but on the other hand, I don't know what to do with it, either. So what brings you over?"

"I know it's early, but I noticed your lights on."

"I was looking up a few things online."

"Well, mind if I tinkle in your abode?"

"What's wrong with your abode?"

"A frog, can you believe it?"

"A sticky frog?" I asked.

"I don't know what kind of frog it was. It scared the 'you know what' out of me."

"What about your son? Can't you ask him to get rid of it?"

"He's still sleeping, which is odd for him. He's usually an early riser."

"Oh?"

"He was out late. I don't know where. I don't ask, but I heard him come in."

"Well, the green sticky frogs are kind of cute, don't you think?" I asked, feeling nervous. "They've got those big eyes."

"Obviously, you never put your foot into a shoe with a frog in it, because if you had, you wouldn't care whether it was cute or not."

"I guess you're right, but my kids love them. We have them sticking outside our windows every night."

I showed her to my bathroom, and when I turned the light on she looked me in the eyes and said, "You have a pleasant way about you."

"Thank you," I said, and went to brew coffee.

When she came out, I handed her a cup and we talked. We talked about small stuff. It wasn't until she was headed toward my door that I asked her the big stuff, whether it's wise for mothers to sacrifice their own interests and desires for those of their children when one day their children are only going to leave and start lives of their own.

"If you really want to know what I think," she said as she started down my steps, "I think a person would do well to immerse themselves in five things in life."

"Why five?"

She stopped midway and looked back up at me. "I don't know, maybe I was standing in a patch of primroses the day I thought of it and primroses have five petals," she said. "But it makes sense, doesn't it?"

"I'd have to think about it," I told her. "Does it work for you?"

"Oh yes, I've always found that when I try mastering more than five things, I start to feel overwhelmed, and when I have less than five priorities on my plate, I feel lonely, bored and lazy," she said with a laugh. By now she had reached the bottom steps but was still holding onto the railing.

"I don't know what a primrose looks like," I confessed from my porch.

"Not just primroses, but buttercups, geraniums, pansies," she said. "They all have five petals. Most flowers do, in fact, what flower do you see right over there?" She let go of the railing and took a couple of steps, then put her butt up in the air and pointed to a cluster of bluish-lavender flowers with trailing stems and evergreen leaves that, vinelike, were creeping along, covering the shady, grassless side of my yard.

I came halfway down my steps to better see. "I don't know," I said. "You're talking to a woman who hardly knows a daffodil from a tulip."

"*Vinca minor*," she said, standing upright again. "They're periwinkles, and they have five petals." She gave me a wave and left for her own yard.

The rest of my misty, moisty morning and cloudy afternoon were spent catching up on sleep. When I woke, I put on a pair of white shorts and a short-sleeved yellow cotton blouse, cleaned the cobwebs off my rusty bike, and set off riding to wherever my thoughts took me.

As I turned onto Casa Ybel Road, periwinkles were covering the ground and got me to thinking in terms of five. I could see clearly how I had fallen into the habit of taking on too many petals up north—volunteering for innumerable causes, serving on this and that board at work and for daycare, heading up two, three, sometimes four committees at a time, never saying "no" and spitting out "yes" like balls out of an automatic pitching machine, offering to bake and bring homemade goodies to every event, staying up until the wee hours, contributing toward endless baby and wedding showers, spending a fortune on gift exchanges at work while bouncing checks at home, claiming for myself all the major titles to promote at work, and with them, all the pressure. Nothing I had been doing was of quality anymore, and I no longer walked, talked or worked with joy.

"No wonder I am what I am," I thought to myself as I rode along Middle Gulf Drive—a woman alone and loving it, pedaling her way across a barrier island in the Gulf of Mexico, with no friends except for Fedelina Aurelio and her son, no work and, sadly, no family for at least a week. "Too many petals and the flower wilts," I realized.

My habit of saying the word "yes" one too many times had worn me thin. My bike tires were thin, too, and needed air, but I wasn't going to worry about that, I told myself as I stayed on the far right side of the trail, letting others pass me by. *I'll start doing that in life, too,* I thought. *Let things pass me by. Let go and let others handle them.* I was in the mood to think, conjure in my mind five things worthy of my attention, but life doesn't always go the way we want and my bike tire went flat. Veering off the trail, I hopped off and leaned the bike against a tree. When I could hardly think of what to do next, I pulled the book, *How to Grow Roses,* from the basket of my bike and, standing under a shady tree, I flipped through its pages, reading notes here and there that Cora had long ago scribbled in the white spaces.

> *Every morning I watch the lilies grow and wonder, what am I doing to grow my own self?*
>
> *There is no such thing as a wasted moment. Every moment of our lives holds significance. Even those we wish we could erase, the moments that made us cry, the ones in which we felt bored, or depressed, or angry. They all mean something, but only if we seek to find meaning in them. Search to discover meaning. Only then will you have no regrets.*
>
> *Don't wait for a man to bring you flowers. Grow your own garden! Flowers don't have to be some untouchable luxury item that you get only once a year, on a birthday or anniversary. You should be out planting your own, surrounding yourself, creating for yourself a world of flowers. Especially when life is dull and its vibrancy fades, it is then you must go out and find your own fragrance. This is not as selfish as it sounds, for a single rose can be appreciated not only by yourself, but by every pair of eyes that glances its way and every nose that stops to smell it.*
>
> *Don't wait for any rose sale. A good rose is worth the price asked for it. But it's better to buy yourself a cheap rose, than no rose at all.*

I closed the book, left my bike against the tree, and started walking in search of a florist. Because I had never gone to a local florist before, never bought roses for myself, I had to ask three different people walking by to lead me in the right direction.

It wasn't that I needed roses—the roses from my neighbor were still fresh and in jars on my desk—but Cora's words compelled me for the first time in my life to buy them for myself! As I walked in the direction of the florist, I could see glimpses of the Gulf of Mexico, and in my mind, glimpses of the woman I wanted to become—a woman who does nice things for herself, and who sets aside a piece of time each day for her own care and well-being.

But as I turned onto Tarpon Bay Road, I could think of nothing more than the excruciating blister forming on my toe. I pulled my flip-flop off, carrying it in my hand and walking with a limp. And then I saw an old red-and-white convertible with silver trim pulled to the side up ahead, and there was a man in the middle of the road, bending over, lifting a turtle by its shell. I stopped in my tracks and felt my throat tighten as I watched him carry it off the road and put it near the shrubs.

"I think they call this serendipity," I said, walking up to him. It was Liam.

"You mean the turtle and me here at the same time together?"

"No," I said, and laughed, "You and me."

"I hope you're not getting sick of me," he murmured.

"No," I told him, and then, as the turtle turned around and headed back for the road again—the direction Liam stopped him from going—I said, "I think you ruined his plan."

"He's a determined fellow—probably late for a date," he told me.

Because I had a curiosity about Liam that wouldn't subside, I could have stood there all day watching him carry the turtle across the road to the other side, and I wondered whether I might incorporate this into my story—the gentlest of things I have watched a man do.

"Question for you—two questions," he said when he came back over to my side of the road. "If you don't mind my asking, why are you holding a flip-flop, and how far are you planning to walk with that limp?"

I told him about my tire going flat and my blister, and about reading the letters his mother lent me—the ones his grandmother wrote—
and how they inspired me to head to the nearest florist to buy myself
flowers.

"I take it your husband doesn't buy you any," he said.

"He used to," I told him, "but not anymore." And suddenly I felt I
had told him too much, had one too many times gone further than I
should in disclosing the not-so-good details of my marriage. "I'm sorry
about the other night," I said, and he looked at me like he didn't know
what I was referring to. "Drinking as I did, and the way I rambled."
His eyes were telling me I didn't need to feel self-conscious, that he had
enjoyed talking with me as much as I did with him.

"You didn't ramble," he said.

"Thank you, but I feel like I did. And about things I'm sure no man
wants to hear—the domestic woes of a woman."

"I didn't mind."

"You're being kind," I said. "I didn't even ask you what I really wanted
to know, what I wondered about after you left."

"And what was that?" he asked.

"Your upcoming sabbatical—what will you be researching, what sort
of a book are you planning to write?" We moved a few feet over so we
were no longer standing with the hot sun hitting our faces, and as we
stood shaded beneath the awning of a sea grape tree, he told me how
he was mostly interested in sacred places, and how every culture and
time period throughout history has these beautiful sites, which are often
marked with trees or stones or mountains or water, and that he wanted
to visit several of them—from the Holy Sepulchre in Israel to Teotihua-
can in Mexico—and research the artistic composition of them, of these
objects of nature, as well as how they became sacred or holy.

"That all sounds fascinating to me," I told him. "You're talking to a
person who has lived in every region of this country, but has never left
the country, never gone to Europe, or anywhere else, only seen those
places in books. What on earth inspired you?" I asked. "I don't mean,

why did you become an art history professor, but what made you want to research sacred places?"

"It's been brewing in me for awhile. Back when I graduated from college with a major in art history, it's what I knew I wanted to do. But before going on for my master's, I wanted to see Renaissance art with my own eyes, walk into the very convent where Leonardo painted his *Last Supper*. And so I went to Europe with nothing but a backpack and a great pair of shoes on my feet. I took trains from country to country—focused on nothing but good coffee in the morning, art during the day, and red wine at night. It was an unbelievable experience to be so carefree. My whole trip was about beauty—mankind's attempt throughout history to create beauty through art.

But then, one late afternoon I'll never forget, I was in Rome and, with a guidebook in hand, I stepped inside the greatest work of Roman architecture and engineering—the Coliseum. I stood there reading its history, feeling the magnitude of the mammoth structure, knowing that at one time there could be some 50,000 spectators in those seats looking down at where I was standing. And the thought of it—of the gladiatorial contests and the animal hunts, all those deaths in a single day—Anna, I can't tell you how small I felt. It was the smallest I had ever felt in all my life. I hope this doesn't sound strange, but I actually saw my size in relation to history—and to all of time—and suddenly, my life felt frighteningly short to me. It was then I knew I wanted to make the most of it, and to study things not only beautiful, but sacred, too."

We stood there under the sea grape tree, talking long enough for another turtle to cross the road, and for Liam to tell me how, in 1749, Pope Benedict XIV endorsed the view that the Coliseum was a sacred site where early Christians had been martyred. I wanted to ask him whether the ground around us might be sacred, too, because standing there listening to him talk of all these ancient places around the world— and the look on his face, of a man pursuing his passion—was putting goose bumps on my arms, and making me feel like I was on sacred ground. Just as I thought that, I felt hot sparks of pain dart across my foot and, when I looked down, I saw I had planted my foot on a fire ant nest and that they were swarming my toes, feet and ankles. Their bites, like miniature fireworks going off on my skin, sent me hopping on one foot like an egret. Liam reached into his car for a bottle of water and poured it on my foot, but the ants were still having their way with me. So he got down on his knees and used his hands like a broom, sweeping the devilish orange-brown specks off my skin, and when we could see no more he let out a laugh.

"What?" I asked him when I had stopped hopping.

"Nothing."

"No," I insisted. "What's so funny?"

"There's absolutely nothing funny about this," he said, "but I've never seen a woman doing one of those Indian rain dances."

"Just don't use it in one of your history lectures—don't tell your students about this, the dance of the fire ants," I said.

"I won't, but I guess you have the title of your novel now."

"The dance of the fire ants? I don't think so. Keep to lecturing and not coming up with novel titles. I had better get going. I really want to continue my walk."

"Are you sure you're okay?"

"Fine," I insisted, though I wanted to tell him that a few ant bites were nothing in comparison to the aggravations I had experienced over the last several months.

"You're a long ways from home," he said. "How about I give you a ride?"

I hesitated, thinking about the blister on my toe, the flat tire on my bike, and how my feet were stinging from the fire ant bites, and then about all the weedy events in my life that had entangled me for months, yanking me to my knees. And I knew that only more trouble comes when a married woman accepts a ride from a single man she is attracted to.

"No thanks," I told him. "I think I'll go sit on the beach and put my feet in the water."

He glanced up at the sky and then back at me. "I don't want to ruin your plans, but those are some pretty dark clouds. Are you sure you don't want me to take you home?"

"You've already helped so much."

"How?" he asked.

I wanted to tell him that when a man makes a woman's heart move like the waves of the sea after a long time of stagnancy, he has done her a service, letting her know her romantic organs are still there, affected by the tides of love and life. "You helped me move my love seat, remember?" I told him.

"I don't mind giving you a ride as well. I don't mind helping you twice."

"No," I reiterated strongly. "I need a good walk. It's good for the mind."

"All right," he said, "but those bites are only going to keep on stinging."

"That's okay. I'm not going to let a few prickling stings ruin my walk," I told him.

"If I were you, I'd ice my foot when I got home. And keep an eye on it. Make sure you're not allergic to them."

"No, I don't think I am."

He got into his mother's 1957 Chevrolet Bel Air convertible, and I started on my way, one foot burning from the blister and the other stinging from the bites, wondering how this all began—our friendship and the way we talked and felt. I knew, as much as I did that the sky was blue and the grass green, that he felt it, too, and when I heard him start the engine I turned and cast a friendly wave. And, because he gave me the sweetest smile I've ever seen on a man's face before, I reciprocated with a wink.

"Oh fudge," I muttered. I didn't mean to wink. I remembered something I once heard, that if one part of the body sins, one should cut it off. I could never cut my eyelid off, nor take back my wink, so I kept on walking, trying hard not to limp. *Move, move, move your feet, gently down the path*, I sang to myself, knowing the car he was driving was about to pass me by, *wearily, wearily, wearily, wearily, life is not a dream.*

"I offered you a ride because I thought it was the gentlemanly thing to do," he said as his car rolled slowly alongside me, "but after watching that limp of yours, I *know* you need a ride. It would be negligent of me to pass you by."

I cringed. "I look that bad?"

"Damsel in distress," he said, nodding.

"Thanks for the compliment," I told him. "I feel more like roadkill mess."

I intended at that point to step into the road, open the door of the car and get in, but before I could do any of that he had already gotten out, run over to my side of the car and picked me up.

"Put me down," I insisted, embarrassed. "I'm not a turtle!"

"No, you're all woman and, once in a while, every woman needs a little help."

"Yeah, but picking me up like this . . ." I said, laughing in his arms, wondering whether I was breaking his back. "It's over and beyond the call of duty for a gentleman."

"Only when the moment calls for it," he said as he gently set me down on the passenger side of his mother's red convertible. I felt as if I were a movie star, fanning my face and rolling my eyes like I couldn't believe what he had just done, nor how my heart was spinning in front flips for this man as he walked around to his side of the car and got in. When he took hold of the silver steering wheel, I sat up straight and took hold of my emotions. "I see you've got your mother's car today," I said.

"I took it into the shop this morning, got it checked and got an oil change," he said. "Now, where's that bike of yours?"

I told him where I had left it, and he pulled into a small beach parking lot to turn around and head us in the direction of my flat tire. We were quiet for a moment, neither of us saying anything. I tried to think of something to say, but at the same time, I felt comfortable saying nothing. And then he turned on the radio and surprised me again.

"Somewhere beyond the sea," he sang along to an oldies' song, "she's there watchin' for me." He sang like he couldn't care less whether his voice was good or not, like he was just having fun, and I felt like a sixteen-year-old girl on her first date, wondering whether or not to sing along as well. "If I could fly like birds on high, then straight to her arms I'd go sailin'," I sang, too, smiling all the while.

"Is this the kind of music you like?" I asked when I started to feel self-conscious and needed an excuse to stop singing.

"Bobby Darin—'Beyond the Sea'—my folks used to play it," he said, staring straight ahead at the road. "But this is my mother's station, and when I drive her car I don't mess with her stations. I'm surprised, however, at how loud she has it blaring when I turn on the car. Maybe it's her hearing. I don't know."

"This car is great!" I said.

"She's owned it forever, at least twenty years," he said. "I suggested she try an SUV, something bigger, safer, but she refused, said she's keeping this the rest of her driving life."

"If I had a car like this, I'd never get rid of it either," I said, putting my nose up in the air like a dog. "Now I see what convertibles are all about. I had always wondered."

"You've got to be kidding me," he said, looking at me as the car rolled to a stop at a stop sign. "This is your first time in a convertible?"

I looked him in the eyes and wanted to tell him it was my first time for a lot of things: for driving anywhere with a man other than my husband, and for singing loudly in front of another person, and for feeling as happy as I had been feeling every time we were together. "I've always wanted to ride in one, but never knew anyone who owned one."

"Well, now you do," he said, "and I'm sure my mother would love to take you for rides any time you show the least bit of interest. She sits on a pillow, you know, to see over the dashboard."

"Does she?"

"Yeah. She'll do anything to keep this car."

"Good for her. When I'm her age, I hope I drive a convertible, too,"

I said, resting my head on the seat, closing my eyes and, to my surprise, singing out loud the rest of the song without a care in the world. "Happy we'll be beyond the sea. And never again I'll go sailin.'"

"So how long do you plan to be around for?" I asked when the song ended and I opened my eyes.

"Long enough to finish the stairs," he said, "and build my mother a ramp."

"A ramp?"

"She's going to need one—so she can wheel her groceries up — but I don't know for sure whether I'll be able to start that this time around. It all depends how long the stairs take. Of course, I could spend all the time in the world fixing her stairs, building her a ramp, but I think the biggest threat to her comes every time she puts her key in the ignition of this car and drives!"

I liked talking about his mother. It was a safe, neutral conversation. The more we talked about her, the less guilty I felt for being with him, and the less I said about myself or asked further about him. He sounded comfortable, too, and I think it was because, like me, he felt guilty talking the way we had about ourselves and to each other.

"You haven't noticed anything strange, have you?" he asked.

"No. Like what?"

"I rode with her to the store the other day, and her stops and starts were jerky, her left turns borderline reckless."

"Did you say anything?"

"I did, but she took it as criticism. I'll wait awhile and bring it up indirectly," he said, and then we spotted my bike against a tree. After pulling to the side, I watched him pick it up carefully as he had both the turtle and me, only the bike was heavier—at least heavier than the turtle—and required more muscle, which he had. I noticed his arms, and they were nice. They were like my husband's used to be when we were in college and he still worked out. As he put my bike in the back of his mother's car, I could hardly take my eyes off his biceps, which were very nice.

"I feel bad. I'm probably disrupting your entire day," I told him when he got back in.

"Not really. I was thinking of checking out the Red Mangrove Overlook. Have you been there?"

"No," I said, "never heard of it."

He cast me a glance, the kind that questions how a person can be living on the island and not be familiar with whatever overlook it was. I gave him a smile back that says, "don't mess with me," I'm a woman with three kids who hardly knows a shark from a dolphin, an osprey from an eagle, a roseate spoonbill from a flamingo, but I know everything there is to know about my three children, from their heads to their toes, and I know all there is about love, the unconditional kind that only a mother has.

"It's over at the wildlife refuge. It's a viewing spot along the drive. I've been meaning to make it over there but never have. I hear you can park your car and get out, walk into a mangrove forest and stand out on a platform. From what I hear there's an incredible view of the tidal feeding flats. Would you like to come with?"

Oh, what is a woman to do? What is a woman to do? She pitters she patters, she does all that matters, oh, what is a woman to do?

"It's up to you," he added. "I could drop you off at your house and then go. It's no big deal either way."

"I don't know," I said. "Are you in the mood for company?"

"I could use some company. Too much time alone is no longer a good thing after awhile."

"You mean that?"

"I wouldn't say it if I didn't mean it."

"Okay, then, I'll go," I said, biting my lips. "I would love to go."

chapter thirty-four

As he turned in the direction of the refuge, all I could think was, *Poor Timothy, if he could see me now, his wife in a car with another man.* The thought made me quiet with fear, as did the possibility of my feelings for Liam progressing, and how it might look like either revenge or "rebound," as I've heard people call it when a relationship turns foul and the wounded instantly flocks to another. But I would know the truth. I would be the only one in the world to know the truth, that what I had for this man beside me in the car was a subtle inner sense, one I didn't fully understand, but that drew me to him, as mysteriously to me as how billions of birds each year arrive where they need to be, tuning into low-frequency sound waves, or barometric pressure, to help them along.

"Mind if I make a quick stop?" he asked, pulling into a sandy, bumpy parking lot.

"Of course not," I said. When I saw the sign for a florist, I looked at him curiously.

"What did you want, a dozen?"

"Oh, come on," I chided. "I know I said it, but I didn't really mean it. I don't need roses."

He looked at me with nonbelieving eyes.

"Yard sale signs," I declared. "That's what I really need. Not roses."

"My mother has signs. I think I saw three or four of them in her shed. I'll bring them over to you. So, what color roses?"

"Oh," I said with a laugh. "I don't know. I think I'd better go in and see for myself."

"It's my treat," he insisted. "A get well gift after all those ant bites."

"That's nice of you," I told him, putting my hand on his and giving it a friendly squeeze—but this is something I have to do myself—and *for* myself."

I was paying for a dozen yellow roses, and peeking constantly out the window at the man who brought me here, when the realtor who had helped my husband and me find our rental home walked in. "Anna Hott," she said. "Buying roses for that charming little house you're in?"

"Oh, yes," I said as she gazed out the window into the parking lot.

"Is that Timothy out there? I should go say 'hello.'"

"No, it's a friend," I said. "My neighbor's son."

"Oh?"

"I had a flat tire, then a blister. And the fire ants came. They bit me all over."

"Oh, my goodness!" she declared, looking down at my swollen foot. "You were attacked!" But then she looked back out at the man in the convertible.

"Did I mention I had a flat tire? He just happened to come along at the right time," I said, and then stopped when I saw the way she was staring at me, telling me with her eyes that *less is more, less is more, less is more.*

"You look great," she said. "What's different, your hair?"

"That or life—it's going well," I said, taking my roses. "I had better scoot."

I got back into the car, and once Liam pulled out of the parking lot I put the roses up to my nose, closed my eyes and took a good whiff. When I opened my eyes, Liam was looking at me. I didn't want him thinking I was one of those egocentrics, always indulging themselves, so I put them on the floor by my feet.

"It would probably be wise if I went home now," I said.

"Whatever you like. If you don't want to go to the overlook with me, you don't have to."

"I do want to go," I said.

"You do?"

"Yes, but I don't know."

"Don't know what?"

I looked him in the eyes the way a mixed-up woman does, hoping, longing that he might tell me what to do, but he didn't and I figured it out on my own. "Let's go," I said. "Take me to the refuge!"

"Great," he said. "Would you like some coffee first?"

"Why, were you thinking of stopping?"

"No, I brought some along. It's in that silver thermos down by your feet. There's a couple of clean mugs on the floor in the back. You might have to reach back."

"I haven't had coffee from a thermos ever, I don't think," I said as I unscrewed the lid. "I do like coffee."

"Does it help you write?"

"I used to think so," I told him as I poured him the first cup. "Way back when I worked at the library, I'd start my day with a huge cup, and I used to think, each morning on my way to work, that I heard inspiration, as if inspiration were a creature hovering over my shoulder, feeding me literary one-liners. I'd sometimes pull my car over and jot it all down."

"So a nice cup of java does stir your creativity."

I poured myself a cup and sipped it slowly. "I'd like to believe that was the case, but then I'd look at what I wrote later and it wasn't that good. My best writing, I've come to realize recently—in the past couple of days in fact—has nothing to do with caffeine highs in the morning or wine lows at night. It has more to do with letting myself feel whatever it is I am feeling—accepting that I'm human, and along with being human comes a range of emotions. When I accept this, rather than hide or try to get rid of the way I'm feeling, I find it easier to write. So to answer your question, coffee does absolutely nothing for me other than help me get through my morning with a little added oomph."

"Oomph is good," he said.

"Yes," I said with a laugh. "So, does coffee make you creative?"

"Sometimes," was all he said.

"So where did you learn to draw?"

"Not in school," he said, and laughed. "I had this professor my first year of college. I told him I wanted to be an artist and he said, ' Sorry son, you chose the wrong school. We have no actual art classes here; just art history.'"

"So you transferred?"

"No—I switched majors four times, from accounting to engineering to business, and finally to art history."

"Well, that's close to what you wanted."

"It was a good enough fit, I thought at the time. Now I see it worked out as it was meant to."

"I can't see you as an accountant."

"No, me neither, but my parents urged me. I used to sit in class, always a seat by the window, and I'd try. I'd try hard to feel passionate about numbers. But I couldn't, so I'd draw. I'd always have a big old cup of coffee, then go to class and sketch. The professors thought I was taking notes."

By now we could hear distant thunder, and Liam said he felt a few raindrops hit his face, though I didn't. I only felt what was going on inside me, and it was a twirling, whirling storm of sorts. But other than Liam commenting that the coffee was good and strong, we were quiet the rest of the way to the refuge. It was a comfortable silence and I felt a familiarity toward him, as if he had been a part of my world forever. And when he cast a smile my way, I couldn't imagine what time was like before him, nor think about a time that would come without him. I only wanted more . . . more of the present, more of him. I wanted to know everything there was to know about him, yet I sensed we already knew and loved one another, as simply and easily as the blue sky, white clouds and spring breeze I had known, and loved, all my life.

As the car stopped at the entrance gate to Wildlife Drive, I turned my face away from the woman at the booth and tilted my nose upward, as if I had spotted something high up in a tree — and then I did, a mangrove cuckoo hiding within a dense clump of leaves! I felt as secretive as the bird, only it wore a black mask, something I wished I had to hide my guilty eyes. As the car rolled slowly onto the narrow one-way road, bordered on both sides by dense wetland woods, I feared red-bellied woodpeckers were watching me go by with another man and that they would wait until my husband returned, then come pecking at my door or drilling on my roof.

"Now that's a feeding frenzy!" Liam said, and I shifted my attention to his side of the car, and a channel with scores of birds feeding and roosting in the mangroves. "Are you seeing all this?" he asked.

By now I felt raindrops falling on my head, and all I could think was, *Rain, rain, go away, Anna wants to stay and play.* But the rain knew what it was doing. It was trying to stop me from falling further for this man.

"Anhingas and tricolored herons," Liam told me in a low voice. "Can you see them?"

I rested my elbow on the center divide and leaned as far as I could to his side of the car, not touching him, but almost. One slip of my elbow could make it happen, send me falling into his lap. My windblown hair was brushing across his face, I knew, as I tried focusing on the birds. But all I could muster in my brain was *one bird, two birds, pink bird, blue bird, white bird, black bird, big bird, small bird. That one has a featherless head. This one shiny black legs instead. What a lot of birds there are. Yes. Some are pink. And some are white. Some are near. And some are far.*

"See the snowy egret?" he asked, and I felt his breath on my cheek, whether he meant for it to be there or not.

"No," I said, turning to find our faces uncomfortably close. "I live on this island. I should know its birds by now, but I don't. Which one is it?"

"The one with the yellow feet," he said. "The one that looks like it's wearing golden slippers."

I leaned further, and this time my elbow slipped a bit, touching his knee lightly but holding my weight, not letting me rest on him. I knew I only had seconds left to hold myself in this pose, pretending I cared about anything out his side, when all I could think about was his breath, warm in my ear as he talked, and my heart, and how fast it was beating, as fast as the wings of an anhinga in flight—continuously, with short, rapid beats.

I returned to my side of the car as the drive opened into the tidal basins and out my window were the saltwater tidal flats and there were reddish egrets in the shallows. I was glad to have my own mind back.

"The overlook isn't far, I don't think," Liam said, breaking the silence. "It should be coming up soon."

"No hurry. When we get there, we get there," I said. "How do you know so much about birds?"

"My father," he said, studying the road ahead. "He worked hard his whole life, was a good provider—always took care of his family. But he never told me he loved me. I just knew he did. He didn't use words to tell us, but he'd give me a pat on the back, tell me, 'Good job, Son.' Shortly after my parents moved to Florida, I came to visit and he took me here, to the refuge. We didn't make it to the Red Mangrove Overlook that day. But we got here early and pulled to the side of the road—just back there, in fact. He pulled out his binoculars and a book on birds he bought at the gift shop. I pulled out my pad of paper and a pencil and the two of us spent a good part of the day here—him watching for birds, and when he spotted one, reading me everything there was to know about it, and me drawing those birds. The enthusiasm in his voice that day—Anna, he was like a boy. Other than bowling for a few years, my father never did anything for himself—never did the guy thing, if you know what I mean. He did nothing outside work and family."

I thought of my own mother and how I missed her, and could feel the pain he might be feeling for his father. "I'll bet you miss him," I said.

"There's so much I'd love to ask him today—things I wonder now at this age, but didn't think to ask back then, at that age. I'd do anything to have one more day with my dad—just me and him and the birds."

We drove further, passing sandbars with birds on both sides. I was sorry to see birds on my side. It gave me no more reason to lean toward him. But soon the road made a gentle curve, and as it straightened we reached a sign that read THE RED MANGROVE OVERLOOK, and Liam pulled the car to the side and got out. I stayed in my seat, wondering whether one day I might regret this four-mile wildlife drive, and stopping at an overlook with a man I hardly knew.

 *chapter thirty-five*

"Have you ever done anything impulsive?" I asked Liam as he came around to my side of the car and opened the door for me. I didn't expect him to take hold of my hand as I got out, but our hands wrapping together felt natural, as if we had been entwined for a hundred years. We stayed hand in hand as we stepped onto the boardwalk. "Holding my hand," I then said. "Taking it like you did, was that impulsive?"

"Premeditated," he said matter-of-factly. "I was thinking about it before I stopped the car." He then pointed out a great heron perched on mangrove prop roots, and it struck me once more what I was doing—entering a mangrove forest with a man other than my husband. My spirits, high and obvious and not at all hidden, like an osprey's nest, had to come down! I squeezed his hand, then let go, slowing my pace and dropping behind him, trying hard as I could to take the extra bounce out of my step. The birds, I decided, were the only ones who should be doing courtship dances today.

"Red mangroves are trees that walk on water," Liam told me. By the time we reached the viewing platform, I couldn't deny the way he made me feel, as though I, too, was walking on water. The tide was going out and there were thousands of feasting herons, egrets and ibises. It felt right to be where we were, tucked away beneath our own mangrove canopy.

"You asked me whether I've ever done anything impulsive," he said, his elbow leaning on the wooden railing, his eyes studying the fish in the water below. "Well, I have, last night in fact." He took his hat off, then rubbed his hands through his hair and looked me in the eyes. "I said 'yes' to that Grand Marnier, then had a few more, and stayed too long."

"I didn't think you stayed too long," I told him, and then asked, "And how was that impulsive?"

"I don't know. Maybe I have to look up the definition of impulsivity—compare it with instinct. Maybe it's instinct. Maybe that's what has me drawn to you."

I turned my back to him and studied the complicated, intertwined branches of a red mangrove. The connection and attraction we felt for one another was as intricate as the mangrove, and left me feeling perplexed. I was a woman holding a couple of powerful titles—married, mother of three—and there were limitations in those titles.

"What are you thinking, Anna?"

I smiled. It was a question my husband never asked me. But then I grew serious and said, "It's been so long since I've had days like this, all to myself, well, I'm not alone—I'm with you." I turned to face him. "But it's been a long time since I've had days when I'm selfish like this."

"Do you view this as selfish?" he asked.

"I don't think you know the real me," I told him. "Usually every intent I have, all my energy, my actions, they go toward my children. I'm truly a twenty-four/seven hands-on mom, and it leaves me no time for myself."

"Then this must feel good."

"Yes," I told him. "I feel like a young girl again, and I haven't felt young like this in a long, long time."

"Why not?" he asked.

"I don't know," I told him. "But I remember the day I cried—felt for the first time like a full-fledged adult, all grown-up—no more youthful

irresponsibility left in me. I was thirty-five and changing two dirty dia-
pers, and also cleaning up vomit, while at the same time holding a teeth-
ing, screaming baby on my hip. *And* I had the stomach flu! There was
more going on, too, all at the same time, but it's a blur to me now."

"None of it sounds easy," he said.

"It's not, and many times it has left me feeling like a crazy woman,
a mixed-up person—a mangrove cuckoo!"

"I've never thought of you as a mangrove cuckoo, and I don't think
you're mixed up at all."

"I might not look it right now," I started to say.

"You don't look it at all," he said.

"Well, I am," I insisted. "I get that way all the time. You just haven't
seen it."

"It's hard to believe," he said. "I see you differently."

"How so?" I asked.

"Well, one of the courses I teach is an introductory course in Renaissance art, and what I always have my students do is look at something,
then write exactly what they see."

"That sounds easy."

"It's not. It's hard. It's hard translating what you see into words. I have
them summarize the overall appearance, then describe the detail of the
object, the composition, the materials used, and most importantly, I have
them describe the order in which their eye is drawn around the object,
starting with the first thing their eye notices."

"That's interesting," I said, wondering why he was telling me this.

"When I first looked at you, Anna—in my mother's hallway that
morning—you know what I felt drawn to first?"

"The ridiculous nightgown I was wearing?"

"No—your eyes," he told me, "and the way in which they danced
and smiled. And later, I noticed your lips, and their form. Most of what
comes out of your mouth is calm and laid-back, and I can tell by how
feminine, how beautiful, your lips are that chattering about others, gos-
siping and rambling on about people, isn't your thing."

"You get an A," I told him, and felt flattered that after all I've gone through, someone could still detect something good in my eyes.

By now he was rummaging through the brown leather pack he wore around his waist.

"What are you looking for?" I asked him.

"My camera," he said. "I'd like to take a picture of you so I can later sketch it and capture . . ." His words stopped as he pulled out a tiny camera.

"Capture what?" I said, standing with my hands awkwardly at my sides and my eyes squinting from the sun that was poking through the branches at me.

"You," he said as he focused the lens. "I want to capture you!"

"Why not just sketch me?"

"I don't have a pencil or paper."

"Too bad. I'd love to see your artwork in progress."

"I do it best when I'm alone. I don't know if this is what writers do, but I let myself go when I sketch. I set myself free."

"How nice, to be able to do that, set yourself free," I said, smiling for his photo.

"I don't worry at all whether what I draw is good or not," he said with his eye to the lens, "and I have no idea whether I've sketched a masterpiece or not. None of that matters. All I care about is that I love to do it. I love to draw."

"That's great," I said, trying not to let human disturbance, the car doors I heard opening and closing on the road, or people walking onto our platform disrupt my stance.

"I'm not a good photographer," he said, fidgeting with the lens. "But when I sketch it later, I'll make it good. I'll draw that smile of yours. A photograph could never do it justice, but a pencil could," he went on, and stopped when an older couple had come out to where we were.

I was standing still as an American bittern, pretending I was a part of the scenery when the man offered to take the picture for him, to take one of the two of us together. We let him, and I was glad to hear that they were from Ohio, not local, and didn't know and could never know who I was, a woman not supposed to be standing here in this mangrove forest as my heart did things it wasn't supposed to be doing. But a woman's heart does that. Sometimes it involuntarily beats too quickly, just as the Gulf waters pick up with excitement every now and then, acting as if it was the ocean.

The beam on my face as I stood there with the sun in my eyes and Liam's arm around me may have told my secret—that I was a perplexed woman, trying to figure out whether it was impulsivity or instinct that brought me to where I was now.

When the couple from Ohio left, and we were once again the only two people standing in the forest, his arm still around me, I knew then what had brought us together. We were like two shorebirds that migrated along traditional flyways, across continents and oceans, to arrive at the refuge where we were now, and our being here together was nothing planned. It was the forces of nature that brought us together, the way those birds navigate by sun, moon and stars, taking advantage of prevailing winds and sensing changes in the earth's magnetic field.

"Are you sure you don't have a pen or something?" I asked minutes later. How could I not want a pen when hanging from the mangrove branches were hundreds of pencil-shaped propagules that made me want to write!

"I don't," he said, searching the pack strapped to his waist once more.

"Well then," I said, reaching into my purse. "It's all I have, so lip liner will have to do." I picked up a dry, tan-colored sea grape leaf off the ground and quickly, sloppily wrote all over it, filling it front and back with words.

"I have to admit," he said. "I've never seen anyone write with lipstick on a leaf before. Mind if I ask what you're writing?"

"Oh, a few things that came to me," I said, dropping my lip liner and the leaf into my purse.

"If that's how ideas come to you," he said, "why don't you carry around a notepad?"

"I don't want to scare it away."

"Scare what away?"

"Inspiration," I told him.

"Is there really such a thing?" he asked. "Or is there only imagination?"

"Inspiration is real," I told him. "It's like watching for wildlife. You need to be at a quiet, comfortable distance or you might disturb it. Sometimes it'll freeze and go away, but I try not to assertively approach it or force it. It shows up when it's ready, as long as it feels secure, as long as my mind is still and in a quiet, receptive state."

"Just like that?"

"Yeah, and I've used receipts, dollar bills and coloring books to write on."

"Is that so?" he asked.

"I would think most writers get their ideas this way, but I don't know for sure. Everyone is different."

"And what do you do with all these objects that you've scribbled all over?"

"Stash them in my desk drawer," I told him, "so one day I can hopefully apply them to a novel." I looked back out at the tidal flats and then at him. "So what do you fear most?" I asked out of the blue.

"You ask good questions," he said, "but do you really want to know?"

"I do."

"Okay, then, I'll be frank. My biggest fear is that history might repeat itself. I don't mean on a grand scale, but in my own life."

"How so?" I asked.

"I know I said I'm content—that I enjoy my own company—but the truth is I don't want to go through my entire life alone. I do like companionship—but here I go, off on another monologue. I just fear I might fall for someone—and maybe I already have—but it can't work out. It can't work out because she doesn't feel the same way, or because she isn't capable of loving me back for whatever reasons she has in her life. And now I'm really embarrassed. I've said way more than I wanted to say."

"You don't have to be embarrassed," I told him. "Not with me. It's refreshing, the way you talk. I don't talk like this often. My husband and I, we don't talk about things like this, about love. Nor do we talk of the environment or politics. All we talk about is the house and what a mess it is and who is to blame and whose turn it is to get the baby her milk in the middle of the night." I bent down to scratch my ankles, which itched where they had been stung earlier by the fire ants.

He crouched down and took a closer look at my ankles and feet. "Are you sure you're not allergic to them?" he asked.

"Oh, stop," I said.

"Stop what?"

"Looking at my feet. I'm embarrassed," I said.

"Why would you be embarrassed?"

"By how ugly my toes are."

"Your toes aren't ugly. Why would you think your toes are ugly?"

"Look at them! They're dirty."

"You're at a refuge. They're supposed to be dirty at a refuge, and even if you weren't at a refuge, a person with dirty feet is a good thing."

"Why?"

"It shows you're real, alive, a part of this world, and in touch with the earth."

"Why do you do that?" I asked.

"Do what?"

Our eyes were locked and I was finding it hard to look away. "Make me feel better," I told him.

"I'm not trying to make you feel better."

"But you are." *It's raining. It's pouring*, I thought to myself, and he must have been thinking the same.

"All right then," he said, looking up. "We should probably get going. I should put the top up on my mother's car." He let go of my foot and stood up.

Rain, rain, go away. Anna wants to stay and play, I thought, and asked, "If it wasn't raining, couldn't you stay here all night?"

"I could," he said.

"Then maybe we should. Rain never hurt anyone. But would they ask us to leave if they found us here after dark?"

"I don't know, but a crocodile might," he said. And we left.

chapter thirty-six

I don't know why I invited him in, but a woman can't always explain her own actions other than by blaming natural laws for the way in which she conducts herself. And after telling him how my husband's throwing darts at my heart made me feel, as well as all the other things he wanted to know about me during our ride back in the car, it felt as natural to let him walk into my house with me as if it was the "freshwater from the river mingling with the salt water from the Gulf," the words I had written in shorthand on the sea grape leaf and that I had handed over for him to read as we walked up my steps together.

"The two don't separate, but form an ecosystem rich with life," he read out loud, then handed back my documented burst of inspiration. The rain had stopped, but the sky to the west of my house was dark and luminous and headed our way.

"If you really want to know the truth about my life," I told him a few minutes later as I rummaged through the medicine cabinet in search of hydrocortisone cream for my feet, "every part of it, lately, has been falling apart. It's why my children are with their grandparents this week. I think I had a momentary mental malfunction of sorts."

"Do those really exist?"

"Yes," I said. "They happen to people who don't have the time or know-how to fix their own problems, people who go, go, go until mentally, physically, they shut down."

"Sit down," he said, taking the tube of cream from my hands. "Let me help you with this."

I sat down, balancing my buttocks on the edge of the tub and pointing my toes toward him, no longer feeling like the frenzied, confused woman from days earlier, but more like a bird sprouting brilliant plumes. As he rubbed lotion into the ant bites on my feet, I no longer cared that my feet were dirty, or that I had no polish on my toes. I opened my eyes once or twice to peek, to be sure my toes were still my own and hadn't turned into the golden feet of a snowy egret, for that was how his rubbing made them feel.

But then he moved his way to the bites between my big and second toe and I started to shake.

"What's wrong, why are you laughing?"

"You're touching my feet!"

"And you're ticklish?"

"It's been a long time since anyone touched my feet," I said. "Timothy would never do this for me. He'd take one look and say, 'You're fine. Give it a day or two. They're ant bites—no big deal.'" It was then that I heard the loudest thunder of my life and, startled by it, I kicked my foot up, smacking Liam directly in the face.

"I can't believe I did that," I told him. "Are you all right? Did I get your nose?"

"Did the lights just flicker or am I seeing things?" he asked.

"The electricity," I said, laughing. "About the same time I kicked you, it went out."

"Then I'm fine."

"You must think I'm a complete wack-a-doo, don't you?" I asked as I got up off the floor where I had landed.

"I don't know. What's a wack-a-doo?"

I gave him a teasing look and went into my bedroom. He followed. "See all those flowers?" I asked, pointing to my writing desk. "Your mother gave them to me."

He walked over and pulled a daisy stem out of the bowl of water. "Odd," was all he said.

"It used to be a daisy," I explained, "but I plucked its petals."

"Some might call that wacky. It's a wacky activity, but it doesn't mean you're a wack-a-doo."

"It's not something I do all the time."

"Good. I was staring to worry."

"I was playing that silly little game," I told him. "He loves me, he loves me not."

"I hope for your sake it ended the way you wanted."

"No," I said, stepping on the petals on my floor. "It didn't. A lot of things in life haven't turned out exactly as I once hoped they might." I went over to my writing desk, opened the top right drawer and pulled out the pages I had printed, the pages I had written so far in this week on my own. "If you really want to know what I was thinking when my eyes were closed, just before I blew out my candles," I told him as I sat down at the desk and he on my bed, "well, I was thinking how I've always wanted to write something significant."

"That's great."

"It sounds great," I told him, "but as much as I love my children, more than anything in the world, motherhood and all my domestic responsibilities leave me little time for my own pursuits. It's a three-hundred-and-sixty-five-day-a-year job of nonstop reacting and responding, Monday through Sunday, from sunrise to sunset, as well as all through the night, without any break." I stopped, then said, "Here I go again. I must sound like a blabbermouth."

"It's your life," he said. "It's not blabbering. It's talking about your life, and it's so different from mine."

I looked at my watch. "Every night, around this time," I said, "when the children are asleep, the floors swept, dishes washed and put away, laundry tumbling about, I take a hot shower to unwind. As I dry myself off, I feel that same burst of motivation, to start something spectacular, something all of my own, and I think to myself, the house is quiet and my time is my own. I should put my nightgown on, sit down at my desk and write."

"Is that what you do then, write?" he asked.

"No," I said. "I don't do anything. I don't read, don't watch television, and don't spend time with my husband. I collapse into bed, telling myself that tomorrow is another day and maybe I won't feel so tired. I've been telling myself this for weeks, months, and years. I'm thirty-six now—no— I'm thirty-seven, and other than being the mother of three of the world's most amazing children, I haven't the slightest idea who I am, only that I must be dull to listen to."

"I don't find you dull at all."

"You're kind," I said, feeling embarrassed for having talked on about me, and fearful that I might start back up again. But it was as easy to talk to him as it had been hard talking to Timothy. And as unhappy as I felt when I first learned of Timothy's act, I now felt that same swing of the pendulum, but in the opposite direction, toward happiness with regard to another person.

"I still feel dull," I told him. "I mean, not right now, not here talking with you, but dull—like I no longer see the vibrancy of life, the colors." I blushed for having said so much. "I'm always overwhelmed, feeling like I can't keep up with the housework, the grocery shopping, the cleaning. It all leaves me feeling like a failure at the end of the day. But like I said, I no longer know who I am."

"I once heard someone say that when you don't know who you are anymore, or what you like, think back to when you were eight, and come up with three words you would have used to describe yourself and the things you liked then."

"Roller skating," I said with a laugh. Come to think of it, I liked writing in my diary more. I kept that to myself.

"Roller skating is good," he said, "but you're supposed to use words like adventure, philosophical, free-spirited."

"Are those your words?"

"I guess they are," he said. "Why are you looking at me like that?"

"That's why you and I get along so well."

"What do you mean?"

"You and I have different circumstances, completely different lives, but virtually, we're the same. We expect things from life. We see life for what it is—an experience—and we want to make the most of it, make it as beautiful as possible. And what's wrong with that, right?"

He got up from my bed and walked over to where I was sitting at my desk and, with a smile on his face and a gleam in his eyes, he picked up a piece of paper—the most recent printed page of my novel. "It's hard being a mother," he read my words aloud, "as hard as a woman climbing all four sides of Mount Everest every day all by herself, a solo expedition, with no time or energy left at the end of each day to celebrate her summits."

It didn't feel right hearing such words coming from the mouth of a man, so I pulled it from his hands.

"I'm sorry," he said. "Is that in your novel?"

"Of course not," I said, feeling my face turn red. I didn't know if it was good or not and didn't want anyone judging what I had written, what I had been feeling.

"So where is this novel of yours? Can I take a look at what you've written?"

"It's getting too dark," I said, glancing out the window at the thunderstorm coloring the trees lime green against the black sky.

"Do you have a flashlight?" he asked me.

"I have candles," I told him, going to my closet and pulling out the jars I had stashed when we first moved to the island and I read of potential hurricanes. When all six of them were lighted, I thought he would have forgotten, but he hadn't. He asked me again if he could read what I had written.

"I'll read a little of it to you," I said, "but it's intimate. My writing is intimate, so you'll first have to tell me more about you."

"Like what? What do you want to know?"

"Something no one in the world knows," I said, aware of the fact that our time together was going to end, that all I would have afterward would be my memories and that even those would eventually fade, making me question whether all this happened or if it was only in my creative imagination. "Tell me your biggest secret. Tell me, and don't leave a single thing out. I won't tell a soul." Only then could I consider handing over my manuscript pages, letting anyone see this aspect of me spilled onto paper.

"I'm not that complicated," he said.

"Oh, yes you are," I told him. "Now don't be shy."

"Okay," he finally said. "There is something nobody knows about me."

"Not even women you've sat next to on a plane?"

"I tried telling this woman in Venice, but she didn't speak English and I don't know Italian."

"Oh, stop," I said with a laugh. "Just tell me."

"If you insist," he said. "I'll tell you what I struggle with most—what bothers me more than anything." And it was then that he told me how he tried to view life as art, tried to see beauty in it all, but hard as he might, he saw nothing good produced from his first marriage—no kids, no masterpieces created together—just wasted time and nothing to show, no gain, nothing to walk away with but regret for having spent that time in misery.

And when he finished telling me his secret, I almost gave my writing to him, like a little girl handing over her coloring book, the one she worked on for hours that felt like years, that felt like a lifetime, but in a change of mind I pulled the pages toward my chest and folded my arms so he could never see them.

"Oh come on," he said, taking hold of a corner of one of the pages and tugging it lightly. "I've told you everything there is to know about me."

"But what you said was beautiful," I told him. "What I've written is not. You're the one who should be writing a novel. And I should be burning mine—ripping it to shreds and dropping it in my candles."

"Have you got it saved on disc?"

"Yes, but I could burn that, too."

"Why would you say such a thing? Why would you burn it?"

"It's stupid."

"I don't believe that. I don't believe anything you write could be stupid. I wish you'd let me take a look."

"I can't," I said, this time more firmly.

"That's fine," he said, his hands in the air, showing the face of an innocent man. "I'm not going to force you. But I would think it would be fun sitting here talking about what you've written."

"No, it's not. I find this hard."

"Okay, but I'm curious as to why you don't want to show me."

I felt my throat constrict. "It's truly no good."

"How do you know?"

"I don't, for sure."

"Well, if you change your mind, I'd be happy to take a look. I would think you'd want to run it by another person, have a fresh set of eyes take a look."

"No. I should stop writing," I told him as I got up from my desk, set the papers on my bed and then sat on top of them. "Move on with my life."

"You think?"

"Yes," I said. "It sounds sad, but I should try."

"If you have to 'try' to stop writing, then you ought to continue."

"No. I don't want the craving anymore, the craving to write. I'd be more carefree without it, without feeling compelled all the time to write. I don't mind feeling compelled. But every time I feel compelled to write, life gets in the way and there's something else I have to do, like change a dirty diaper, feed a hungry mouth. I guess if I ignore it long enough—the craving to write—it'll go away."

"Not if there's a story in you that has to come out," he said.

"I'd love to believe that, but I only have these few measly pages that I'm sitting on."

"There's got to be something you like about those pages."

"No. And what a waste of my time."

"Creative endeavors are never a waste," he said. When he sat down next to me on my bed, I got up and walked over to my desk, opened the top right drawer and put the pages back in. "What does your husband think of your story?" he asked.

"He doesn't know I'm writing one."

"I'm sorry to hear that," he said. "And I don't know if you realize this or not, Anna, but you just told me one of your biggest secrets in life."

"I did not," I said.

"In so many words, and by the look on your face, you did," he said. "You let me know in a roundabout way that writing is the most intimate part of you."

I stared him in the eyes, wondering how he knew so much about life, and about me and the things that were churning in my head. I wondered even more how much I knew of him, and what he was thinking, and whether he truly was thinking what I thought he was: that he wanted me like I wanted him. "Maybe I'll work on my story more," I said. "But I still can't get over how nice it must be to be you, to have all the time in the world for thinking profoundly and sketching."

"I wouldn't change a thing."

"No, I'm sure you wouldn't," I said, and then picked up a decorative pillow sitting on my bed and whipped it across the room with a smile on my face. "But what if you fall in love with a woman that you meet at Stonehenge, or one you see trekking up to Machu Picchu in Peru?"

"I don't think I will," he said, giving me a peculiar look. "I'm not going to any of these sacred places in hopes of meeting a woman. I'm going for research, and I'm going to have a million other things on my mind, like what I am going to put in this book I plan to write—you're looking at a man who hates to write. Sorry, but it's true—my other deep, dark secret, and I hope it doesn't make you dislike me."

"You'd be an impossible person to dislike," I said. "You're the kind everyone loves."

He looked at me oddly again and I feared I had said too much, but then his eyes told me it was okay—what I had said—and, like an irrational creature, I said more. "What if you meet a woman while you're traveling—visiting the Coliseum—you're going there again, aren't you?"

"I'm not going to meet any woman," he said quickly.

"Yeah, but let's say you do. Let's say she's sitting there all by herself, smack in the center, in the dirt, crying at the profoundness of it all."

"I'd look at her like she was a wack-a-doo," he said, "and I'd walk on by. I think what would affect me the most is if, one day, I'm walking on the beach and I see a woman, a mother of three, laughing out loud, playing with her kids, but I can see in her eyes that she is crying on the inside, crying because her husband doesn't appreciate her."

"Would this woman that you're talking about be here or somewhere far away?"

"Here," he said, looking me straight in the eyes. "On Sanibel."

"Oh," I said, "so there is a woman in this neck of the woods that you care about."

"Yes, and I'm getting to know her, and there's something about her."

"What?"

"I don't know. It doesn't matter. She's married."

"What a shame," I said. "And you—you're free, completely free. Like I've said, it must be nice to be you." I wanted to reverse time, take back my comments, my tone of resentment, and the look on my face. If this were the story I was writing, I could do all of that. I could delete the entire paragraph and start over, but it wasn't a story. It was life and there is no taking back the words that escape our lips. Then again, we do author our own lives. To a certain degree we can control what happens next. At least, we try.

I got up from where I was sitting beside him and walked over to the small screened porch attached to my bedroom. "You probably think I'm a ding dong," I said as I stepped out. "I don't blame you if you do."

"I haven't heard anyone use the words 'ding dong' in a long time," I heard him say from inside my room. "I was thinking more along the lines of 'ding-a-ling.'"

"You're mean," I called in to him as I stared out at the dark limbs of the banyan tree.

"I should go," he said, poking his head out.

"You don't have to."

"Thanks, but I should, don't you think?"

"I don't know," I said. "Let me think about it."

# chapter thirty-seven

I listened to the sound of the whip-poor-wills and looked good and hard at the ever-expanding banyan roots and how simplistically complicated they were, and then I looked back at Liam and took hold of his hands, pulling him out onto the porch with me, so close that we were as interlocked as the roots and branches surrounding us.

"What should we do, Anna?" he whispered.

When I felt his lips, his breath in my ear, I no longer cared about whip-poor-wills or rubber tree plants, husbands or housework. My only care was him, and all I wanted was to stand intertwined as we were all night long out on my back porch.

"We could dance," I said.

"Dance?" he asked.

"Doesn't that sound nice?" The night was dark from the thunderstorms. There was no one but the owls to see us, and they were too wise to be sitting around staring at a midlife couple dancing, unless they were debating how foolish we were to have let happen what was.

"Do you have music?" Liam asked.

"The electricity is out," I reminded him. "Don't you sing?"

"Only in the shower," he said.

"Well, let me think," I told him and then said, "do you mind if it's a music box?"

"No."

"Okay then. I'll be right back."

I hurried into my bedroom and over to the red roses music box that I got when I was a young girl, the one that chimed to the tune of "It's a Wonderful World," and I wound it tightly as it would go, then returned to the porch, setting in on the ground since my white wicker table was now regrettably under the house and intended for sale.

"I see birds of blue, red roses, too," it started to play, and he sang the words to my favorite song. I peeked up at the sky, hoping to find a full moon—an excuse for acting crazy like I was, but the storm clouds were hiding it. Regardless of its shape we could repel each other no longer, and he pulled me close and started humming instead, and that was nice, too, because then we started to dance.

Hidden away in the shady forest, tucked within the leaves of the rubber tree plants and the aerial roots of the banyan, like two birds safely isolated in their own rookery with no land predators, we danced with no others to see us but the owls and the osprey and the pileated woodpeckers. And "hoo hoo hoo" would they possibly tell?

"I don't know how your husband could have done what he did." Liam muttered in my ear.

"Well, he did," I said.

"You're everything a man could want for—beautiful—inside and out."

He used his finger and wiped a tear rolling down my cheek, and we danced until the music box stopped. Then we rewound it—first me, then him, and then we took turns. We did this so many times that we no longer minded letting it stop because we went on dancing to the sound of distant thunder. When that settled down, there were the night critters— less romantic to the ear, but we didn't care—and when they stopped their croaking, it was the sounds of our own two hearts, faint but as powerful as the distant lapping waves we could hear hitting the shore not far from my tiny house on stilts. We danced so long I started to fear the light of day, and what early risers on the road might say should they walk by and spot us nestled within the branches of the banyan tree.

"I've hardly known you a week," I said to him, his arms wrapped tightly around me. "Funny how some things take a lifetime to figure out, and others a mere second." I wanted to believe there were laws, universal ones, to explain this sort of thing. That somewhere in my past I had a thought and took an action, and that simple thought and action brought me closer to him, and he, too, in time had thought of me, a woman who would love him the instant she heard his voice from her window. There are those who would tell me we were meant to find each other, and that we were right where we belonged.

I wanted to believe it all, that our coming together was part of a mysterious natural law of physics, but it was hard. Nowhere in the files of my mind could I recall a time when I wanted or wished to fall in love with someone other than the one I had married. I didn't intend for this to happen. It wasn't a choice, to feel this way for a man I could not have, to be dancing with him the way I was, our feet slowly swaying back and forth naturally, instinctively, like two birds' courtship dance, putting no thought or logic into it, into who they love, but letting it occur.

We danced a long time, until my perspective changed. "Why do you do this to me?" I asked him.

"Do what?" he asked.

"I no longer feel like a miserable woman with throbbing feet, living in a tree house," I whispered, "but more like a snowy egret wearing golden slippers and doing a courtship dance in a mansion by the sea. Pinch me," I said, and knew by the whereabouts of the moon that it was sometime after midnight.

"Pinch you?"

"So I know this is real and that I haven't turned into a bird, that I'm still a woman," I told him. "A rational, logically thinking woman, and not some loony bird without capacity to reason."

"You're all woman," he reassured me. "You don't have to worry."

"I can't help it," I said. "I'm starting to worry."

"About what?" he asked.

"Us—we can't go on like this all night, you know."

"No, we can't," he agreed. "What do you want to do?"

I pulled myself away from him, far enough so I could look him in the eyes, and there I saw my own wants and cravings staring back at me. "I'd love to wake up in the morning next to you and drink coffee in bed."

"That's it?"

"Yes, and talk intimately and profoundly until eleven."

"Why eleven?"

"I don't know," I said. "But doesn't it sound good?"

"It does," he agreed. "Let's do it."

"We can't."

"Why not?"

There were a million reasons swarming in my mind, but only one emerged. "Your mother," I said. "What if she found out?"

He shrugged his shoulders and kissed my neck. "She'll ground me," he said. "For the rest of the week."

"That's all we've got, the rest of the week."

"Then we should make the most of right now," he said, pulling me close again, his breath in my ears sending shivers down my spine.

"I'll bet you say that to all your women."

"No," he said firmly. By now we were cheek to cheek, our feet hardly moving, hardly dancing at all anymore. "I've said more to you than I've said to anyone in a long time. You're different."

"How do you mean?"

"I don't know how to explain it."

"Where did you say you were born?" I asked him.

"Chicago," he told me, kissing my cheek and my neck.

"Then no, it wasn't at our births that we met," I said.

"But it sure stinks, doesn't it?" he asked.

"What?"

"How we mutually feel the same way for each other, when you belong to someone else."

"I will never belong to someone," I said, more loudly than I intended. "I belong to myself!"

He pulled himself away and ran his hands frustratedly through his hair. "I have no right being here."

"But you are," I said.

"Call it what you will, but it's against the grain for me to talk for more than a minute to another man's wife."

"I may not be his wife for long."

"But you are now."

"Yes," I said.

"Are you one hundred percent positive you're leaving him?"

Suddenly the reality of what I was doing struck me the way a bolt of lightning had the tree out back the month after we moved in, cutting it in two. "I don't know," I told him honestly.

"Then what should I do right now? I don't want to overstay. What do you want me to do?"

"Will your mother come looking for you?"

"Only at four, when she wakes up," he said, looking in the direction of her house.

"Then stay until four," I told him.

"Then what?"

"Then we'll listen to the mourning doves."

chapter thirty-eight

BELVEDERE

Give me a piece of that fudge, will you?" Fedelina asked when I stopped reading. "It's too early, and bad for my teeth, but I don't have to chew it. I can melt it in my mouth."

I got up and sliced a piece of the fudge. After handing it over I went back to my chair and sat down.

"So he stayed the night? My Liam stayed the night with you?" she asked as she pressed the fudge between her two fingers until it softened, and then put it into her mouth.

I looked down at all I had written, at all that was coming next. "You really want to know?"

"Yes," she insisted, and I continued to read.

# chapter thirty-nine

Through the passing of the storm and into the morning sun I could have stayed dancing the way we were, his arms wrapped around me, our feet moving back and forth slowly, but the phone rang. On the second ring I opened my eyes, returning to the reality of my life, of who I was and who I was not, and who I had chosen for my husband and who I had not. On the third ring, I closed them once more, imagining a life with Liam. By the fourth ring I had pulled away and ran fast as I could to pick up the telephone and say hello to my husband.

As I answered all his questions, "yes," I've pulled myself together, "yes," the house is picked up, "yes," I'm ready for everyone to come *home again, home again, jiggedy jog*, there was something I wanted to ask him—why are you calling me in the middle of the night, and why are you awake at this hour? But I didn't want our conversation dragging on and I wasn't in the mood for an argument. As I answered my husband's questions, I took hold of Liam's arm and silently tried to get him to stay. But he didn't. In the yellow room the next morning there were roses on my desk that were starting to wilt, an unopened orchid standing at a tilt, petal-deprived daisies floating in water, and a lonesome mother missing her sons and daughter. But there was no man having coffee beside me in bed, and I would forever imagine what might have happened between Liam and me had my husband not called instead.

I climbed out of bed and went to my window, feeling gloomy that our dancing ended as it had, and that I was not, nor would I ever be—despite him having made me feel like I was—the bird that seems to be wearing golden slippers, or the princess in glass shoes.

The morning outside was gray, everything was gray, and I felt gray, too, as I stood perched at the sill, my eyes wandering over to my neighbor's house, thirsting for the slightest glimpse of her son, while determining how I might spot beauty in this gray day and in my bleak future, knowing Liam and I could never be. I was about to walk away from the window and the colorless day when Fedelina, with her big straw bag in one hand and a pillow in the other, came out of her house and down her steps. She tossed the pillow into her convertible, then propped herself atop it like little Miss Muffet sitting on a tuffet. But instead of eating curds and whey, she backed out of her long, curvy driveway, veering too far to one side, scratching the side of her red convertible against the branches of her hydrangea bush, and then turned onto the bumpy road and disappeared.

The lavishly blooming white shrub looked fine, not damaged at all, but Fedelina's car had to be scratched. If it wasn't, it would be the next time she came into her driveway with those branches extending as they were.

"I should tell her son," I declared. "I will go over there now, before she gets back, and tell him what I saw and that I'm worried about his mother's life—the lives of others, too—the way she drives so far to the right."

I dressed, and as I headed out my door and down our porch steps, I thought about my neighbor, who I cared for immensely, and her son, whom I also cared for. I couldn't decide who I cared for more, since I cared for them in different ways. But her son I would hardly see anymore, whereas she, I would see every day out my window.

I no longer wanted to go snitching to her son about the way in which she drove. Instead, I would do her a favor while she was away—cut away the branches closest to her driveway—I decided as I walked over to the trunk where she kept her gardening tools. I took hold of the pruning shears, not intending to cut much away from something not belonging to me, but once I started, I got carried away, moving inward, too, snipping away at dead blooms hidden within. It didn't take a horticulture degree to decipher which ones were dead. I found the activity of snipping profoundly therapeutic, and couldn't stop until suddenly I wanted some for myself—lavish, white, live blooms for my bureau! I wanted them as badly as I had a piece of her son, and I wondered, if Liam was my husband and this hydrangea shrub was in my own yard, would I desire them this much?

I was fully submerged, deep within the branches and feeling one with the bush, when a voice startled me. "I'm afraid to ask what you're doing," he said. It was Liam. He was wearing a black T-shirt, jeans and reading glasses, which made me nervous, reminding me of a professor I had in college, one who was serious.

"I'm trimming dead blooms," I answered properly, too properly for having danced cheek to cheek the way we had the night before.

"Good thing you're not a barber."

I poked my head out from the branches. "And why is that?"

"Your customers would go home bald." He made a face and looked at the excess lying on the ground. "By the looks of things, you've cut more than you had to."

I wanted to tell him the reason for doing what I was—that I wasn't crazy—that he should look at the side of his mother's car when she got home, at all the scratches, and thank me for sparing more damage.

"Why are all those branches sticking out of your pockets?" he asked.

"I'm taking a few home for myself," I said, wanting to tell him that the orchid his mother gave me wasn't opening, and the roses were wilting, and the daisies were now petal-less and waterlogged and the periwinkles all over this island were stressing me.

"I don't know that I recommend that," he said, his voice formal and a bit too cold for Florida, and for the way in which he had whispered warmly into my ear the night before.

"Recommend what?" I asked.

"Taking something that doesn't belong to you, wanting it for yourself when it isn't yours," he said. "So when is your husband coming home?"

"Tonight," I answered, knowing now the reason for his frigid tone, "Late tonight." The thought of my family returning, and all that had happened during my week alone, suddenly made me question whether I was thinking like a normal woman thinks.

"Did I mention I leave tomorrow?" Liam said.

"You do?"

"Tomorrow night. That's why I've got to finish these stairs today!"

"Don't let me keep you."

"A ten- or fifteen-minute break will do me good." He sipped from the mug he was holding and made a face. "This coffee is weak. I'll bet if I held it up to the sun I could see through it. I'm not a fan of weak coffee. It does nothing for me, you know?"

I saw a look of anguish in his eyes I hadn't seen before. "How was the rest of your night?" I asked.

"When your husband called, I came back, took a shower, made coffee and drew. I drew all night," he said, walking away from the branches and from me.

"What did you draw?" I called out to him.

"A woman," he said, with his back to me as he gathered his tools.

"What kind of woman, what was she doing?"

"She was standing on the platform over at the Red Mangrove Overlook, looking out at the birds."

"Was it me?" I asked. "Did you draw me?"

But he had started hammering, and I don't think he heard me ask that. I tried minding my own business, going about my work in the bush, fully enjoying the hydrangea experience, but it was hard—hard not to keep looking out at him, at what he was doing, instead.

"It's wonderful, isn't it, that you drew all night?" I asked when he stopped hammering.

"To tell you the truth," he said in a voice that was glum, like the day, "I'm tired."

"Why not take a nap?" I asked, stepping into the open.

"I'd like to, but I've got to finish." He walked over to the shed and went inside. I followed.

"I know it's hard," I said.

"What?"

"Life—when there's all these things you have to do, and only a couple of things you want to do but can't."

"What are you talking about?" he asked, looking at me like I was cuckoo.

"Taking a nap," I reminded him. "You said you wanted to take a nap but had to fix your mother's stairs. I've got things like that, things I want to do but can't."

He still looked at me like I was kooky. "Like what?" he asked.

"Really want to know?" I asked.

"Wouldn't have asked if I didn't."

"Fly away with you," I told him, and just as I felt like laughing, he looked up from the pile of tools he was sorting with a serious look on his face.

"Then why don't you?" he asked.

"Oh, come on," I said. "I couldn't."

"Why not?" he asked.

"I'm a mother, and like I was saying, the first night we talked, what choices do I have left in life?"

"I see what you're saying, but a person always has choices," he said.

"As much as I *don't* love my husband, I *do* love my children with all my heart," I said. "I don't know how I can leave their father. They love him. They love us together. Then again, having gotten to know you, and the way you make me feel, I wonder whether my kids might benefit from seeing a happy mommy—oh, I don't know. I'm getting confused, but can't help it."

"You are a thinker," he said.

"Did I mention I almost majored in philosophy in college?"

"No, you should have. It explains a lot." He picked up three yard sale signs and handed them to me. "Here they are," he said.

"Thank you," I said, taking them from him. "I chose literature instead. And Timothy—I chose him, too. When I think back, there were so many choices. I wish I had appreciated them more, given them more discernment. I look at things too seriously, don't I?"

"It's your life! You can never take it too seriously. Most people don't take it seriously enough. They go about, never questioning discontentment. They live with it like it was the color of their eyes, something they can't change. Me? I can't do that, Anna, I expect more from life. Call me a revolutionary, but if there's something I hate about my life, you better believe I'm going to set out to make radical changes."

"It's not always that easy," I said. "It might be for you, Liam, but you don't have children."

"I would think children want to see their mother happy."

"Preferably with their father."

"But that's not fair to you," he said.

"Mothers don't always care about what's fair or not for themselves. There's a part of me that wants to teach my children about forgiveness, only I don't know that I can, so I instead will teach them about endurance, and how marriage endures through good times and through bad."

"Yeah, but don't you want to teach your sons the consequences of cheating on their wives, and your daughter that she deserves better?"

"I don't know," I said. "Is there better?"

"Anna," he said, and by now he was standing up and close to me and there was nothing but the yard sales signs separating us. "Never, in my miserable years of marriage did I cheat on my wife. I divorced her, and then started to date, and that was only after we went for counseling and tried all sorts of things to make it work. And let me tell you firsthand that not all men cheat! For him to have cheated on you, a woman like you, Anna, the mother of his children—he's a real dog and you deserve more in life, and I'm here if you're considering a change."

I turned my face so I wouldn't have to look at him. "Oh, that's hysterical," I said. "You—an art history professor leaving for Stonehenge, and me—a stay-at-home mother who can hardly make it to the supermarket."

"You think you're better off staying where you are, in an unstable marriage with some dog who cheats?"

"Maybe," I said, wiping tears from my face.

"It's your choice, Anna," he said. "It's your choice."

"Not really," I told him, and by now I was feeling foolish. "You and I, Liam, we're a whim, we're a fling, a good memory, a reminder that my heart still beats, but a foolish thing, the two of us, and probably one day nothing more than a regret I'll have and, for you, a name you can add to your list, a woman you knew from Sanibel, like all the other women you are yet to love from around the world—all those sacred places!"

"Oh, come on, Anna," he said. "You don't believe that. Somewhere in your deep-thinking, contemplative mind you know there's got to be a way to make it work between us—if not now, someday soon."

"Nope, there's no way," I said like I believed it, and stormed out of the shed, dropping the signs and picking them up, but still storming the best I could. Once I knew he was following at my heels, I went on, "Unless we could reverse time and I met you earlier, but then I couldn't imagine not having my kids, or having other kids instead of them, so no, it could never work."

"Why?" he asked me.

"Why what?"

"I don't know," he said, pulling his hat off and tossing it to the ground, rubbing his hands through his hair. "Why do bees love honey?"

I gave him a look that said, "you're not making sense," and with that he returned to his hammering and I to my snipping, receptive to any unfurling wisdom the flowers might have for me and trying in my mind to see things differently, to see them the way his mother saw things. And to think, before meeting Fedelina, I knew nothing of flowers, other than "roses are red and violets are blue." Suddenly I knew more, that I should do with my life what I was doing with the shrub—cut out the bad, the dead blooms, starting with my marriage. "I will leave Timothy once and for all," I mumbled.

But what would I tell my children? That, hard as they might try, all of the king's horses and all the king's men, couldn't put Mommy and Daddy together again? I closed my eyes and held a branch tightly, wishing it had knowledge to share with me. When I opened my eyes, I decided that cutting my husband out of my life wasn't the answer. How much easier might it be to add rather than cut . . . add what? Add beauty!

"Bye," I called out to Liam, my arms full of good blooms.

"Where are you going with all that?"

"Home," I said. "I'm taking a few for myself."

"Don't forget your signs. You need help putting them out?"

"No thanks," I said.

"I'll leave them at your steps."

"Thanks," I said. "Bye."

As I carried the blooms up my stairs and into my house, I knew that, like the hydrangea branches, Liam and I didn't stand a chance at rooting, and I felt remorse for loving that which wasn't mine, and for taking flowers that didn't belong to me. Still, I dropped them into jars of water, wanting to believe, hoping one might root.

The rest of my day I spent organizing the junk under my house into piles, and sticking prices to the items for the next day's yard sale. I worked well into the night, and shortly after dusk there was a knock at my door. It was Fedelina.

"There's something I need to ask you," she said, a grave look to her face.

"There is?"

"Yes, and be honest."

I felt like crossing my fingers behind my back. I could never tell how I had fallen in love with her son.

"Promise me you'll be honest?" she asked again, and I gave a nod of my head.

"Good, because I need to know," she said, turning to the side, showing me her profile. "Is my mouth drooping?"

"Is your mouth drooping?" I repeated back to her.

"Yeah, right here," she said, pointing to the left side of her face.

I stepped up close. "I don't think so. Why?"

"Oh, I looked in the mirror, and it looked to me like it was."

"I don't think so," I said, giving it a good look. "I don't see it drooping."

"Then it's the way I'm applying my lipstick," she said, and when I gave her a peculiar look, she added, "I've had a couple of minor strokes in the past. That's why I'm asking."

"Oh," I said. "What does your son think?"

"I didn't ask him. I wanted to ask you first."

"Put no trust in me," I told her. "Please get yourself checked."

"I don't feel like moving up north, or touring assisted living homes. I know my family wants that. It's why my son is here, checking up on me as he is. He's leaving tomorrow, you know," she said.

"Is he really?"

"Yes—and that's a good thing. I don't want my children sticking around, worrying about me. They've got their lives and I've got mine." She was rummaging now through her straw bag and I was glad she wasn't looking into my eyes, detecting that which mothers detect, the eyes of a girl in love with their boy. "You wouldn't happen to have any lotion, would you?" she asked. "My hands are dry and they're driving me crazy. This itching! It doesn't stop."

"Over there on the windowsill, help your self," I said, pointing.

The look in her eyes went from warm to suspicious. "My oakleaf hydrangea?" she asked.

"I felt bad for it—all the dead blooms! I wanted to help."

"That wasn't necessary," she said quickly, setting it down next to the other ten jars. "Hydrangea—they can thrive on very little attention, Anna."

I could feel the guilt eating away at my cells for taking what didn't belong to me, and for letting my heart yearn for another man when it should be yearning for my own husband. I could learn a thing or two from the hydrangea, I thought sadly to myself. If they can thrive on very little attention, then I should, too. I shouldn't have allowed myself to get so lonely, to the point of doing what I did—cutting from branches that don't belong to me.

"Anna," she said sharply, and I obediently looked her in the eyes. "I hope you're not being falsely optimistic, romantic in your thinking that one of these ten jars of water is going to grow roots. Is that what you're hoping for, dear?"

I nodded, unsure whether we were talking flowers, or if she was alluding to me and Liam, and whether or not I believed our love might take root.

"I don't mean to burst your bubble," she continued. "I've had friends in the past, a long time ago, who cut branches from shrubs and tried what you're trying. It worked for some, but they had to leave their arrangements in water a long time before they could grow roots of their own. But, more often than not, it does fail, and the branches would have been better off where they were, where they belonged before the cut."

I gave a loud sigh and shook my head, wanting to tell her that I already knew that Liam and I didn't stand a chance. "What was I thinking? It could never work," was all I could say, for I still didn't know whether I was sensitized and perceiving flowers differently due to our prior conversations, or whether she was on to me and trying to caution me with regard to my love for her son.

"I'll be seeing you," she said, heading for the door.

"No time for coffee?" I asked.

"Already had my cup."

I was glad when she left. I had other things to think about, like my yard sale in the morning, and where to put the signs announcing it, and my husband's return tonight. I went to the dryer, pulled a warm sheet out, shook it, then went to the sofa and tucked it in.

chapter forty

Early the next morning in the little yellow room there was a window. Out that window were cars honking, doors opening and closing, people talking and knocking at my door. Then into the room came my husband's voice like a frustrated squirrel, saying, "I thought you said the sale started at nine."

"I did. That's what I put in the paper."

"Then why are people showing up now?"

I pushed him lightly out of my way and shrugging my shoulders, I hurried past. "Welcome home," I said. It was the same thing I had said to him when he marched into my room around three-thirty in the morning and announced his return.

"What's all our stuff doing outside?" he had asked me then.

"I'm having a sale."

"You think you went to extremes?"

"Some call it 'cleansing.'"

"Cleansing? Our house is empty. Should I be concerned?"

"Why should you be concerned?

"A man comes home to an empty house. Are you planning something?"

"What would I be planning?"

"I don't know," he said. "Leaving?"

"Don't be ridiculous," I told him.

"So I shouldn't be concerned?"

"If you want to be concerned, you can. I did go through your closet. If there's anything you're missing and still want, you'd better look downstairs."

"Should I do that now?"

"No. You can do it in the morning. The sale starts at nine. It should be a good one. I'm hoping to make a lot of money."

"It sounds like your week was productive. What else did you do?"

"It's almost four in the morning," I reminded him.

"Fine, where do you want me—couch or bed?"

"Couch," I said.

"Story of my life," I heard him rant as he went down the hallway. "May as well buy a hammock, hang it outside."

"Welcome home," I said softly, and could have said more, gone after him with my words. But I felt like an owl that had been hit by a car. While he was away, someone cared for me, brought me back to life, and I no longer had it in me to clack at people who upset me, or puff myself up like I used to. And besides, I was glad he had left for the couch. I didn't feel like listening to him snore.

By the time I got downstairs, carloads of shoppers already had our belongings piled high in their arms, ready to cash out. I accepted the on-the-spot bargaining they did with me because I was eager to get rid of the stuff before Timothy noticed ties, shoes, or other things he wanted to keep.

"This lady wants to buy your leather journal," my husband said to me an hour into the sale.

"Two bucks," I told him.

"You bought that in San Francisco," he said. "It inspired you, remember?"

"That was years ago, and see?" I said, taking it out of his hands and thumbing through its pages. "It's still blank. My mind is overtaken by other things now." I handed it to the shopper.

"I don't think you should sell it," he called after me as I walked away.

"Let it go. It's time to let go," I said without emotion.

"For two bucks," I heard him say sarcastically, "My wife is selling the dream she once had, her dream of writing a literary masterpiece."

"Oh, please," I said, rolling my eyes at him. "A bit dramatic, don't you think?"

I wanted then to tell him I wasn't the same woman I was back when I bought the journal, back when life was simpler and it was the two of us, with no places to fly off to, no children interrupting our every sentence—those newlywed days when we had only a mattress on the floor to sleep on and our dreams to wake up to, back when we didn't have to wake at the crack of dawn like farmers. I think he already knew he was no longer married to that woman with the pot of coffee and the dreams, but in some ways he's married to someone better—less egocentric, more compassionate, and there's three people in the world she loves more than herself—but somewhere in the midst of this beautiful, motherly metamorphosis, she got stuck in a cocoon of martyrdom.

"I'm not the same woman you married," was all I said. "People change."

It was starting to feel like a long time that we were standing there, like two bulls looking into each other's eyes, ready to charge, and I didn't want him probing further, asking me how I had changed. He was about to, I could tell. I didn't feel like weakening, crying on his shoulder, disclosing that beneath the mommy costume I had been wearing for years was a woman longing to be in an adult relationship with a husband she could grow with, change with, trust! I was glad when he turned and walked away. I couldn't help myself. I made sure he wasn't looking when I picked up the journal that the lady had put back down, and wrote in it the first thing that came to mind.

I craved for us, as a couple, to delve into the depths of the seen and unseen, sharing our reactions to the world, and getting to know better the spiritual forces that have the miraculous power to bind two people together for the duration of their existence on Earth. These were my original expectations, and what is wrong with being a high achiever when it comes to the person you are going to spend the duration of your physical life with?

I closed the journal and returned it to the table, but would have to sell it at a discounted price now. Who wants to buy a journal already written in? There was a lot going through my head at once. When her children are away, a woman finds she still has her brain and all its functioning parts, and she is capable of loving, thinking, figuring things out, and of remembering all the expectations she had of marriage in the first place. I almost picked the journal back up again, wanting to write more, but when I suspected that Timothy, watching me from afar, might recognize all of this on my face, this part of me that hasn't changed— my creativity, my desire to write, lying dormant within but still there as strongly as during our newlywed days together in San Francisco when that brown leather journal caught my eye—so I left the journal and walked away.

We both kept busy for the next hour. He was picking out clothes, and things he liked, and carrying them back into the house, while I was loading furniture into pickup trucks, fitting toys into the backs of cars, and dealing with seasoned bargainers who wanted to buy the belongings of my life for mere pennies. When business finally slowed and I looked up from the wadded-up bills shoved into a coin box, I saw that Fedelina had come over and was talking with my husband.

I stepped closer, pretending to care about folding sweaters on the clothing table. I wanted to hear what they were talking about, and was hoping she was talking sense into the man, telling him his wife wasn't nutty and that she didn't need her kids taken away for a week. All she needed was a little help around the house and short rests here and there.

But I know they weren't talking about that. Husbands don't like hearing about sleep-deprived, overwhelmed wives.

"A man I was talking to the other day told me he was having marital problems," Fedelina was saying to Timothy, "and so I asked him, 'Do you fight a lot?' He said, 'No, hardly ever.' 'That's your problem,' I told him. 'You both need to say everything, get it all out and let the other say it, too. Oscar—he and I were together a long time. Want to know our marriage secret?'"

"Sure. What do you charge?" Timothy said.

"Nothing," she said as she leaned toward him. "We fought daily. That was our secret."

"Really, that's it?"

"Yeah and right after the fight I'd say, 'Do you want a sandwich, Oscar,' and he'd say, 'Yeah, bologna.' I'd speak my mind, he'd speak his and then we'd both move on. We were good at moving on."

"Thanks for the pearls of wisdom."

I walked over, wanting to tell them how hard it would be for me to joke about a sandwich after a thick slice of my heart—the slice I had fed to Timothy—had been half chewed and spit out.

"Hey there, Fedelina," was all I said.

"Why hello, Anna. I was telling your husband my marriage secret. Have I told you?"

"You did," I said matter-of-factly. "How long did you say you were married for?"

"Five decades, can you believe?"

"My God, that's long," I said. "But life is long, too. At least sometimes it seems so, doesn't it?" I turned my attention to a lady who wanted to buy the heart earrings Timothy had bought me for one of our anniversaries.

Moments later, after she left with the hearts already on her ears, my husband came up and asked, "Where's your ring, Anna? Did you sell that, too?"

"Of course not," I said.

"Then where is it?"

"I lost it somewhere in Tarpon Bay," I told him.

"Tarpon Bay, that's interesting."

"Yeah, I went canoeing while you were gone. It slid off accidentally."

"I didn't know you liked canoeing."

"I do now," I said as I put my hand out and let a woman drop quarters into my palm.

"Should I be checking our banking account to make sure our money is still there?"

"Yes, and brew some more coffee while you're at it, will you?" I asked, and was glad when he went upstairs. I found it easier to warm my face into a smile and walk over in friendly mode to Fedelina, who was flipping through a box of photo frames.

"The orchid you gave me hasn't bloomed," I told her. "It hasn't opened at all."

"Give it more time," she said. "It will."

"What if it doesn't?" I asked. "Nothing in my life is blooming."

She let out a loud sigh. "What are you saying to it?"

"To what?"

"The flower that you want to bloom, how are you talking to it?"

"I'm saying, 'What's wrong with you, you'll never open, will you?'"

"There you go," she said. "You have to be careful in what you are saying to yourself, Anna, what messages you are giving you! Talk to yourself as if you were a flower, wanting it to bloom. Talk to the flower, too, and it will bloom!"

"I think I've got a buyer for a lamp over there," I told her. "I'll be right back."

"I've got to get going, dear. I'm taking my son to the airport," she said.

"Are you going to be okay? It's a long drive home."

"My God, Anna," she gasped. "I live for these moments when my grown children need me. I spent most of my life training them to solve problems, handle their own needs, and I guess I did a darn good job as a mother, sending them into the world as fully capable, independent adults, because believe me, they don't need me often. So when they do—even if it's just a ride to the airport—I see it as a selfish opportunity."

By now the sale had picked up again, and the area under my stilted house was swarming with people. After answering questions, taking money, helping load things into bags, Fedelina was gone, but her car was still there. I watched in the direction of her house like a woman actively birding, determined to spot some rare species before it flies off for the season. They wouldn't leave—he wouldn't—without coming to say good-bye, and all I kept thinking about in my mixed-up mind was how I might go on without him.

"Life is a pilgrimage," I thought to myself, wishing I could find my journal once more to write it all down, the ideas that were coming as I handed over a stuffed toy turkey to a man, giving it to him for free so I wouldn't have to count money and disrupt my parade of thoughts. "And I am a woman capable of enduring, but also of leaving certain hardships behind should leaving become necessary, journeying toward a better life, one of true love."

And then another man came up to me with my music box in the palm of his hand, the one Liam and I had danced to.

"'It's a Wonderful World,'" he exclaimed when it stared to play.

"That's right," I told him. "But it's not for sale. I don't know how it got down here—my husband, maybe."

"Oh come on," the man said. "It's my favorite song."

"It's everyone's favorite song," I told him. "And it's not for sale."

"I'll give you fifty dollars."

"Nope."

"Seventy?" he offered.

I shook my head. "It has sentimental value. It's priceless," I told him, taking it from his hand. It was then that I spotted the man who had made it sentimental and priceless to me in the first place—Liam! He was kneeling on the ground, flipping through the pages of an encyclopedia set I had as a schoolgirl.

I walked over to the man I happened to love and knelt down beside him, pretending I cared about the page he had opened in the encyclopedia—a page about leaves. I tried focusing on all that was written about them, that when they fall off annually they are called *deciduous*, whereas, when they remain for two or more years, they are *persistent*, and the plant is *evergreen*. But after reading more than I wanted to know about the arrangement of leaves on a stem, I said to him, no pun intended, "You're *leaving* today."

He didn't say anything, but kept on reading and, because I would go anywhere with him if I could, I kept going, reading about the intricate parts of a leaf, and how the arrangements of them on a stem seem to form a mosaic, in which each leaf fits into the space between neighboring leaves without overlapping. The leaves are placed that way to prevent overshading.

"If I were to close my eyes right now and wish for something," I told him when we reached the bottom of the page, "I'd wish to *leave* with you."

"Is there any way?" he asked.

I thought for a moment and told him, "When I was a little girl, I'd flip through the pages of these encyclopedias, looking at all the pictures and reading all the fascinating facts."

"Nice, simple reading for a little girl," he said.

"The pictures, and the facts, became possibilities I saw for myself in the world, and I believed! I believed I would one day do it all, everything from walking through the Amazon to becoming a zoologist."

"I think it's wonderful that a set of books gave you an ability to aspire."

"Well," I said. "Unlike you, I don't think I'll see most of the places I once looked at on the pages of these books, or be all the interesting things I read about, but my children will do more, be more. That's what every mother wants—for her children to do more than her!"

"Then why are you selling these books?"

"I'm not," I said then. "I've changed my mind."

"What about your husband? Have you changed your mind about him?"

"Why do you ask?"

"Because if you are, if you're planning to leave him, it would give me something to aspire toward, the possibility that some day soon we could be together—that's why I asked."

I shook my head and looked back down at the page still open, the page having to do with leaves, but I saw no facts that told me decisively whether I should *leave* my husband or not. Then my mind roamed the four corners of the Earth, searching the possibilities for how it might become a realistic option in my life, a choice that was sound, an opportunity worth taking—me flying off with Liam to faraway places, like two migrating birds, stopping to rest at refuges as we went. But I was no flying creature with wings. I was a mother and a wife.

"I'm not sure that you fully understand," I told him, "what I'm going through— the responsibilities that I have here."

"No, but if I could walk in your shoes for a day, to fully understand, I would," he said. "But I can't. I can't possibly imagine. Despite all of that, what do you want to do?"

"I already told you. I told you exactly what I want to do—fly away with you," I said with a laugh, and then I grew serious. "My children are coming home. I need to get a grip."

"Anna," he said, "you're more in tune than you think."

"No I'm not," I said "I'm all mixed up."

"You're the most contemplative person I know."

"Then where do I belong?" I asked him, and it was then that I spotted from the corner of my eye my husband coming down the stairs with two cups of coffee. "Because I feel like I belong with you."

"As much as I don't want to accept it, you're right where you need to be, where your children need you, perfect and with a purpose, like a leaf on a stem," Liam said, hitting the page of the book with his hand. "The problem is—that guy coming toward us is shading you, covering up who you are."

When my husband spotted us nestled on the ground, sharing one book in both of our hands, I quickly flipped through its pages as if searching for something. "I will never forget," I quickly whispered to Liam as I pointed to a picture of a wading bird, "how you made me feel—like a bird as beautiful as this." And when Timothy walked over, I hoped he might think the look of desire in this other man's eyes was for the set of encyclopedias and not for me.

"Why don't you give him the entire set for fifteen bucks," Timothy said to me.

Liam got up and stretched his legs. The two of them were similar in height, just right to stare each other in the eyes. "I do want them," Liam said, glancing down at me. "I've never wanted anything as much, but I think the lady is unsure, and I've been brainstorming how to convince her that I might make it all work."

"They're worthless in today's Internet world," Timothy said. "Take the whole set for ten. You're only doing us a favor, getting rid of them."

"Generous of you," Liam told Timothy, and then looked back at me, still on the ground holding the book. "But encyclopedias will never be worthless, not if they can help one boy or girl to think about the world and imagine."

"Look, I've got to tell you," Timothy said, giving Liam a peculiar stare. "I'd rather go on a business trip, and bring pictures home for my kids to see, than have them look through these dusty old books. If you want them, they're yours and you can have them for five bucks."

"No thanks," said Liam. "What I'm really interested in is that music box over there." He walked over to the table where it sat.

"Timothy," I said, following him. "I didn't bring that down."

"No, I did," he said. "What do we have it for? It's a piece of junk."

"Doesn't it work?" Liam asked.

"It works," I declared, trying not to look him in the eyes out of fear it might give away our secret.

Liam picked it up and wound it gently. I stayed where I was, at a comfortable distance from these two men—one I would grow grumpy and old with, and the other I would soar through the sky with every single night for the rest of my life in my mind.

"I'll take it," Liam said. "How much do you want for it?"

Timothy looked over at me. "Don't ask me," I said, shrugging my shoulders. "To me, it's priceless."

"Okay, then, a dollar," Timothy told him.

Liam already had his wallet open and was pulling out a bill. "Here," he said, handing it to my husband.

"You're killing me—this is a yard sale. I don't have change for a hundred! Take the piece of junk. It's yours for free."

Liam picked the music box up, winked at me, and said to my husband, "You know what they say."

"What?" Timothy asked.

"One man's junk is another man's treasure."

I wanted to wink back, blow a kiss to this man I had only known for one week out of my entire life, this man that I loved, but I had to let him go, let him get on with his life, leaving my yard for the far corners of the Earth.

"I have to get on, too," I muttered to myself, returning to the yard sale, gathering the pieces of my marriage, *falling down, falling down*, while building it up with *silver and gold, silver and gold*, working overtime trying to love the man I had vowed to stay with until death do us part. As I held my hand out, letting a woman drop dimes into my palm as payment for a set of old wineglasses, I knew it was time for me to accept the choices I had made in life, and the circumstances to which they have brought me. It was time for me to find beauty in my own yard, I thought to myself, time to spot the daisies.

But as I carried the box of glasses out to the woman's car, I tried to figure which of us might have it harder—Liam, encountering and falling for countless women from around the world, or me, trying to love one man for the rest of my life. I went about the rest of the sale feeling sorry for myself—growing old with someone who, by default, is there in my life—and feeling sorry for my husband, the one who would have to grow old with me. It was agonizing, trying not to think about Liam and what might have been.

But I never wanted to beat myself up, give myself a black eye some-day, over the memory of our week together, thinking that my love for him was a mistake.

At the end of the day I hurried over to a pile of junk and retrieved my brown leather journal that never sold, the one that I bought long ago in northern California. Late that night, after my husband was asleep and snoring on the sofa, I stayed up until the wee hours of the morning writing fast and furiously, so as never to forget the details leading up to why I did the things that I did, and why I fell in love with another man.

But when I closed the journal and climbed into bed, I could still hear in my mind the music box playing "It's a Wonderful World" again and again. And I could hardly stop my feet from moving. They wanted to dance.

chapter forty-one

BELVEDERE

I stopped reading, then walked over to the counter, pulled a tissue out of the box and wiped my eyes.

"You've never stopped loving him, have you?" Fedelina asked me.

"In all these years not a day has gone by when I haven't thought of him." I hesitated and then said, "After he left, I wanted so badly to believe that the love a mother has for her children is strong enough to carry her through life. I didn't ever again want to think about the other kind of love, between a man and a woman." I sniffled and blew my nose, then told her the real reason I was crying and couldn't stop. "In the story, my children are about to come home again, barge through my front door and into my arms. In real life," I said, "they're gone. My children are grown and gone. My son called this morning to tell me he wouldn't be home for Thanksgiving. He met a girl at school who lives in California, and he's spending the holidays with her family." I took a big breath in and let it all out. "I'd do anything to have them back—pay a million bucks to have them small again. I feel like I have nothing without them."

I feared she might refer to the falling-out we had years earlier—the one that was still coming in the story—a difference of opinions that made me retreat from her yard, stay out of sight and look the other way when she waved to me, but she didn't bring that up or tell me, "I told you so."

"I know it's hard. It's an emotional transition at first," she said instead. "When children start doing what they're supposed to be doing, what we want them doing—living their own lives—they're like the seeds of a dandelion. All of a sudden they're separated from the parent plant and carried off by the wind, but don't worry, Anna. They'll be back!"

"You think?" I asked, and could hardly talk. I already felt embarrassed for crying like I was. I didn't want to cry any more.

"I had seven, remember? And trust me, one by one, they return. I didn't always recognize these people knocking at my door at first, the adults my children had become. The world changed them, but a part of them was the same. Make sure you hear that part."

"What part?"

"The part that has them drifting back as adults, craving a new sort of time with their mother. Listen for it closely."

"I will," I said. "But what do I listen for?"

"Their coming back to you," she said. "It'll be subtle, like a soft buzzing sound. It's not like when they were three and falling down at your feet screaming out your name, but they do come buzzing back, even though it's subtle and brief."

"I'm not saying I want them moving back home, living with me into their thirties and beyond. I wouldn't like that."

"No, I'm not talking about that. I'm talking about how, when your children turn into adults, your relationship with them starts over, and it's exciting. You get to know them and they want to know you, but let me warn you, and I know because I've been through it, this is *your* time, Anna! You need to do special things with your life and yourself now. So when they come back, grown and changed, you, too, have grown and changed."

"You're probably right," I told her, feeling much better. "Maybe this *is* my time to start something new with my life."

"Adult children love seeing that," she went on. "They love seeing their parents out in the garden, doing what is necessary to keep their lives beautiful."

I wanted then to tell her that I would try. That I wasn't fond of gardens without children, but that I would try doing something beautiful with this new phase of life I was entering. What exactly, I did not know, and I wanted to ask her more, like, how does a mother with grown children go about pulling herself from the rut she is in?

"Read more to me, Anna," she said, and I decided I could ask her later.

"Aren't you feeling tired?"

"A little," she said, "but I'm curious as to what happened next, after the yard sale."

"Okay," I told her. "If you fall asleep I'll leave. I'll come back in the morning."

I fingered through the pages of the manuscript to where I left off, hoping she would fall asleep and not hear what I had written next, about the disagreement we had long ago, the one that sent us down diverging paths.

chapter forty-two

In the mornings following the yard sale three little children chit-chat-tered away as the birds chirped through the windows of the yellow room. The house that was clean the week before was a mess again, and I could no longer see my dreams of writing or hopes for love, or figure out where I had left them. "It's okay," I tried telling myself. "The love a mother has for her children is all she needs to sustain her through life."

As I sat out on the porch steps early one morning in the middle of spring—a big old book of Mother Goose nursery rhymes opened in my lap—I felt content with the children and challenged by the harebrained questions they were tossing my way, like, why did the farmer's wife chop off his tail with a carving knife?

"Because she was crazy," I told them as their eyes grew big. "All the characters in these nursery rhymes are a bit crazy."

They were fine with my answer and I turned the page, knowing that one day they would ask me more, like, why do we remember you crying on the kitchen floor, and giving Daddy all those slams of the door?

"Peter, Peter, pumpkin eater," my son said next. "Why did he have a wife and couldn't keep her?"

"That's a good question," I said, searching my mind for an answer. I was glad when he turned the page in the book. "She pitters, she patters, oh, what does it matter," I read, but their attention span was waning, and the boys grew more enthusiastic about catching love bugs in plastic sandwich bags than in hearing me read. I closed the book of rhymes and let them capture as many as they liked, since the state of Florida didn't need so many love bugs and the circle of life had no use for them. And because Timothy had a work-related conference call, and there was nowhere in our home that a person could go and not hear the ruckus three children make. I left the children outside while I hurried inside and grabbed a pen and piece of paper.

When I came back out again, the children were holding hands, spinning and singing, teaching their sister "Ring around the Rosie," so I sank into the swing chair that hangs from the beams of our house. With the early morning sun touching my face, I felt like a girl with nothing better to do than to swing up to the clouds, swing up to Heaven. It felt nice, in those tens of seconds that my children were doing their own thing, to think my own thoughts. And when Liam came to mind, I tried pushing him out. I had done this countless times since my children returned. It would be too painful for me to think about the kind of love I felt for him, so instead I thought about the love I had for my children, and of all the things I wanted to teach them about life. As I watched the three of them drop to their knees in the childish game, I knew then what I wanted them to know, and that is that sometimes we all fall down!

But when I heard Timothy's voice through the window, growing softer. I put my feet to the ground and stopped the swing. Holding my breath, I tried to hear the words upstairs. I had to. Once a husband fools around, his wife can never again be the oblivious type, but when his voice grew louder and I heard mention of sales numbers, I put my feet up and let the chair swing.

I lived for these moments, sitting outside with my children, and something about the way in which my children's voices were blending with the chirping of the birds inspired me and got me to thinking like

Cora, that I should write them each a letter to let them know how much I loved them, so out of all the things they might question in life, they would never question that! And since they were now blowing bubbles and hardly noticing me at all, I got up from where I was sitting with my pen and paper. I sat down on the bottom wooden step so the sun was warming my face and wrote what came to mind.

Dear Son,

You are like the cardinal in the tree that makes me smile,
No, you mean more to me than the cardinal in the tree that makes me smile.
You are the child who makes me sing.
You are like a ruby-throated hummingbird that makes me smile.
No, you mean more to me than a ruby-throated hummingbird that makes me smile.
You are the child who makes my thoughts flutter.
You are like the dolphin in the bay that makes me smile.
No, you mean more to me than the dolphin in the bay that makes me smile.
You are the child who makes my heart leap.
You are like a treasure on the island that makes me smile.
No, you mean more to me than a treasure on an island that makes me smile.
You are the child who makes my eyes glisten.
You are the manatee in the canal that makes me smile.
No, you mean more to me than the manatee in the canal that makes me smile.
You are the child who makes me cherish each moment and move slower through life.

I put my writing down and joined the children where they were, this time, singing "London Bridges Falling Down," while trying to think up another letter for Marjorie, and one for Thomas. But then Timothy came down and loaded his suitcases into the car.

"It's only a week this time," he said after kissing the children.

"And two weeks after that," I reminded him.

"What do you have planned while I'm away?"

I felt my "poor Anna" look spread across my face, letting it answer for me that while he was away I'd be sweeping, mopping, cleaning, grocery shopping, cooking, putting to bed kids who won't sleep, comforting nightmares and observing night terrors, and basically walking around like a sleep-deprived zombie.

"You should win an award, darling, for the look on your face. I wish I had an Oscar to give you. No one deserves one more."

"Oh, stop," I said.

"It's true. You're too pretty to look so miserable all the time."

"Overwhelmed," I said. "I'm not miserable. I'm overwhelmed."

"You're life isn't so bad, Anna."

"I never said it was."

His face perplexed, he hugged and kissed the children, said his good-byes and got into his car. These were the moments when I found myself missing Liam the most. I missed the man who talked to me, listened to me, laughed with me and wanted to be with me. And I missed that "me," too, and tried not to think about it. I didn't want to cry. All those tears hitting my pillow each night did me no good as they were absorbed into the feathers. What a shame, because if all the tears I shed over Liam could be put to good use—collected into barrels and transported to the areas of this earth undergoing drought—there'd be no more dried-up crops, unusable land, farmers going broke, lawns turning brown, or flowers wilting.

Once Timothy's car pulled out of sight, the children ran over to my neighbor's yard and began circling her magnolia tree. I stood where I was, watching them while interrogating my heart as to whether my love for the man who planted that tree had been real, or only to fill a void.

"You children like butterflies?" Fedelina said, coming out her front door and down her flight of steps. "Would you like to see my butterfly garden? C'mon, I'll show it to you."

By the excitement in their voices, one might think the ice-cream truck was coming down our road, and I took advantage of Mrs. Aurelio entertaining my children. It gave me a few more seconds to myself. And once I reached the conclusion that my love for her son was real—pure in and of itself, a rare sort of love, as rare as a red-throated loon, which I have never seen with my own two eyes, but read about a couple of nights ago in the encyclopedia set I never sold the day of the yard sale— I headed over to his mother's yard, granting my heart permission to go on longing for Liam, if only in my mind.

But then I stopped short, hiding behind a rubber tree plant, listening to that which she was saying to my children.

# chapter forty-three

"If you want beautiful things to appear," she was telling them, "it's quite simple. All you have to do is attract them."

"So," I said, coming out from where I was hiding, and putting an end to the lesson on life that she was giving to my children. "You're one of them."

"Hi, Anna. One of who?" she asked me.

"You know, who believe life can be perfect simply by following a few simple steps, and that if you want good things to appear, you've got to think good thoughts and abracadabra, life is good?"

"Well," she said. "I don't know if I'm one of 'them' or not, but positive thinking does go far."

I shook my head. "Sometimes," I said, "life just happens—it rains, it pours—regardless of a positive outlook."

"What's your point, Anna? What are you trying to say?"

I rolled my eyes at her. "I refuse to believe that I once had a thought, or didn't have a thought, or did something, or didn't do something, to attract into my life a husband who cheats." I felt my face turn white as snow. It was the first time I had blurted out to her the bitter truth about my marriage, and the tone in my voice told her I saw no possibility of it blossoming again. My words had a chilling effect within me, starting with the valves of my heart—freezing them like pipes on a wintry day— and I stiffened in the way I was standing, crossing my arms like a cold person does.

"Oh, Anna," she said.

"So where's this butterfly garden?" I asked her, wanting to change the subject.

"Actually, it's a parsley plant," she told me, "but it attracts them the same." She squatted down, pointing to a terra-cotta pot beside the shed where the boys were counting the fluttering creatures. Marjorie had her finger pointed and her eyes were begging for one to land on her. "Give me a couple of months," she went on, "and I'll have a real butterfly garden. I'm having a *Lantana camara* put in next week."

"A what?"

"A plant belonging to the vervain family, a perennial, and it blooms all year in south Florida. Butterflies go wild over its orange and yellow flowers. And soon I'll be putting in scarlet milkweed. I've heard the monarch, and two other kinds, lay their eggs on it. But I'll tell you, the butterfly I most desire to attract and am willing to wait until fall for is the zebra longwing. Ever heard of it?"

"No," I said, feeling irrational for how I reacted, and aware now that she hadn't been teaching my children any universal law. She had simply been teaching them how one goes about attracting butterflies into a garden.

"The zebra longwing is Florida's state butterfly," she told me.

"And how will you attract that?" I asked, softening my tone.

"Passion vines—the largest native passion vines I can plant. If you want butterflies to appear, then you've got to know which plants to grow—the ones with flowers in which they can find nectar." She reached down and tore a browned leaf off her plant. "My daughter called this morning," she said. "She called to tell me her son failed his first year of college and that he's moving back home again, and her marriage is ending. "Mom," she cried. "What did I do wrong?" And I know I should have kept my mouth shut, Anna, but I told her, 'You gave your children everything. You made their world too beautiful.'"

"There's no such thing," I said right away, "There's no such thing as a mother giving her children 'too beautiful a world.'"

"I don't know about that," she said. "My daughter never said 'no.' Children today want for nothing—at least my grandchildren wanted for nothing. They were playing two and three sports at a time, taking piano and golf, getting whatever they asked for at the store, video games galore, then going off on elaborate spring-break vacations with their friends, driving new cars, and having thousand-dollar birthday parties. Where did my daughter learn to be this type of a mother? It's like she's Santa Claus. She didn't learn it from me, Anna. My children each got a cake and two presents for their birthdays."

"Yeah, but every mother wants life to be better, more beautiful for her children than it was for her."

"But where do we get this notion that giving our children everything they want means giving them a beautiful life? Maybe this is why there are so many eighteen-year-olds like my grandson unable to get by in the world, and why grown-up kids are moving back home to live with mommy and daddy. Back in my day, eighteen was a full-fledged adult. There was no question. I don't mean to go off like I am," she said. "I just think life is too easy for these kids today, and then, once they leave home, everything is too hard for them."

"No," I said, shaking my head. I could feel my body tightening, my defenses rising. "It's a big, bad world out there. They're going to find out sooner or later what life is really like, so why not give them a perfect childhood? Give them whatever you can?"

"It's a matter of opinion, I guess, but what I think parents ought to give their kids—what kids want more than anything—is to grow up in a house where their mother and father get along. But it's hard nowadays because these children are ruling the homes. Fathers are not allowed to raise their voices and spankings are unheard of. I told my daughter for years, every time she called me up after a fight with her husband—and their fights were always pertaining to the children—I told her it's okay for them to hear the word 'no.' The word 'no' is not going to hurt them. But let me tell you, Anna, my son-in-law slept on the couch for years, and those kids slept with her in the bed. And sometimes, she would go into their rooms and sleep with them. They couldn't sleep without her."

I nodded. "Yeah," I said. "Mine sleep with me, too."

She hesitated, and then said, "Now where does that leave the husband? My Oscar wouldn't have allowed that. The children slept in their beds, and we together in ours."

"Maybe it's a generational thing," I said. "I don't know, but I never thought, before having children, that I'd let them sleep in bed with me. But then, after carrying each one nine months, it didn't feel right to be putting them in a room down the hall, in a crib. It happened naturally and now, well, all three of them fall asleep with me, but lately I carry the twins into their own room once they're asleep. I feel I'm raising more affectionate kids this way, and I researched it. This was the norm for centuries. In fact, entire families slept together in one room, one bed. It's all they had and they never questioned it."

"If you really want to know what I think," she went on, "it didn't surprise me at all when my daughter told me her husband was divorcing her. My son-in-law, Anna, he was a neglected man—I witnessed it with my own eyes. And now he's gone and the children are coming back— expecting her to give them everything, even an apartment of their own so they can move out again. She did everything for those children and never had an ounce of energy left for him. I used to tell her, when they were younger, go on date nights—you need to go on date nights, but would you believe she wouldn't? She didn't think it was right to get a babysitter, to leave her kids for a single night."

I shrugged my shoulders. "It's been awhile since I've gone on any date night," I told her. "Why should we hire babysitters when everyone is a pedophile?"

"Oh, Anna, you don't believe that, do you?"

"I do," I said. "It's what we're told. It's what mothers today are told."

"I feel bad for you mothers today," she told me. "I truly do. You have things to worry about that we never thought of in our day."

"It's a scary world," I said.

"I guess it is," she said. "But despite all of that, I think it's sad—sad that women are treating their children like royalty and their husbands like servants."

I laughed and laughed and couldn't stop.

"What's so funny?" she asked me, but I would never tell her that my own children were at a higher point in the hierarchy of love than my husband, and for no other reason than that they were cuter and easier to love. For I had loved them from the moment I learned I was pregnant, whereas my husband, well, I didn't start liking him until the seventh date, and loving him until well after he proposed, and even then I questioned whether my love for him could last a lifetime. I'd throw myself into the mouth of a shark to save my children. I don't know whether I would do that for my husband, or not.

"I don't know why I'm laughing," I told her. "None of this is funny to me."

She walked over to a white lattice lying on the ground. "I don't want to overstep boundaries," she said then, "but I wonder, if wives today would put their husbands before their children, put them up on a pedestal, show them a little love and respect, well, I wonder if all these wilting marriages might stand a chanced at reblooming."

"That's ridiculous," I said. "And let me tell you, I refuse to believe that anything I did or didn't do would have prevented my husband from going astray."

"I didn't mean to upset you, Anna," she said.

"I know you didn't, but there are bad things that happen to us in life that we have no control over."

"You're right," she said. "I can't change the fact that the caterpillars ate away at my *Senna polyphylla* plant. And I can't change my past, or how I ignored my symptoms for so long: the unusual thirst, the frequent desire to urinate, my blurred vision. But I try to focus on what I can do now! I stopped smoking a pack a day. I'm choosing healthier foods to put into my body, eating more fiber. I'm staying active and doing what I love—working in this garden every morning."

"Good for you," I told her. "But it's hard when you can't trust the man with whom you've fathered three children."

"I do feel bad for you," she said. "I've always believed there are two kinds of men in the world—those who cheat and those who don't."

"And luck, or lack of it, has me married to one who does."

"Yes, and you're miserable, aren't you? I've seen it all along—the way you hardly talk of him, or the faces you make when I mention him. I see you out my window, laughing with those kids of yours, but when he's home you hardly crack a smile."

"It hasn't been fun," I said. "And I don't know what to do."

"I'm thinking out loud, Anna," she went on. "My plant, the one with the caterpillars, may still die. I don't know, but I want to be sure I did absolutely everything possible to give it a fighting chance. I probably shouldn't say this, but do you think you're doing everything you can to save your marriage? Have you tried loving him more?"

I never hit an old lady, never hit anyone in all my life but for the single spanking—a light one, more of a love tap—I gave my son, so soft, but hard enough that it made me cry more than him the day he said what he said to me, but as my neighbor bent over, legs locked, buttocks in the air, trying to lift the lattice, I felt more offended and disrespected than I had the day Thomas called me "dummy Mamma."

I wanted to tell her she should keep her opinions to herself, and that she knew nothing about my husband or my marriage except for the quarreling from our windows, my snide remarks here and there, and the look of misery found on my face. She had no right telling me in her roundabout way that I was responsible for my marriage going dry, and that if only I cared for him more, loved him more, things would be different. I wanted to give her a piece of my mind, but then I saw her face turning red, like the red of a red-breasted robin, and her throat was turning red, too, which is never good, and her legs were starting to wobble. It was hard seeing a woman her age turning red and wobbling, as it was hard to accept my marriage turning sour and toppling.

"You should bend at the knees," I told her. "Like this." I took hold of one end of the wooden lattice and, together, we lifted. "Where do you want it?"

"Over there, against that tree," she said with a nod of her head. "It's for the butterfly garden I was telling you about. Once I add those posts over there, it's going to be the trellis I plant my passion vines on."

"I hope it works," I said. "I hope you attract lots of butterflies into your yard."

I stared at her, wondering whether I should get hold of her daughters and report the overexertion of labor and opinions I was noticing of her in the garden, or her symptoms of loneliness, like her butting in to things that were none of her business. Had I a good marriage, I would have brushed most of what she said off as nothing more than senior nutty nonsense—old ladies say nutty things—but since my marriage was bad, and I lived next door, kept my windows open and fought with my husband nightly, I was taking everything she said personally.

"Anna, would the children like some lemonade? I've got lemonade upstairs."

"No," I said, and could feel my bottom lip snap shut. "I've got housework to do. We've got to go."

If she had asked why my lip snapped shut, I would have told her that, like the snapdragon flower, it snapped because I felt threatened, and didn't like what she had said to me. I rounded up the kids and left her yard without looking back. Once inside my house, I started to boil water for the children's lunch. But as I waited for the noodles to cook, I couldn't help myself. I flipped open the book she had lent me and read a quick letter from Cora.

chapter forty-four

My Dear Daughter,

Have you ever wondered how sunflowers can grow tall and stand upright with all those heavy petals? I was sitting in the park thinking about this today and realized that flowers in general can only stand because of their stems. I don't think mothering, work, relationships and so forth can stand without a stem and, to me, that stem is spirituality. And if one of the petals, say "work," doesn't pan out, the petal falls off but the stem—God—is still there.

chapter forty-five

In the days following I stepped not a foot into my neighbor's yard, but could see from afar her chrysanthemums no longer mingling with the iris but having words with the gladioli, her birds of paradise telling secrets and the colors of the hibiscus intensifying, and the narcissi with their toxic sap threatening all the other flowers. Even the hydrangeas, I decided in early June as I quickly packed the children into the car and pulled out of my driveway, had heartless, boastful looks. And when I returned hours later, I couldn't help but notice her gardenias in a pot, and how resentful they looked.

It was hard forgetting about all my neighbor had said to me, how in a roundabout way she implied that this is the house that Anna built. This is the marriage that exists in the house that Anna built. This is the frazzled grump that destroyed the marriage that lives in the house that Anna built. But as I labored up the stairs to my house, bags of groceries hanging from my wrists, crying children on my hips, I couldn't help but think of what Cora had written—about spirituality being the stem that holds it all up—and for the first time in a long time I cried out for the Spirit of God to relieve my exhaustion as I put the groceries away, cooked dinner for, bathed, washed and dried the heads of, brushed the teeth, and dressed in pajamas three finicky bodies, all the while praying for the strength I needed to make it through these after-dinner hours—the witching hours leading to bedtime. When they were fast asleep, I started on all those other nonglamorous, nonselfish, nongenius, menial tasks— like washing dirty dishes and folding clothes—plowing full force ahead like a farmer with a day's worth of work to do out in the field, only the sun had gone down. As I picked up wet towels from the bathroom floor, I asked for the spirit of God to breathe life and energy into me. The very next morning, I thought of Cora, waking an hour earlier to grow those flowers, and I introduced into my life a new petal—writing consistently, rain or shine, clean house or messy, tired or rested. I had written the week my children were gone but not at all since they returned.

As my alarm went off at five o'clock in the morning and I touched my feet to the cold floor (no matter how far south of the Mason Dixon Line one lives, floors are cold at five in the morning), I thought of Cora in the early mornings, walking out to that patch of dirt, and I prayed. "Lord, help me," I said. "I pray for strength, I pray that whatever I do in these morning hours will delight you and I ask that you hold me up." I nudged a pillow beside Marjorie's body so, if she woke, she'd think it was her mama still beside her in bed and then I tiptoed across the room to my desk. There, I went about the writing of my silly little story about flowers, an overwhelmed mother and the lonely gardener who lived next door.

And one morning, glancing at my children tossing and turning in my bed, I was overtaken with emotion at how big they were getting and could hardly focus on the story I was writing. It was then that I walked out onto my porch. In a spot with a view of the children I sat on the floor scribbling a letter to Marjorie on the page of a coloring book.

Dear Marjorie,

I've never been into bird-watching until I had you,
And now I spend my life doing nothing but watching you.

To me you're like a little bird,
The kind through our windows you've heard,
A newly hatched osprey wanting to fly,
A screeching owl demanding "why"
A growing pelican I struggle to keep fed,
And a noisy woodpecker that wakes me from bed.
I've never been into collecting shells until I had you,
And now I spend my life collecting things for you.
To me you're one of those rare and unique shells,
The kind one finds along the shore, then likes to show and tell,
A rare junonia I will cherish forever,
A jingle shell attached to my hip wherever,
A conch shell I hold to my ear as you importantly blab,
And sorry, darling, but sometimes you're simply a crab!
I've never had time for smelling flowers until I had you,
And now I spend my life smelling them with you.
To me you're every bit as beautiful as the flowers,
The kind I could look at and hold for hours.
A morning glory that wakes me each day,
A rose that reminds me to rest, then play,
A periwinkle that keeps my priorities real,
And an orchid that cares about how I feel.
I've never had, but always wanted, a parrot of my own,
And now I spend my life teaching you how to talk.
To me you were already a beauty before you had feathers,
The kind I want to fly with through good and bad weather.
A bird I can nurture in my nest for awhile,
A bird I can train using my own innate style.
A bird that will one day leave my nest and say good-bye,
And then return to tell me of her soaring through the sky.

Time goes by quickly when everyone is doing what they're supposed to be doing. The children, for weeks, had been sleeping until seven. The birds were chirping and the woodpecker pecking away at the trees and not my roof. Timothy was gone, too, for days at a time! And I was waking at five, finding joy in the process of writing, discovering for myself the sense of lavish indulgence that comes from doing anything solitary and early in the morning, before the sun rises. I knew what Cora meant when she said that a woman pursuing her passions might feel and look as if she is only playing frivolously. Blind faith made me believe it was a story worth telling, and that no mother in her right mind would consistently sacrifice two hours of sleep to do something that wasn't worthwhile.

And then, one morning, even the orchid Fedelina gave me finally did what it was supposed to do—opened—and its brilliant, plum-colored lip said "good morning" to me! "Good morning to you," I said back to the enormous lavender flower as I sat down to write. In the days following, I wanted to tell my neighbor—despite her assertive opinions that overstepped boundaries—of its opening, and to give her another "thank you" for sharing with me the letters from her mother, and to tell her how the last one I read had inspired me to reintroduce into my life the spirituality I let go of long ago when the winds of life picked up, scattering me in different directions. Yet an opened orchid was nothing she hadn't seen before, and the concept in that letter from Cora—about spirituality being the stem that holds everything up—wasn't new to me. It was only reworded and packaged differently, as are most of life's philosophy and inspirational sayings, but, like seeds, it fell upon my ears at a time when my insides were ripe.

Every so often, as I typed away, I would look out my window and see her, there before the sun, dropping seeds into the dirt, and it reminded me of all the menial tasks a mother does for her children.

All those menial tasks a mother does for her children will one day be significant, just as a pianist practices hours upon hours, years upon years, and no one hears all those times her fingers hit the keys. They only hear the concert. And the writer puts in untold hours of solitude at her computer—

and no one sees all the work that goes into it as she types away before the rest of the world wakes, year after year. They only read the novel.

No one but me saw Fedelina dropping those seeds into the dirt, but every car that goes down our bumpy road will see her flowers. And no one in the world—but God—would know of my behind-the-scenes toiling over my children all the years of their lives thus far. They would only see the finished products, the masterpieces I was creating—the adults that I raise.

I almost jumped up from my desk, wanting to forgive my neighbor for the blatant things she had said, to run down there and let her know that, with spirituality as my stem, I was finding that the petals—the priorities surrounding me—were easier to keep up, and that they complemented one another as if they belonged in a circle on a stem.

And if one of the petals isn't meshing with the whole, it can be plucked and replaced with another.

I was thrilled that, for now, my petals were flourishing, and that ideas for the story were coming while playing with my children, biking or wading in the water near the Lighthouse Beach. I got my full cardiovascular workout easily and pleasurably once I decided to participate in the childrens' activities, pulling the wagon, a chariot behind my bike, or chasing them in the sand. And I tried as we went, using nature, to teach my kids a few things. "Red coquina, blue coquina, orange coquina, too," I would say as we sat where the water meets the sand—my children learning their colors from the shells in my hand.

"Never kids," I told them as we hopped over the clear jellylike blobs washed ashore. "Never in your life should you be spineless like those jellyfish, you hear?"

Motherhood in and of itself inspired me, as did going to the beach. In our hands we carried home pails filled with seashells, and in my mind I brought ideas and things I wanted to write but couldn't—not

until the children were asleep, and then from nine to eleven, and again
the next morning from five to seven, I'd let it all out. When they awoke
my writing would end and we'd sit in our favorite spot, halfway down
the wooden steps of the house, with that great big book of nursery
rhymes. And there I'd read until the sun was too hot or we reached that
one with the farmer's wife who cut off their tails with a carving knife,
and we'd put the book down and go inside, for my kids had never seen
such a thing in their life, and adamantly didn't care for "Three Blind
Mice."

We'd go back out in the early evening—me pulling all three down
Middle Gulf Drive in the wagon, always the same course. I figured, why
turn here or change to there when it's already good with regard to the
children liking the walk and me getting inspiration. It was always at the
same point in the walk that ideas started coming, dropping from the trees
like coconuts, or falling softly at my feet like sea grape leaves. I never
had paper, but I'd gratefully accept the ideas, jotting them down on any
writable object found in my purse, be it a grocery receipt or a dollar bill.
Sometimes I would leave my purse at home and decline ideas, turning
them away since, like a dream, I could only retain so much. But when
they were really good, worth holding onto, I could feel my mind swelling
and would walk faster. The children loved it when Mommy walked faster,
but mostly I would tell the ideas to stop, for there is a limit to what a
mother's mind can hold in a single walk with three children. Many ideas
were lost when Marjorie started to cry of thirst or the boys began to
fight. But motherhood, I learned in those mornings spent outdoors with
my children, complements, not deters both the creative and physical petals. And spirituality holds them all up!

"This is the day that will have Mama crying," I announced to my
children as I parked the wagon under the house and lifted each tired,
sandy, dirty child of mine from the wagon. "The day she will want to
relive when she is old."

It had been a perfect day. The birds were singing louder than usual,
the children were getting along, and my mind was bursting at the seams

with ideas. I couldn't wait to get us all upstairs and the children into one big bath, so I could write it all down before I forgot it like a dream.

"Anna," I heard a familiar voice call out as the children and I were halfway up the stairs. "I haven't seen you in awhile."

I looked all around, knowing it was Fedelina, but I couldn't see her.

"Over here, in my window."

"Oh, there you are," I said.

"I haven't seen you people in weeks. How are those wonderful kids?"

"Good," I said, not meaning to be brief, but how does a woman explain—without sounding crazy—that her time spent with the kids on the beach was so inspiring that she was holding all these ideas in her head, the way one holds a firefly in her hand, and if it wasn't all put into a jar quickly it would soon slip through a crack in the fingers, or lose its light and die?

"It bloomed," Thomas shouted out of the blue. "The orchid you gave to Mama, it bloomed!"

"Did it really?" asked the woman who had grown it from seedlings, and who gave it away as a gift. "And what color is it?"

"Um, um," he said with his face squashing into my thigh.

"Lavender," I whispered into his ear.

"Lavender," he shouted.

"That's wonderful news. I thought maybe it died and you all were hiding from me."

"Of course not," I told her.

"Well, I've missed seeing you all," she said.

"We've been out every morning. Where have you been?" I asked, only seeing bits of her through the branches of a tree and the darkness of her screen. "You're doing okay?"

"In with a foot infection," she said. "Would you believe I injured the bottom of my foot without knowing it, because I stepped on a thorn while barefoot in the garden?"

"You're kidding."

"No, I won't be doing that again—walking out there without shoes. Good thing I gave myself a pedicure. That's how I noticed it."

"I'm sorry to hear that. Will it be okay?"

"Oh yes, I'm fine now," she said. "And I already have my calendar marked for future pedicures. Not how I like spending my money, but I now see the value. Medicare is there to cover the cost once I have issues, but keeping myself healthy—taking better preventive care of me—is all mine. But I don't want to bore you. That's all that's new with me—nothing too exciting."

"I'm glad you're feeling better." I was still shy from when she last rained her strong views on me.

"Anna," she said then. "By chance, are you going to the grocery store this week?"

"I usually go once a week," I said.

"What about the bank?"

"Maybe."

"The post office?"

"I don't know. Why do you ask?"

"No specific reason. My daughter said to me on the phone the other day, 'Mom, why don't you move closer to me, then whenever I go shopping, you go shopping, and when I go to the bank, you go to the bank.' In other words, she was telling me I could go along with her wherever it was she had to go, and wasn't that nice? I could help with the kids."

I made a face, but don't think she saw it from where she was.

"So I was wondering," she continued, "how often you shop and when you were thinking of going next."

"I don't follow any routine. I have no idea when I'm going next. I just go."

"Well, call up to me in the window and I can be down in a flash."

I couldn't imagine anyone going along, running errands with me, expecting adult conversation as my children hung from the sides of the cart like talented monkeys. We were a mess in the store, but had a system—a-tear-open-a-bag-of-lollipops system—that worked well for me as long as I got big enough lollipops, the kind that take at least one hundred licks to reach the center. Fedelina would only stop me en route to the lollipop section, questioning the sugar mothers give to their children these days, or judge me for the frozen, packaged and processed dinners I was tossing into my cart.

"The only place I've got to go to right now," I told her, "is inside, to get these sandy kids into the tub."

"Enjoy it, Anna," she said through her screen as I reached the top of my stairs.

"It's nice to be needed. Trust me! It's rather sad when you're not needed anymore."

chapter forty-six

I started the bathwater and got the children in, feeling guilty for holding a grudge, and for not having gone next door all those weeks to find out where my neighbor had been, to see how she had been doing. But my days had been busy with kids, my mind preoccupied with the story I was writing. Having kids and writing a story does that to a person, the composition takes over a good part of one's mind, even when not with the kids or sitting at the computer, writing.

Some friendships are like annuals that last no more than a season, but sure put on a good show. And there are the perennials, which are great, but you have to resign yourself to certain times of the year when they will be dormant.

I scribbled a few thoughts down on scratch paper, then dried the children off and got them into their pajamas. It was then that I considered adding another petal to my life—one called "others" with which I care for the lonely, or make time again to chat with rose enthusiasts living next door. But with three children all crying at once and relying on me for their every whim, reality was not in favor of me adding more priorities to my life.

Down on my hands and knees, I scrubbed the floor of the laundry room, feeling bad for my neighbor's loneliness but not knowing how to fix it, or my marriage. When Timothy walked in, I don't know why I found it so easy to be mean to him.

"Why don't we get the kids to bed, and you and I have some time together," he said over the noisy dryer, which was on the brink of breaking again.

"Can't," I said. "I've got cleaning to do."

"You always say that. Is your cleaning more important than us?"

"Lower your voice," I scolded as I got up from the floor and slammed the window shut. "Our neighbor is going to hear you bickering with me."

"I'm not talking loud at all."

"Then talk in a more laid-back tone," I said, looking out toward her house, trying to make out whether or not she was in her window.

"You should have married a perfect man, Anna. That's what you want."

"No, I want a bigger house. That's what I really want."

"A bigger house? You loved this house. You're the one who insisted we rent it."

"Well, it's closing in on me now. The smallness of this house is driving me crazy. It's impossible to clean."

"I'd think a bigger house would be harder to clean."

"Didn't your mother teach you how to lower your voice?" I asked as I went to the dryer and opened its door, so the house would stop shaking. I stood there in the stillness, making a mental note to teach my sons how to lower their voices, wash their clothes, cook a nice dinner, clean the whole house, and bring flowers home for their women. If I don't teach them all of that, one day my daughters-in-law will look at me with both shame and curiosity as to why I didn't teach their husbands these things when they were boys and still trainable, and how I let them get to manhood like this.

"I'm sick and tired of that dryer," I said as I emerged from the laundry room, bustling from wall to wall of our house, adjusting all the lopsided pictures the rumbling, tumbling dryer caused to hang crookedly.

"Can you imagine what a hurricane would do to this place?" Timothy found it amusing to ask.

"Our house would be the first to fall," I said. *And down would come baby, bough, cradle and all.*

"But on the bright side," Timothy added, "the dryer puts Marjorie to sleep and the rosarian next door might think we're up to no good."

I could feel my mouth open as wide as a megamouth shark's. "Oh, hush," I said.

"Okay, then tell me this," he said, his voice a whisper. "How long has it been since you've held my hand, rubbed my back, since you've touched me in any way, or asked me about my day? It's always about the kids. Either the kids, or you—you and your turmoil, your hardships."

I could stand it no longer. I ran into the kitchen and pulled the book with all the letters from Cora from the cabinet, then I grabbed a flashlight and hurried out the front door of our shoebox of a home, letting the screen door slam behind me. I kicked an enormous conch shell good and hard, sending it off the porch, before I sat down on the wooden steps to read another letter from Cora.

chapter forty-seven

Dear Fedelina,

When you were a child, you would drape a blanket over our kitchen table and sit beneath it, making believe that it was a castle. On summer days I'd fill a pot with water and watch you drop your dolls in. You wanted to give them a swimming pool. It was only pretend, but this is the sort of play that has little girls imagining, fantasizing about the day they might become mothers themselves and living in a mansion. But the old lady who lived in a shoe probably never dreamt of living in a shoe, or of having so many kids she didn't know what to do. And she never dreamt of growing old. But she did.

Life doesn't always go the way we plan, and we either become resentful victims of our lives or we shift the way we view things in order to see the good. I've chosen the latter and no longer care so much about the house that I live in, but rather in what I see when I look out my window. Are there trees filled with red-bellied woodpeckers and nests full of ospreys? And when I leave through my front door, where does it lead? Should I go for a stroll, will I find nearby hideaways—nature's kingdoms?

A woman reaches a certain point in life, Fedelina, when she no longer cares about living in a castle, or how many glass slippers she owns. At least, I don't. My feet are bad and I hardly wear shoes. What I care about now is, how many prayers do I have in my soul, ideas in my mind and memories in my heart? And, have I loved? Have I loved the Lord, my God, with all my heart, soul and mind, and have I loved another person abundantly and to the extreme? Whether they loved me back or not, I do not care. But did I love extravagantly—for what a great sport it is—to love extravagantly in the sense of the action verb.

It's not how many rich people I have as my friends, or how much money I have in the bank, but do I know the words of Jesus, have I read the great literary masterpieces of our time, are the melodies of Mozart waltzing through my mind? Filling ourselves this way is important and goes into the makeup of a woman. When you're feeling underdressed and poor in worldly ways, you've got to ask yourself what you're made of. What are little girls who turn into women, made of? Your house may be a dive, darling, but your soul is a mansion. When you're feeling down and out, step outside your physical house and take a walk! I do this all the time, and the things I've discovered—well, I'll tell you about them soon.

I know what you're thinking—it's hard for a mother to go for a walk all by herself. But a mother's hug is like a flowering shrub that perfumes a room with a single branch. In other words, even as you're out taking a walk, your children will still feel your presence. And a mother's fragrance can be noticed six feet away. It's why a mother is able without guilt to put a little space between her and her children. But a rose is only as good as its last watering. It doesn't matter that it rained a month ago, or that a mother may have taken a half hour to herself a week ago. The roses need more rain now, and you mothers are only as good as your last break.

 *chapter forty-eight*

I didn't finish the rest of the letter, but closed the book and thought about all that was driving me crazy. The way the walls of the house were closing in, and how there wasn't a corner or closet I could go where it was quiet, where I might hide—sit by myself without distraction, without mess or conflict or cleaning that had to be done. Even at night, in my own bed, my kids are kicking and strangling me. I'm never alone, and then he comes home and expects me to dote over him when what I really want is time to myself—which he gets lots of on the plane, in the car, and at the hotel. Then again, I wasn't sure how alone he was at those hotels, so I switched instead to thinking of my week alone, and how it did me no lasting good, because here I was, finding myself exhausted again. Maybe Cora was right in what I just read, that a mother is only as good as her last watering, her last break.

Maybe, had I done some of those things the other mothers did— joined that book club with the group of ladies once a month, or taken the time to read a book alone in my room at night, or taken off on that inspirational retreat, taken more long baths, made time for weekly pedicures, pampered myself at the spa every once in a while, or taken off for a simple hour or two, to where? I don't know, *ride a cock-horse to Danburry Cross, or London Town*—would I still have broken down like I did? And would I still be feeling as I was now, like a piece of seaweed, washed ashore and shriveled up?

"I don't think it's who I'm meant to be," I said out loud as I turned the flashlight off and closed the book with the letters from Cora. "That miserable, motherly, martyr who does nothing for the care and well-being of herself—the woman who goes about bemoaning her life."

It was then that I looked out at the trees and spotted a pair of eyes through the branches of a gumbo-limbo tree. They became still, as did mine, and I stood there a couple of seconds, holding my breath, hardly moving. It was Fedelina. She was lonely and I was scathed, and any time two negatives are gathered together there is great company. I almost said, "Hi" and asked her how she was doing, but I didn't. I almost went inside to console Marjorie, who I could hear crying, but I didn't do that either. I got up from where I was sitting and, with the book clutched tightly in my hands, I jogged down my steps and stood in the sandy road, staring at my lit-up house on stilts. It was small and people driving by might mistake it for a birdhouse, but it was glowing with charm, and falling asleep inside were the world's three greatest children. I realized there, standing in the road in front of my house, that every so often a woman needs to step away from her life to see from afar how beautiful it is.

From there, I went to the beach and sat down in the sand, listening to the waves. Then I turned on the flashlight and read the rest of that letter from Cora.

 *chapter forty-nine*

A mother wonders which of her own experiences she ought to share with her children. She doesn't want to tell them everything about life because doing so might impair their own journeys of discovery. But there is something I want to share with you that I have never told anyone before. I'll tell you how it happened so you can try it, too. I don't know why I've kept it hush-hush.

One night, a long time ago, I was lying in bed, unable to sleep and working myself into a tizzy over everything that had gone wrong in my life. It was back around the time your father died, when everyone was dying or barely enduring and America was crying. We were struggling financially, moving into cramped quarters to survive. All of those big worries, as well as little ones—harsh words people had said to me, or the way they looked at me—kept creeping into my mind night after night. And nighttime has a way of turning even little things into big, dark, tormenting shadows.

So one night I tried something unique—something I have gone on to *do through all the years of my life. As I lay awake in a dither, desperate to escape the worries in my mind—I took several deep breaths in and out, and tried imagining what the door to my soul might look like. Well, I could see no door, but I did fall asleep. And so I tried it again the next night, and guess what? I fell asleep again. It was aiding me into sleep, and I continued the activity thereafter until, one, night, a door appeared in my mind. I won't tell you what it looked like because everyone might have a distinct door of their own. I tried opening mine, but it was locked. And so I knocked. I knocked and knocked on the door to my soul. And then it opened.*

You might be thinking your mother is a strange bird, but I swear this to be true, that when the door opened the Holy Spirit welcomed me in and led me through the corridors of my soul. And down every corridor there were rooms, and in each room was a different purpose. We didn't go into them, but I could see that the rooms to my soul were infinite. It's why I told you, darling, that your house may be a dive but your soul is a mansion!

The next night I knocked again and the door was opened. I asked if there might be a way to get rid of all the negative thoughts keeping me awake and the Holy Spirit took me past a window. Out that window was a fiery forest, and for the first time in my life I saw my thoughts for what they were—mere thoughts and nothing more. The fiery forest was the world outside my soul—the issues of the physical and the mental, and all the things I let bother me. But now, as I looked more closely, I saw how ridiculous it is to let them bother me, for they are not me, nor can they ever be within me. It made me cry, thinking of how long I let my worries roam like out-of-control rodents, biting at my heels and getting in the way of my intimate walk with the Spirit. I also knew then that everything that happens "out there" is only "out there," and of a differ-ent realm. None of it can ever enter my soul because it is guarded and protected by the Holy Spirit.

When I turned from the window, I saw a great light and fell down, but the Lord picked me up and, as He held me, I saw the Holy Spirit standing to the side, communicating with the Lord about something but I do not know what—I couldn't understand their way of communicating. But I knew the Lord loved me because He let me know, and from there a lot more happened.

I knew that, the more I did this, the more I would see and get to know, so I went on doing this and can only say that since then I have seen and gone into all kinds of rooms to my soul, including one where Jesus was hanging on the cross with blood dripping from his body. It was an emotional experience, and written words could do it no justice, so I'll simply write that I asked Him whether there was another cross so that I might climb up and be closer to Him, but He told me it wasn't necessary, because He was doing this for me. When I fell to my knees, crying about everything in my life, the cross was suddenly empty, and Jesus walked into the room and gave me His hand. More things happened, but I'll stop here because each person's experience and relationship is unique. I'll only say that when I woke up the next morning, I still felt myself holding Jesus' hand. That was when He told me in the "meditation" or "dream"—whatever one wants to call the experiences I've been having—but He let me know that He isn't only in my soul but in my life, my everyday life, too, and is holding my hand through it all.

The door doesn't only show up at night. I can be at the park, or in line at the market—wherever—all I have to do is think of it and it is there. And I hardly have to knock anymore before it opens and I feel them present—the Holy Spirit, the Father and Jesus. They are real and alive and living within me. I get it now, whereas once I didn't.

I could go on and on, Fedelina, about the walks I've been taking through my soul with the Holy Spirit and Jesus in my life, but I won't. I will say this, however. If you find yourself caught up in the branches *of the fiery forest, full of despair, knock, darling, and the door with be opened. Ask and you will receive. Seek, and you will find. You will find what you are looking for and you will see more than what you were looking for, or at least I did. I saw that which I had always heard about as a child, but now know for sure lies within me—the kingdom of God—and after the first time I caught a glimpse of it I was never the same again. It is there, darling. You are not hearing this from a friend of a friend, nor a friend of a friend of a friend. You are hearing it from your mother, that the kingdom of God is within you! And you are, literally, a walking temple of God!*

I pray, Fedelina, that you knock. Knock and the door will open.

chapter fifty

BELVEDERE

"Did you ever try it?" Fedelina asked me, and I stopped reading.

"You mean did I ever knock on the door to my soul?" I asked, and then admitted, "Yes. The first few times I fell asleep before seeing a door, but then one night one appeared and the experience that followed was very powerful."

"I'm glad," she said. "I've done it, too. The activity has put things into perspective for me. I stopped letting things bother me as I once had, you know, things people say or do."

"So how do you like my story?" I blurted out. I was desperately craving feedback at this point, and when she made a face I feared she didn't like the parts about her—and the little spat we had.

"How do *you* like your story?" she asked me.

"I don't know," I told her, unsure how to articulate that writing a novel, editing it slowly over time, revising it day after day, is like chiseling away at tiny rocks. After a while all you see are the tiny rocks, not the fact that all those tiny rocks are part of the Grand Canyon.

"Bring me the fudge, will you? It should be over there on the counter somewhere. And please, Anna, have some with me."

It wasn't the answer I was looking for, but I walked over to the counter and studied the two kinds I had bought. "You like black walnut?" I asked her.

"Hate black walnuts, can't stand them. Why do you ask?"

"Well, I don't want to eat the one with black walnuts if that's the one you like." I still didn't understand where she was going with this. I only knew she had something in mind. I sliced myself a piece of the black walnut fudge, and gave her a slice of the other, then sat back down in the chair that faced her.

"Anna," she said as she pressed the fudge between her fingers, softening it like putty before putting it to her mouth. "It's okay that you like black walnuts and I hate them. It's okay for us to differ. We're still friends."

"You're right," I said, licking my lips and making a mental note to add to my story that it's okay to disagree and still be friends, that there was no need for reacting as extremely as I did, for avoiding her. I walked over to the sink to wash my hands, and I knew her response was her way of letting me know what should be added to that part of the story. "There's something I need to ask you," I said then. "Would you mind if I moved forward in getting this published?"

She made a face, and I knew she either had fudge stuck in a tooth, or she was struggling with her answer. "I don't think it's ready," was all she said, shaking her head.

"You don't?" I asked, and I could feel my creativity shriveling up and falling to the floor. "You mean you don't like it?"

"I didn't say that," she said. "I think it's a wonderful story. But Anna, there's something missing, something big."

"I'm not done reading," I said, wondering whether she saw fear on my face, fear that winter was coming and everything in my tree was about to fall to the ground. "Whatever it is that's missing, maybe it's coming."

"I don't think so," she said. "Call for the nurses, would you please?"

"Are you okay?"

"Fine," she said. "I'd like to have my blood pressure checked. My face feels hot. I need rest."

I felt an instant state of situational depression descend upon me because the manuscript I had put what felt like infinite hours into writing wasn't getting more of a "wow" response, that she hadn't once told me what I needed to hear, that she loved it, or liked it—especially all the parts about her!

"You'll be back in the morning?" she asked me.

"Yes," I said, but could hardly talk.

"Good. Let me think about it," she said. "I do want to hear more in the morning."

In the skies outside Belvedere Nursing Home there were sparrows circling and cranes whooping, but there was nothing good soaring through my mind, no ideas flapping or bursts of inspiration swooping down upon me. And because nature always inspired me in the past—was always the stimulus that put my mind where it needed to be, into a state that was ripe for receiving ideas—I set off walking down the long country road.

Indiana's fall-blooming crops were pretty but left me feeling disappointed with myself for reaching the fall of my life without having produced a worthy piece of fruit. And Fedelina's lackluster response to my novel made me question whether inspiration exists, or if there is only imagination. The thought of inspiration not existing produced within me a deep loneliness—the kind one might feel when alone in a house at night with nothing but the thoughts in their mind, because they don't believe in the soul.

I was looking at the cotton and the corn in the fields as I walked, wondering whether it really was blind faith that had kept me plowing ahead hour after hour, chapter after chapter, year after year, or if it was only stubborn determination.

"I'm not doubting you, Lord," I prayed, "but I'm questioning whether inspiration is only imagination, and blind faith simply compulsion, and creativity the arousal of the mind."

When I finished my prayer, I looked up and saw a sign for a corn maze. After paying the five dollars, I set off through fourteen acres of dead ends, crying my eyes out as I went. My mind and soul were at odds with each other, questioning which one was to blame for having wasted all those years working on the same darn story, a ridiculous story, and wondering whether I had made a mistake, entwining spirituality with creativity and thanking the Lord each time a sentence or paragraph fell into my hands like a blossom from a tree.

"Where are you, Lord, when I need you the most?" I asked out loud, two hours into the maze and unable to find my way out. I didn't want the farmers sending helicopters out in search of me. I didn't want to be the laughingstock of Indiana, or of the world should I decide to release my novel, so I got down on my hands and knees and once again prayed to God, telling Him how scared I was at the thought of Him not existing, and how full of fear and alone I would feel in walking through the labyrinth that is my life.

Three hours later I found my way out, refused a complimentary hay-ride, but bought a homemade soy candle instead. As I started walking back toward the Belvedere Nursing Home, there was a tractor stopped ahead waiting for a bird—a whooping crane—to cross the road.

"The bird forgot it has wings," I said to the farmer on the tractor.

"They have no fear," the farmer said back to me with a grin. "The birds have no fear."

All I could think for the rest of my walk was what that farmer had said, that the birds have no fear, *no fear, no fear.* So why should I? I knew then that I would fearlessly plow full force ahead, read the rest of my story to Fedelina, and then ask her what might make it better.

"Whatever it was," I mumbled to myself, "the receiving of inspiration or the activity of imagining, it drew me closer to God."

Early the next morning, after my own dark night of the creative soul, I returned to the nursing home and to her room. I didn't feel like talking about pancakes or asking her how she had slept. I only felt like reading. And then, about asking her what might make it all better.

chapter fifty-one

I went about the rest of my summer setting the alarm and writing for two hours every morning. And one morning, as I was brewing coffee, I noticed through my kitchen window that things were starting to happen in Fedelina's yard. I grabbed a crayon and a picture one of the boys had drawn for me, and on it I wrote what I saw:

There were new varieties and colors, new flowering stems growing in her yard.

Later that afternoon, carloads of seniors were coming and going, and this got me to wondering whether she was ill and whether I should bring flowers— no, chocolate . . . no, an apology— but then, a couple of evenings later, I saw her hurrying down the stairs with one lady, two ladies, three ladies trotting behind, each of them carrying straw hats, dried flowers, glue guns and more, as if they were volunteering for a bazaar, creating items for an arts and crafts festival. And they were laughing.

It was hard not to notice all that had been going on in that yard of hers each day, and soon I noticed a routine. Ladies would pull into her driveway every Tuesday night, talking about a thing I did not under-stand—"Mah-jongg" was the word they always said, a word I heard at least once through my window every Tuesday night, after the kids had fallen asleep and I had turned on my computer to write.

I found it difficult to write with my windows open on Wednesday nights. More women with white hair, these wearing oven mitts and car-rying pans of steaming potluck-style foods would arrive, so I closed my window, not wanting to smell the food or listen to the ladies having fun.

Thursday nights were the best for writing. I would turn on my com-puter and, as I waited for it to warm up, I'd look out my window and watch my neighbor, all dressed up, carefully descend her steps. "I can't talk now, I'm late," I heard her say on a cell phone one Thursday. I had never seen her talk on a cell phone before. "Yeah, my e-mail class, that's where I'm going now." Whoever it was she was talking to was probably as surprised as I to hear she was taking an e-mail class. "It's easy. We're attaching pictures. It's a nice way to keep in touch with grandchildren, but I'll call you later. If you were on e-mail, I'd e-mail you later."

And then I'd watch her back out of her driveway like a teenager, talking on the phone and pulling too far to the right, the branches still scratching the side of her car. Thursday nights she left for the movies. I know because I heard her once, talking with a friend who had come to pick her up. They were going to someone's house to watch *Grumpy Old Men*, which one of them had rented. I saw her on Saturday mornings going down her steps, carrying different orchids each week. She must have joined the orchid society, and was probably president by now.

Her orchids were gorgeous, and got me to thinking again as to who I was. "An unhappy wife," I said out loud as I swept the last remnants of a morning at the beach out my front door and over the side of the porch while the children were at the table eating. And I no longer wanted to be an unhappy wife. I wanted to be something beautiful, like an orchid or a white ibis, or a wife in love with her husband.

It was then that I noticed my neighbor dragging a suitcase down the steps, and there was that look on her face, the one that says "I'm no longer lonely," and it inspired me. If she, at her age, could sidestep her way out of loneliness, than I could do something about the stagnant relationship with my husband.

Despite the time gone by without us speaking, I left the kids inside and hurried toward her, wanting to tell her of the impact that the look on her face and all the activities I saw through my window were having on me.

"Let me help," I said. "You shouldn't be doing that by yourself."

"I'm fine, really," she said.

"Looks like you're going on a trip."

"Nashville, Tennessee," she declared. "Grand Ole Opry."

"You have family there?"

"No," she said. "I'm going with a group of friends. We're taking a motor coach."

"Good for you," I said as I helped put her suitcases in the back of her convertible, wanting to tell her that I admired her. "Do you need help watering your flowers while you're away?"

"It's not necessary," she said as she opened her car door and got in. "Nature waters them for me, and I won't be gone that long, but thanks for offering."

chapter fifty-two

I stood there waving until I could no longer see her car, and then I got on with my day: finger painting inside with the children, making homemade dough, gluing glitter and eyeballs to seashells. After all of that I looked at the clock and it was only nine-thirty in the morning, and I started to fret over what else we might do with our day. Fretfully, the hours passed, and I was glad when I put the children to bed and could start to write.

The next morning I woke early, as I had grown accustomed to doing, writing by candlelight my story about a woman who suddenly wanted more than anything in life for her marriage to rebloom. I did this, staying up late and waking early to write, for the remainder of summer, no longer caring whether it was good or not. The writing was mine and I enjoyed the process. It satisfied me to the point that I didn't stress at the end of the day if the laundry wasn't folded or the floors swept. As long as I knit together a nice sentence or organized a good paragraph, I could close my eyes and feel that which comes from being productive.

But the last day of summer I wanted to be different, a day the children and I would remember. I woke my usual two hours before the world, but not to write. Instead I washed and dried their clothes, laying them out warm and in a row on the sofa, then filled cups with juice, giving Marjorie the pink, Tommy the blue and Wil the green according to their favorite colors. I then poured cereal into bowls, set spoons beside them, and placed shoes by the front door. The children were still asleep, so I showered, dried my hair for the first time in months and got dressed.

And they were *still* sleeping. I scurried around the house, wiping counters, emptying the garbage and smashing with a paper towel the small black bugs—the newcomers—that had invaded my pantry shelves. I dumped a box of rice and stopped myself from doing more. I could do more tomorrow. I could do everything tomorrow.

Tomorrow, when the boys start preschool and Marjorie goes to the two-morning-a-week program for younger children, everything from folding laundry to writing during the day to grocery shopping and prepping for dinner would become simpler, more possible, and I would feel more like the person I once was, a woman both sanitary and sane.

I poured myself a cup of coffee and sat down outside, on the top step, dreaming of tomorrow. I would bring them to school, come home and do all the things I had been longing to do but never had time for, like floss my teeth. I would start caring for my marriage, setting it up as one of my petals and nurturing it in ways I never had before. If Fedelina could add all those things to her life, alleviating loneliness as she did, then I could try a few things of my own—what did I have to lose? But I would do all of that tomorrow, after dropping the kids off at school.

First, I would enjoy today—take them to town, get their pictures taken inexpensively at a superstore, have lunch and watch a matinee. And if everyone was behaving, we'd breeze through the children's department, picking out desperately needed T-shirts and shorts for school. Then, if the sun wasn't too hot, we might stop at a park. Timothy could meet us, and together we'd watch our children play to their hearts' content on this last day of summer. And it was a beautiful start indeed, one of those mornings when everyone was getting alone fine. The daisies were mingling with the pansies, the morning glories entwined around weeds, and even my husband and I were talking kindly to one another. It all had me feeling as royal as any Queen Anne could be.

"Hi," Timothy said as he sat down next to me with a cup of coffee in hand.

"Hi," I said back.

"So what do you and the kids have planned today?"

"Special things," I told him, "all sorts of special things."

"As long as you don't spend money," he said. "We only have eighty dollars in our account."

"What?" I asked, bursting with self-pity. "How can I do the things I had planned if I can't spend money?"

"I don't know. You'll have to figure it out," he said.

"Not even a little?"

"Not even a dime," he said. "We bounced three checks last week."

"All I bought were groceries." And oh, how I had been craving a good loaf of rosemary bread from the local gourmet market, with olives on the side and a bottle of sparkling pomegranate juice to go with it.

"Doesn't matter what you bought," he said. "You still bounced three checks. We can't keep doing that. Don't spend a penny until Thursday. You've got to respect me on this."

My mouth closed shut like the beak of a black skimmer.

"I can't spend money until Thursday?" I asked, fighting back tears. I could hardly talk about how overwhelming I found it to be a woman, a consumer in today's world, a person with material desires and needs, yet no longer having an incoming salary of her own.

"Better yet, Friday," he declared. "And I think you know what I'm about to say."

"No," I corrected. "I never know what you're about to say."

"It's time you return to work," he told me.

I could hardly talk. I no longer felt any passion for work. I wanted to write, and to focus on other things, like keeping house, making great dinners, picking my children up from school feeling refreshed! And I wanted to work on our marriage, on figuring out what had gone wrong, on making it better, or trying.

"Why are you making that face? The kids are starting school. It shouldn't be a shock to you. I can't do it any longer, living on one income like we are."

I could hear the kids waking, the television on, the refrigerator door opening, the carton of milk dropping to the floor, my sons feuding and Marjorie whining. It took me a long time, but I knew now who I was as a mother—nutty and crazed and always in a dither, but a woman falling in tune with the beautiful chaos. I no longer knew who I was outside the cuckoo's nest that was our home—a woman who no longer knows how to walk in high heels or spray her hair or pull nylons up without ripping them or carry on adult conversations with anyone over age five and under age eighty.

"I'm sure you knew this was coming," he said.

I felt as if I no longer knew how to use my mouth, as if I had a beak instead, and I was glad when an osprey in a nearby nest started making noise and the children came running out onto the front porch to find us.

"We're going to the post office," I announced to my kids. "We're going to buy a stamp, one stamp. A stamp costs thirty-four cents, so I need you to dig through your piggy banks, put your pennies together and count out exactly thirty-four, okay? Can you do that?"

They hurried inside, kids on a mission, and I went, too, a woman driven by a dream, believing what I wanted to believe regardless of how unrealistic it was. I went into my bedroom, turned on my computer and printed the letter I had been working on for months, the query I had written with regard to my story. I needed an agent. All writers need agents. But I wasn't done writing the book and didn't believe I deserved representation, so I addressed the letter to my editor friend instead. She worked in acquisitions, and they always say it's not what you know but who you know. I always disagreed, choosing to believe the opposite, that it's what you know, but I was now desperate and would try anything, even those theories I felt were not right.

My old editor friend, despite having seen me picking daisies in my nightgown that day, would tell me the truth about whether the story I was working on was anything the world might want to read. And if it wasn't, she would reject me softly, using the gentlest words.

chapter fifty-three

BELVEDERE

I had stopped reading the day before when I noticed Fedelina's eyes closed. I didn't say good-bye, but left her room quietly and returned to my hotel. When I returned early the next morning, I was surprised to find her bed—Fedelina in it—parked in the hallway outside her room. She wore a brightly colored cotton gown and had pretty decorative combs in her hair. "I know what will make it better," Fedelina said when she saw me.

"Make what better?" I asked.

"Your story."

"You do? What?"

"The butterflies," she said. "You've got to see them. They're in the court-yard. The nurses are going to wheel me in there. I told them I wanted you to see them."

A couple of women, along with their daughters, showed up next. They introduced themselves to me, told me their girls were homeschooled, and that they volunteered at the facility a couple of times a month.

"It's so many lessons at once," said one of the mothers. "The girls see

living history, and hear with their own ears the stories these women have
to tell."

Then one of the young girls walked over to Fedelina's side, kissed her
on the cheek and, with the formality of a reporter, asked a question. I
wondered whether she had the maturity to come up with it on her own,
or if her mother had prompted her to ask it.

"You have lived a long time," the girl said to Fedelina. "I'm curious,
what's one of the biggest changes you've seen in people as a whole throughout your lifetime?"

"That's a good question," Fedelina told her right away. "I'll talk in
terms of flowers because, as you know, it's the easiest way for me. Back
in the old days, when I was growing up, people knew flowering shrubs
needed time to grow a solid root system before producing blooms. Today,"
she went on, "people want to purchase plants already in full flower. They
expect the instant landscaped look. They want things in life, and they want
them right away. And another thing," she said, "You gals today have more
choices than my generation had. It's good, but harder, too. Along with
more choices comes accountability for the way our lives turn out."

"Thank you," the little girl said quickly, and I wondered whether she
understood it all. I did and was rummaging through my bag for a pen,
wanting to write it down, add it somewhere in my story.

"And women today," Fedelina started up again, "especially my own
granddaughters, they're emotionally consumed with looking young."

"What I'd give to look thirty-six again," was all I said.

"I was thinking the same about eighty-six," Fedelina said, and we
laughed. "But it's harder in some ways for you women living in today's
antiaging society and probably easier, too, with all those products and
things you can do to put off wrinkles and reduce the signs of aging. When
I was younger, if you really want to know, I'd mix laundry detergent with
water and rub it into my face as an exfoliant. Back then, for me, that was
pampering my skin, so I'm not opposed to modern science and doing what
we can to look our best. But in my day, we hardly talked of it. I guess
we welcomed wrinkles with wisdom."

"Now there are support groups for women with wrinkles," said one of the mothers. "Anywhere you go, it's not uncommon for it to come up in informal conversation, and for women to commiserate together."

"You see this dress I'm wearing?" Fedelina asked us, pushing the blanket down so we could see it. "I always wondered why old ladies wore these things, and now I know. They slip right over the head. No buttons, no zippers, and they come in a zillion different colors and patterns. They're so darn comfortable. That's important to me at this age, you know. At my age, comfort is more important than how I look."

"Are you comfortable?" one of the school girls asked, and I felt bad for not having asked her this myself, and sooner.

Fedelina reached for a tube of lotion beside her on the bed, took the cap off and started rubbing it into her arms. "No," she said, shaking her head. "Not all the time. My skin is dry. I've got itchy spots on my buttocks, knees and elbows. I have tingling in my hands, and pain. It's worse at night. I have trouble digesting my food, but constipation is the worst. Everyone does his or her best, and it's like a team effort to keep me comfortable. I'm grateful for all the effort. I don't want to disappoint the nurses and my family, especially all you girls who come to see me."

"You could never disappoint us," the girls told her.

"She's a beautiful person, isn't she?" I said to them.

"Thank you," Fedelina said to me, and then focused her eyes on the girls. "You are beautiful, too," she told them. "You are living, breathing masterpieces, created by God. Don't let the world trick you into thinking you are not beautiful, because you are, and true beauty never fades, never dulls."

The nurses took her bed and, like an organized procession of people, we started to parade through the halls of Belvedere Nursing Home. Fedelina was quiet but had a look of pride and festivity in her eyes as if she were riding on a float in the Macy's Thanksgiving Day Parade. I think she got a kick out of the entourage surrounding her, and she started blowing random kisses to women in the rooms we passed. They were waving back, and a few called out her name.

I looked at my old neighbor being wheeled through this final stage of her life, and promised to pay older people more attention—because tomorrow I will be old, too, and what might I give then for a young person to show up and ask me my story!

"My friend Anna, here, she's a writer," Fedelina was saying to the girls, "and I'm one of the characters in her story!"

"Everyone has a story," I told the girls. "Whether you build an empire from the ground up or raise a child, your lives are worthy books of their own."

We rounded a corner, turning down a hall that had no rooms and was quieter. "We're about there, aren't we?" Fedelina asked me, taking hold of my hand.

"The butterfly garden?"

"No," she said. "The end of your story."

"Sort of," I told her.

"What do you mean 'sort of'?" she asked.

"I don't have an ending," I told her. "I could never think of one that was good."

By then we had reached the indoor courtyard, once a patio, but over time it had been transformed into a haven featuring a walking trail, a trickling fountain, and fragranced flowers and plants. The little girls opened the gates for us and I, along with the nurses, pushed my friend's bed in.

"This is remarkable," I said to the volunteers.

"It's brought a lot of joy to this facility, and it all began with Fedelina's flower boxes."

"What do you mean?" I asked.

"The ones she insisted on bringing with her the day she moved in. She hardly brought anything else, just flower boxes, and the nurses thought she might be losing her mind. But she wasn't. Turns out she had a plan."

I shook my head, as amazed now as I was the day I heard about it on national radio. She had recruited children from local schools to come by and help her turn those flower boxes into a haven for fluttering butterflies.

"A woman is never too old for flowers," Fedelina said. "If I were younger, if I knew then what I knew now, that old people like me still crave beauty in their lives, then I would have worked to implement such courtyards in facilities nationwide. But I didn't know back then . . ."

"Know what?" asked one of the girls.

"That one day I'd be old, really old. I had no idea then what being old was all about. It's just an extension of being young."

We broke up laughing, but as I watched the girls prance about, their arms extended, hands opened wide, waiting and hoping for butterflies to land on their palms, I knew that later I would give more thought to what Fedelina had said about what being old really was.

I extended my arms like the girls and let butterflies land on my palms. "You know what amazed me most about you back then, when we lived next door to each other? And what still amazes me now?" I said to my friend.

"No, what?" she asked.

"You have a way of showing me that getting old isn't all bad."

"Did you imagine it all bad?" she asked, and I gave her an honest nod, "yes."

"This garden," she said, "is designed to sustain the entire life cycle of the butterflies. But metamorphosis is not finished, Anna, with the production of a butterfly."

"It's not?" I said, looking at the winged creatures gathering on my palms, then back at my friend on her bed.

"No. One might think this is the end. After all, what more is there after becoming a butterfly? But let me tell you, Anna, the butterfly is the beginning. Metamorphosis is a cycle."

I thought about it a moment. "Thank you," I said then, tears welling in my eyes.

"For what?"

"I have an end to my story."

"Well, we haven't reached that point yet," she reminded me. "Why don't you read more?"

"You mean when we get back to your room?"

"No," she said. "Right here, read to me right where we are."

"Okay," I said as I sat down on a black cast-iron bench and pulled out the manuscript I had in the bag that had been slung over my shoulder all this time. I started to read where I left off last, about my children and me, and their last day of summer.

chapter fifty-four

The post office was closed when we got there. After all the effort it had taken, counting pennies and getting ourselves dressed and out the door, I decided we would stay, sitting on the curb, waiting the fifteen minutes until the post office opened. It was nice knowing, after our summer spent without looking at clocks, that I was capable of getting us all ready and to a destination early in the morning. I felt more confident about starting the school routine.

Then one child had to use the bathroom. Another fell down and scraped her knee. And the last, I saw from the corner of my eye, was pocketing large landscape rocks. From the corner of my other eye I saw that the first child had peed in his shorts. My daughter was screaming bloody murder over the sight of her hurt knee. And my remaining son had clenched his fists and was grunting at me in an ill-tempered fit when I told him to empty the rocks out of his pocket. It was all making me think that I had a hundred children, not three!

"In the car, all of you," I scolded. By the time I had fastened their seat belts, the post office doors had opened and I was tired. I could do without the stamp, and my children could go on without having experienced a field trip into the post office.

"Whoopee," I said out loud as I put the key in the ignition and started my car. Then again, I should get us all out, go in there, and buy the doggone stamp. Or I could buy it tomorrow, alone. I could come back and stand in line silently, full of peace, a pleasant look on my face, with no one tugging on my hands or pressing my nerves. I could leisurely stuff my query into the envelope and lick it lackadaisically, or I could do it all now, get it over with— Oh, how I hated my indecisiveness. I sat in the car, fretting over what to do.

"We're going to rest," I announced to the children. "We're going to sit right where we are and rest for ten minutes." I was aware of weariness that had to do with writing past midnight and again before sunrise. Writing at those hours would be simple if I weren't mothering three children from sunrise to midnight.

With their seat belts fastened I no longer cared that their mouths were rambling, or that they were whining and giggling in the backseats. As long as they weren't getting into things, I could close my eyes and fall asleep. A mother gets her sleep wherever she can, even in the post office parking lot.

But then, like a cat about to nap, I gazed out my window, my eyes homing in on a patch of dirt alongside the building. Hard as I tried, I couldn't look away, for I instinctively knew what I needed to do in my life, and the thought had me pawing at my eyes. Rather than send my query out in the mail, I would dig a hole in the dirt, drop my writing in, and fill it up—I saw no other option. There was only so much of me to go around. I needed to work on my marriage, my husband needed my help in generating income and my children needed a mother, not a walking, talking, sleep-deprived, dream-chasing zombie.

"Sometimes a mother does that," I whispered to myself. "She tosses her aspirations into the dirt and walks away, leaving them behind. It's not that she doesn't have the passion or desire to cultivate them, but that there are other things demanding her care and people who cannot flourish without her."

My children were bickering in the backseat, and the sound of it made me cry—not ordinary tears, but rather droplets of passion-filled dew that watered my dream, my desire to write, which now, like seeds, I was mentally, emotionally and spiritually letting go of, tossing into that dirt. I would walk away from it for one year, two years, or however long it might take until my life cleared and I found myself a woman strolling along, frolicking in the rain, tiptoeing through a garden with more time and less pressure.

But then I could feel my creativity, like a strong wind twirling within me. My thoughts were spinning like the noise in my car. Inspired by the chaos coming from my children, I grabbed a broken crayon from the floor and, on the back of a grocery receipt, I calmly wrote a letter to my first son, because I had already written one to my second son, and one to Marjorie, and it had been in my subconscious all this time that I didn't want anyone to be left out. And besides, I was feeling emotional about them starting school in the morning.

Dear Child,

When I look out my window I see an osprey soaring through the sky,
　　But when I look at you I see you doing more.
When I pull you in the wagon we see a turtle diligently digging a hole,
　　But when I look at you I see you doing more.
When I take you to the shore I see a big boy building castles out of sand,
　　But when I look at you I see you doing more.
When I take you for a ride at night, I see the lighthouse lighting up the Gulf so bright,
　　But when I look at you I see you doing more.

When I push you on the swing, we see the trees reaching up to
Heaven,
But when I look at you I see you doing more.
When I look at you, my son, I see the things that you can be,
And I also see bits of me.
I see all the things I wanted to be, the things I wanted to do,
But then I see more.

When I had finished writing the letter to my child, I glanced into my rearview mirror and saw a car run through the four-way stop sign and turn into the post office parking lot, jerking into a space behind me. I recognized the red-and-white convertible and the woman driving it. It was Fedelina, and she was getting out. With tears streaming down my face, I felt caught in the act. I considered telling her that she had changed the way in which I perceived my life, that her garden idioms were rubbing off on me, and that I was sitting here crying over my children as well as for dreams that were like seeds planted in the earth. But how ridiculous, I thought as she came up alongside my car. She was a busy lady and there was purpose to her walk.

"Why, hello, Anna," she said, stopping at my opened window.

"Hi. How have you been?"

"Good up until a week ago," she said.

"What happened a week ago?"

"My claim was denied and I don't know why. It's not the first time. Last time, would you believe, they wanted a prescription for eye drops that didn't require a prescription with the pharmacy. Who knows this time?"

"Didn't your insurance company send you an explanation?"

"They did. I had to use a magnifying lens to read it, and I read it over and over again but still don't get it. I feel like a struggling schoolgirl. I'm so frustrated."

"Sorry to hear that," I said. "How was the Grand Ole Opry?"

"Wonderful," she said. "I felt so alive on that trip. Now I just feel tired. I was up all night, hoping there might be a better explanation of benefits waiting for me in my P.O. box today."

"Did you try calling a representative of the insurance company?"

"I will today."

"Good. They should be able to talk you through it, give you a thorough explanation. It's probably something simple."

"Let's hope," she said, looking out at the parking lot filling with cars. "I better get in there before the lines start. I've got a lot going on today."

"I only came for a stamp, but . . . " I lowered my voice. "Someone in my backseat needs a change of clothes. I'll come back later."

"Don't be ridiculous! I'll go in and buy it for you. Just one?"

"No," I told her. "I can come back later."

"Let me help you," she insisted, and hurried inside. A few minutes later she returned, holding a stamp in one hand and a large, padded envelope tucked under her arm the way one clutches a purse.

"Thank you," I told her. "You spared me from what would have been an all-day, hair-pulling field trip."

"I do remember," she said.

I smiled at her. Despite her opinions that day in the garden, I missed the pleasant things she used to say to me. "Other than your claim being denied," I said, "life is going well?"

"I have nothing to complain about. And I've been waiting for this," she said, taking the padded envelope from under her arm.

"What is it?"

"A couple of more letters my mother wrote. Two, I've never read before. After all these years they've shown up. My cousin found them tucked in with some old papers in a trunk she hadn't opened in years, and they had my name on them. I can't wait to get home and read them, Anna."

"Wow," was all I said.

"If you're at all interested, I'll let you read them. I know you enjoyed the others."

"Yes, I did. I'd love to."

"Good, then why don't you come by sometime?"

"You're the busy one," I said with a laugh. "You tell me when a good time is."

"They start school tomorrow, right?"

"Yes, so don't be alarmed if you hear a few hallelujahs coming from my yard."

"I'm sure you're looking forward to a little private time."

"I am," I told her, "although I do have to find a job—nothing too stressful—but a job that pays, a job I enjoy." I smiled, waiting for her to give me a glimmer of optimism, a fact about roses.

"Well," she said, "I had better get going. I'm meeting a group of ladies for a breakfast in ten minutes."

"Don't let me keep you," I said.

"Stop by sometime, Anna. If you see me out in my garden, come on by."

"I will," I told her. "Maybe tomorrow, once I get the children off to school."

chapter fifty-five

The next morning I walked up the steps of my stilted house alone. There was no child riding on my hip, or tugging on my hand, or whining at my heels. But there were two lizards dancing in circles at my feet, and a bunny staring at me from afar, and a sticky frog attached to the railing. It all made me cry, for there was no one for me to point these things out to, no children for me to share it all with.

I was a teary mess by the time I reached the top and there, sitting at my door, were a plant and an envelope with my name on it.

Hi, Anna,

This Trimezia martinicensis *is for you. Don't let that name intimidate you. It's a subtropical walking iris. I figured, what better gift to give a mother whose children are headed off into the world, even if it's preschool. I used to divide my clumps of iris by taking the whole mass out of the ground, breaking it into smaller pieces, and planting a few small ones. Of course I always gave some to friends.*

Anyway, it's called a walking iris because it sends up a spike with a baby plant on it. The baby plant falls to the ground, still attached to the mother plant, and often roots. The plant appears to be walking!

You're probably wondering, Anna, what that has to do with your children going off to school. Well, like the walking iris, as children step out into the world, so does their mother. A mother stays attached to her children by way of her heart, soul and mind, as they go off, rooting lives of their own.

I thought I'd leave this for you, because I forgot when I saw you yesterday at the post office that I had some appointments in town today. If I'm not too tired when I get home, I'll stop by with a copy of one of the letters from my mother. Hope you enjoy your first day all to yourself, no kids.

I went into my house, made myself a cup of tea and sat down at the kitchen table, but there was a silence to my house that made me nervous, the kind one hears at a circus during the trapeze act, and I found it hard to focus. My own voice was coming through loud and clear, and I found it disturbing that all it was telling me was that I should be cleaning, washing floors, folding laundry and finding a new job. Because I didn't feel like hearing all of that, I got up from the kitchen table and went over to my neighbor's yard with my cup of tea. And, because I knew she wouldn't mind, I sat down on the stone bench amidst all the flowers. There I sat, doing nothing, thinking hardly anything, but looking with my eyes and smelling with my nose and getting up every so often to touch with my fingers the beauty of her flowers, the beauty of my life.

chapter fifty-six

BELVEDERE

I kept watching out my window the rest of that day, hoping to see you in your garden," I told Fedelina when I came to the end of all I had written in my novel so far and closed its pages. "I wanted to thank you for the plant."

"I know," she said.

"I knocked and knocked at your door the next day. I swear, I even looked in your windows," I went on. "I figured you left, went on a trip."

"It's okay, Anna, forgive yourself."

I turned my face from her and tried focusing on all the butterflies, but I was crying now and couldn't hide it. "Forgive me. I'm sorry I didn't help you. I didn't think, didn't know! I didn't know until weeks later, when your daughters came to pack your boxes. That's when I found out what happened."

"Diabetic shock," she said. "A stroke, too."

"I would have come to see you," I said, wiping my eyes. "I would have come to the hospital, had I known."

"I know," she said. "But I was in poor condition, and before I knew it my children had me transferred up north."

"You didn't want to go back north."

"No, but the best time to move an established rose is when the rose is dormant," she said. "And it was more convenient to have me in their neck of the woods. They were busy with jobs, had their own lives. It was best for them."

"But you loved your life, your garden."

"Yes," she said, "which only proved what I already knew, what you and I talked about, that no stage of life lasts forever. It's all a big meta-morphosis."

"I see what you mean. The best stage for me was when my children were little. At least then I knew they were coming home from school each day. Back to what we were talking about before, I'm lucky now if they come home for spring break!" I wiped my eyes on my sleeve. "I know I need to start doing things for myself, but it's hard. I'm not crazy about the stage I'm currently in."

"You're in a transition stage, like a pupa, suspended under a branch, hidden in leaves or buried underground," she said.

"That's exactly how I feel, and I'm ready to get out, move on to a new phase," I confessed.

"And you will."

"I hope," I said.

"You will!"

"I don't know. I've been stuck in this rut since Marjorie left for college."

"Oh, it can last a few weeks, months, even longer, but keep in mind, if you've ever watched a butterfly work its way out of a cocoon, you'd know it's a real struggle. It has to be. It's the struggle that pumps blood into its wings so it can fly. Did I tell you what I did the first morning alone in my house after my youngest left home?"

"No."

"I sat in my pajamas at the kitchen table, smoking a cigarette and reading the paper, drinking coffee, and wondering, is this it? Is this all that is left to life? And then," she said, "I became a certified master gardener!"

"You became a master gardener? Just like that?"

"Well, nothing is as easy as it sounds. I took an intensive training program. I learned everything about botany, soils, vegetable gardening, annual and perennial flowers, insects, diseases and weed control. Whoever thought, after raising seven children, that I'd then spend several years planting and maintaining public gardens?"

"How rewarding."

"Oh, it was. I made horticulture presentations to civic and garden clubs, and helped with community beautification projects."

"Wow," I said, shaking my head. "I did not know you were a master gardener."

She laughed. "So when, Anna, are you going to start doing what a mother of grown children does?"

"I don't know. What does she do?"

"She looks around at the garden she is in, which, by the way, is usually overgrown. Then she goes about creating a master plan for a new garden, something more suitable to her liking."

"I don't know for sure what I like," I said.

"You've got to ask yourself a simple question."

"Oh, no," I said. "Not, who am I?"

"No," she laughed. "But what do you want?"

"What do I want?"

She nodded.

"And then what?"

"Then you put your gardening gloves on, and get down in that dirt and dig."

"Dig?"

"For the dreams you once had, the ones you buried."

"You make it sound easy."

"Nothing is easy," she said. "And let me warn you. Once you start, you'll probably find yourself pulling weeds—all those things keeping you down, hindering your joy. And you might come across worms and pests and layers of memories, as well as dried-up stuff that you never intended to let dry up."

"Nice," I said. "And then what?"

"Then you pray," she said. "Don't forget to pray."

If she weren't so frail-looking, if her eyes weren't starting to close like she was falling asleep, I would have jumped into her arms and given her a hug, for her tidbits on life—hers and her mother's—had been what helped me through, before and now. That was the reason, one of the reasons, I had come all this way to see her.

"I want to find closure," I said then. "I've been working on this same doggone manuscript all these years, tweaking here, adding layers there, and voilà, this is it—all I've got to show after all these years of toiling."

"Yes, there comes a time when you must declare yourself done."

"You have no idea," I told her.

She looked at me oddly. "But it's inspired by real-life events, like your knowing me."

"That's true," I said, worried by her reply. Her not liking it, opposing it, would have me crawling out of here on my knees.

"What are your intentions for this book?"

"Well, I was thinking it might be a book others would like to read, so I was going to send it out into the world, find an agent."

"And what will you do if it's wildly accepted?"

"I don't know, build a mansion by the sea and live in it, then write another."

"And what if it gets rejected?"

"Burn it," I said, "and spread its ashes out over the Gulf of Mexico, vowing never to write again. But don't worry—after a period of mourning, I'll move on. There's got to be other things I could try, like painting, or learning the piano. I've always wanted to play the piano. I could move into a town house and buy one of those ten-dollar battery-operated pianos for children that I see all the time at the drugstores." I stopped there.

"Anna," she said, "will you ask the nurses to bring me back to my room now?"

"Of course," I told her. When we got back, I went to her window with nothing but cornfields outside and closed the blinds, thinking to myself how gloomy it all looked.

"Open them," she insisted.

"You like them open?"

"I love them open. I love that view," she said.

"What do you like about it?"

"I look out at all that land," she said, "and think of the stages of growth, the cycles of life. Fall, even winter, serves its vital purpose."

I opened the blinds and looked back out, trying to see things differently, the way she saw them. And when I came back to my chair and sat down, she said to me, "I see the vulnerable state you're in, Anna. You've toiled, you've sweated, you moved onward with this story despite your fatigue and insecurities, and you did all this because you were led by blind faith. You are a writer. You wrote a story," she went on. "But it's a story about me! At least, a large chunk of it is about me!"

"Yes," I admitted.

"I don't mind that it's about me, but nowhere in the story do you mention what I think is the most powerful thing a mother can do for her children—and I remember saying it to you when you asked one day, when you asked whether I had any secrets regarding motherhood and marriage."

"In my book, I said you claimed you didn't have secrets or advice, but you did."

"Yes," she said. "And if you're going to use me as a character, I hope you'll include it somewhere."

"Okay," I said, reaching for my pen, touching it to the paper. "I'm ready. What is the one thing a mother, a woman can do?"

"Pray," she said. "I prayed and prayed, and still pray today, for each and every one of my children. Why do you think I spent so much time in my garden? It was the place that brought me closer to God. And it made me want to pray!"

"I see what you're saying," I told her. "But I didn't mean for it to be a book on spirituality. It's supposed to be about the stages of life."

"It's your book," she said. "You do what you like. But if you use my name, put it in! I think adding a spiritual side will only make it better—breathe life into it—but you're the writer, not me. What do I know? All I know is there's a butterfly on your head—a monarch."

"Is there?"

"Yes."

"Well, there's one on your stomach," I said, pointing. We watched it until it flew away, and then she said, "Are you ready for the other thing I see missing from your story?"

"There's more?"

"Yes," she said, pulling a piece of paper from the side of her bed. "This is the other letter from my mother, the one I was going to share with you the day of my stroke. Read it to me, will you?"

"I would love to!"

"Read it to me, then catch your flight. Go home and get your story published."

"You mean that?" I asked.

"I wouldn't have said it if I didn't mean it."

chapter fifty-seven

Dearest Fedelina,

I look in the mirror and wonder who the old woman is staring back at me. But I know that yellowing leaves are part of the normal aging process. Days like this, when I'm mourning the vibrant colors that once were, I force myself to look up. And then I spot a cardinal sitting in a branch above me. I listen closely to its chirp. It sounds like this: "Pretty, chirp, chirp, chirp. Pretty, chirp, chirp, chirp."

The birds sound lovely, but to tell you the truth, I miss those days when the parade came down my street, filling my yard with the sounds of bands and the clapping of hands, of children laughing and of babies not napping. Older women standing on the sidelines, watching us go by, used to yell out to me, "Those were the best years of my life! They go by fast! Enjoy," but I was too busy keeping children in line, marching this way, heading that way, mending costumes, tidying the streets, picking up confetti and candy wrappers, to think about my children marching on ahead of me one day.

But children grow up and yards become quiet. And it's sad when there are no reasons to roller skate, or floats to decorate, or candy to hand out, or little girls dancing about, and there is nowhere I can think of to march to, no routes to pursue, no band I can join or clap to.

I take my pen and paper and go down to the garden, where I sit like a flower stripped of her petals. How quickly it all happened, as though driven by a gust of wind—you were off and married and moved away. It's hard going about my days with the most precious part of me—you, my daughter—off and into the world, and I see now why it is wise for a woman to have a few things going on in her life so that when petals blow off she still has other things surrounding her.

For months now, my thoughts have been going round and round like dust devils in my mind—swooshing up memories of when you were small. Not big moments, but little ones, like the morning I filled a pan with soap and water, and watched as you twirled through the yard after your first bubbles, kicking your heels in temper as they popped.

Life's sweetest moments do pop quickly, but I have to believe, Fedelina, that there are always more waiting to be had, for us to breathe life into. My problem lately has been that I see no more bubbles heading my way, and no children to blow them toward me. Everyone tells me, "Just wait for the grandchildren to come running your way!"

Until then, I'll force a hyacinth bulb into a glass of water and keep it by my bed. Hyacinth means "remembrance" and they are poisonous (wear gloves when working with them). At the sight of it each morning, I'll know that reminiscing is okay, but that living in the past can be poisonous. It's hard not to worry, to think of you every day, and so I ask myself, what is a mother to do? I tell myself, all she can do now is pray, and so I *will* each and every day—it's what a mother who loves her grown children can do.

I've filled every white nook and cranny of this book, written over pictures of flowers, folded and tucked stationery notes throughout. What more do I have to write or say about flowers, or life, that hasn't already been said? I only hope one day you open this book, How to Grow Roses, and discover it is more than a book on roses, because in it your mother wrote all her crazy little inspirations about womanhood. It doesn't contain everything about life, as I once wanted it to, but I have a hunch that one day, if you don't already, you'll know more than me. They say that's what happens when daughters grow up and have little girls of their own.

Mums

P.S. Just as you fear your mother is about to rot into nothing, here I am now, out in my yard looking at the ground around me, at all the work to be done. It has been a frigid fall, and I feel winter life approaching. But there is always work to be done in one's garden, no matter the season, and we shouldn't let a frost line stop us. So I've decided to pick up my rake and clear the ground. Then plant new things. I think I'll grow some roses. Roses grow everywhere in America.

chapter fifty-eight

When my buttocks were sore from the stone bench I was sitting on, and I no longer felt like reading about that stage of my life—the brief and passing whirlwind I had experienced when my children were small—I closed my recently published first novel, wiped my eyes and looked around to be sure no one was looking. I didn't want to be one of those authors caught reading and crying over their own book. It's why I didn't tell them my name when I bought it earlier this morning at the island bookstore, or that I was the author, and that I was returning for a visit after all these years, to visit the stomping grounds of both the best and toughest days of my life—those days when my children were sprouting and my marriage crumbling.

Everyone has their own story to write, sing or paint, but it had been a while since I had read mine. Now, as I fingered through the pages of my book—one I started long ago, and kept tucked away all those years in my desk drawer—I was finding it hard to believe that this was the yard in which it all began, the inspiration for this story, this silly little story about flowers and an overwhelmed mother and the master gardener living next door. There was no champagne, no release party, when it first came out. I wasn't publicity-crazed and didn't go about setting up book signings. No one sent me flowers. And so I bought my own—roses, of course. But I had no desire for hoopla and craved neither fame nor praise, nor discussion of this book. Unless I was a Hemingway, or a Stein, or a Tolstoy, I would never be proud. Writing it brought me insight and pleasure, along with grief. Reading it would do me no good, but leave me cringing at the parts in which I could have done better—the things I could have done differently in my life. Once a book is released into the world there is no going back, no changing the things you wish you could change, no spending more time with the chapters you knew you should have spent more time with.

It's the same as when a loved one dies. There are no last kisses to be kissed, hugs to be hugged, words to be spoken—no going back, apologizing for what once was or wasn't. It's why I found it hard to talk about this book, why my mind went blank when people asked me what it was about. It is hard for me to tell, even to my own children, that which is fact from that which is fiction, and hard for me to accept the truth, that Fedelina Aurelio never lived to be so old—only in my book! In real life, she had a stroke that morning, the morning I took my children to school, and shortly afterward her children moved her to Indiana, to a nursing home. I never had the opportunity to visit her the way my book describes because she died shortly thereafter.

The news of her death hit me hard and left me sad for the longest time. I did take a trip to Indiana, to visit with her daughters and tell them about the way in which their mother had inspired me. They were surprised, saying she always claimed she had no secrets with regard to raising children, marriage or living life. Maybe she didn't, but we agreed that she did have experience, which is where the secrets hide, waiting to be uncovered in a conversation or set free from the rubble of memories.

After meeting with those beautiful girls of hers, who were there beside her every morning of her brief stint at the nursing home, I returned home eager to interweave what they told me about their nursing home experiences into my story. But when I sent it out into the world—to agents and publishers nationwide—they rejected it, one terming it the "silly little story about flowers." It was then that I saw in my mind a tree, a barren tree, for the first time. So I went to work, adding more, layer upon layer of embellishment, starting with those letters from Cora that weren't really from any Cora. They were from me. I thought up all the things I wanted my own daughter to know about life, and then I did historical research. Adding those letters to my story was like putting leaves on the tree. I added more things, too, like making Fedelina a master gardener. She wasn't really, but she could have been with all the passion she had for her garden. Suddenly there were flowers in my tree. And because I wanted birds, too, lots of birds so that none would be lonely, I added to my story Fedelina's trip to the Grand Ole Opry, and her computer class and game night, and anything else I could think of. She never did any of that. But showing her living out her life in a lonely state wasn't how I wanted my story to go, and I wanted to believe that a person has choices in life, and that when one is lonely there are options, things they can do to pull themselves from the stagnant swamp. I stepped away from my manuscript for several months, but knew from a distance that the branches of my tree never moved and that they needed to move. I went back to work, adding more spirit and the part about prayer. It was the wind that made my story move.

And when I saw in my mind that my tree was as beautiful and full of life as it could be—when I reached the words, "The End"—I was done, and felt both happy and sad, and older, too, for having gone through all of that. A writer doesn't only pick her themes like apples from a tree; she prepares the ground, plants, grows, harvests, nurtures and processes those themes, too. It took a long time, and the process of writing it was hard, but I never wanted to look back one day and ask myself, *Why didn't I plant a Royal Poinciana?*

Now, sitting on a stone bench in the yard that once belonged to my main character, and with a view of my own old yard where the children played, I opened the novel once more. Reading it was like biting into an apple from a tree I had grown myself. I had two of my own copies from the publisher somewhere at home, but the day they arrived in the mail I found it hard to open them, and never did. Doing so would only spook me, I had decided, from seeing my heart and soul poured into words. I had questioned for months whether a heart and soul are meant to become words. There was only one thing I felt sure of when the book was released, and that was my adamant opposition to the publisher when he wanted to change the title to *Mrs. Aurelio's Son Knocking at My Door* or *Knocking at the Door to my Soul* or *Letters from Cora* or *The Flower Letters.*

If only Fedelina was still up in that old house of hers, or out here pulling all these weeds, I thought as I dropped the book in the grass, leaving it for someone else to read. Then I could walk over and ask the reader what she thought the title should have been.

There had been a subtle breeze all morning. I waited for it to pick back up again and, when it did, I let it carry me over to my old yard, and to the time in my life when I was hardly seeing all the beauty that was there. It was as if I had something in my eyes, clouding my vision. The grounds were full of memories of when my children were small. There were thorns and thistles, too, reminding me of the man who had tried dulling my colors with his betrayal, crumbling my petals with his impurity, wilting me with his forbidden act.

He said he felt remorse, said he wanted to start fresh. So for my sake, and that of my children, I stopped cursing the ground their father walked on and I forgave him for the thing he had done to me. And because my neighbor did indeed tell me one day—whether I liked hearing it or not—that women need to put more care and nurturing into the well-being of their marriages, I went to work. My husband and I went to work. We worked on everything, starting at the roots deep within ourselves, raking through the disturbed soil, fertilizing, nurturing and caring for the ground around us. We worked until the stench was gone, the impurity raked away, and the water clear. It was when the water was clear that I felt myself loving him again, truly loving him, pure and simple. But then he did it again—pursued his pleasures once more, dulling my colors, crumbling my petals, wilting me for good with his wicked ways—and raining on my parade!

And so I left him. A mother does things for the sake of her children. I left him for my sons. I left him for my daughter. But first I loved him, and they saw this, too. Thanks to the advice from my neighbor, my children saw a mother loving a father, a wife caring for her husband—at least trying! And when he yanked at my roots once more, pulling me from the Earth, tossing me into the dirt, I waited for a breeze and found in it the energy to get back on my knees and crawl away. My children saw that, too. They saw their father, an adult, bearing the consequences of his sin. It was a lesson they needed to see so that one day they will know what not to do, and what not to let someone do to them.

And then they saw more. They saw their mother in her darkest days of dormancy. All I kept thinking while I was down was that, hopefully, my children would see that not everything in life is always going to be a beautiful blast of color. But it was also for them that I knew I would have to reemerge. It was for them that I looked up to the Lord and made sure they saw this. And then my stem emerged from the dirt and grew tall and strong, and to my own surprise my petals opened again, and my colors returned more brilliant than ever before.

I saw the marvel in my children's eyes, and knew then what a mother is supposed to do, show her children life in all its stages and that not everything is going to be blooming at once. Sometimes it feels as if nothing is blooming or will ever bloom again. A mother can only use words to tell her children so much. It's how she lives her life that teaches them the most.

I worked hard to support my family—did what I had to do to put food on the table—and in the very little selfish time that I had through the years, I wrote. I wrote for comfort. I wrote for pleasure. I wrote to make sense of it all. This is not the only novel I had tucked away in my drawer. There are more, several more, and it's time now to pull them out, get them published, and write more. It's quite common for a mother to put her own passions aside, tuck them in a drawer, but it's my time now and writing is what I want to do.

My old house was vacant. There was a "For Rent" sign out front and no furniture in the windows. I sat down on the bottom step and pulled the letter I had been writing to Marjorie out of my purse. I was always writing a letter to Marjorie, or Thomas, or Will.

chapter fifty-nine

My dear daughter,

What mother doesn't want to teach her children everything there is to know about life? I've written a book, I've written you letters, but deep within me, I know that nothing I say or do is going to prevent or protect you from the infinite problems of life, which like waves from an ocean keep coming at you one mammoth challenge after the next. No sooner do you deal with one than you are hit by another, until one day you find yourself no longer seeing the beauty of it all. It's as if you're walking around with sand in your eyes.

But fueled by motherly love, here I go unfurling my most intimate wish for you, that when life does this to you, when it has you no longer seeing beauty or believing in good, that you cry out to the Lord. He is the only one, I have found, who can wash my eyes clean. And because problems are a part of living, as infinite as the grains of sand on the seashore, I find myself crying out to Him almost every day.

What more can I say, just that everything takes a certain amount of work; that if you think getting what you want in life is easy, then you may as well walk over to your neighbor's yard and steal one of her flowers when she isn't looking, because life isn't easy, nor is growing a garden, but once you start recognizing the pests and learning how to control weeds, and all the other basics there are to learn, then the effort you put into your gardening becomes more pleasurable.

But, because not everything will be blooming all the time, it is my prayer for you that each and every morning of your life, and in every season, you wake to birds singing out your window. And when there are no birds, or window, that you wake up singing yourself, and when you have nothing good to sing, that your soul will sing for you, to remind you in some roundabout way that this is the day that the Lord hath made and only He can turn your bad days good, making you feel as if you're flying above those waves on the wings of a Great White Heron.

And if nothing else, then, I pray that you will spot the wildflowers hidden within the weeds. Look for the wild petunias and think of them. They bloom for one morning or day, and then die. We don't know the number of our days so, like the wild petunia, why not make each current day we do have spectacular?

It's hard being the mother of small children, and harder the mother of teenagers, but the hardest of all is to be the mother of adult children who are no longer seeing the beauty in life. When her children are grown, a mother can only do so much. She can no longer scold or punish them, cradle them in her arms or sing lullabies to them at bedtime. She hasn't the power to change her children's lives. All she can do is try not to judge. but pray and hope that she gave them when they were younger the tools needed to step out into their gardens and do their own work—to become master gardeners for their own lives!

Well, that's all I have to say about life. It's all I know. I'm just your mum. I look forward to our next visit, and to hearing about all that you know, too!

Love, me

# chapter sixty

W hen I had nothing else profound to say about life, and no longer felt the need to stare up at my little house on stilts, I walked back over to Fedelina's old yard, to the magnolia tree her son had planted in the ground twenty years earlier. The tree was now taller than the roof of the house, and as I stepped beneath its shaded canopy I nervously glanced at my watch. Any minute now I would meet up with the planter of this tree.

The thought of seeing him after all these years had me circling the trunk of the tree like a squirrel, and I didn't know whether I would jump into his arms at the sight of him, or run up the tree and hide. My children had asked me countless times since the release of my book if I ever loved anyone other than their father, but I've told them only what I want them to know. A mother has that right, to tweak reality, add a fictitious flair and get creative with the stories she passes on to her children. And an author has the right to declare fiction from fact.

"It was only a week out of my entire life," I muttered beneath my breath as I reached down and picked a daisy. "I don't know why I'm feeling as nervous as I am."

When I stood back up again, there he was—the man I watched through my bathroom window twenty years earlier as he planted this magnolia tree for his mother.

"Oh my goodness," I said, smiling into his eyes, but he looked right through me as if he didn't know me at all—and he didn't. We had only met briefly—that time in the hallway—and then I had watched him through my window, and he had no idea I was up there. The rest was all a product of my imagination, a story I wrote the week my husband was gone, and my children, too. A story I worked on around the clock, morning, noon and night without rest, attempting through my writing to paint a picture of the love my husband might have had for the other woman when he cheated on me. But I knew, in the end, that my husband never in his wildest dreams had such love for anyone as what I had for Liam, if only in the expectations of my mind and the longings of my heart.

"Congratulations on your book, Anna," he said formally. "You must be proud."

"No," I said, and it was true. When I thought of pride, when I thought about what mattered to me most, it was my children. They were the masterpieces I helped to create, the statues I sculpted, and the gardens I nurtured and grew. "Writing brings me insight and pleasure—along with grief—but I'm not 'proud' of my writing, no."

"I must say, I wiped my eyes when I saw it was dedicated to my mother," he told me then.

"She really did inspire me," I said. "Seeing her out there in the garden like that. And she was always so nice."

"Did she really say all those things about flowers?" he asked me.

"Some of it, she did," I said, my face turning red with embarrassment. "The rest I came up with on my own. I hope I don't sound like a total wackadoo. But I will say your mother still inspired me. Having lived a short time next to an amazing woman, having watched her at work in her garden, did something to me."

He looked at me strangely. "It made you want to write a novel?"

"No," I said. "I always knew I'd write a novel, long before I met your mother. I guess seeing her out there each day got me to thinking about what I want to be doing when I'm her age."

"And what's that?" he asked.

"It's hard to articulate," I told him shyly.

"I don't believe that," he said. "I would think it would be easy for you to articulate. You're an author."

I laughed and had to look away, for his blue eyes were making it hard for me to think. But then I spotted specks of blue at my feet, and those specks of blue were as beautiful as his eyes. I felt like blowing a trumpet at the sight of them, for it was spring and there were morning glories everywhere!

"What's wrong?" he asked me.

"Your mother did tell me something interesting about morning glories," I said, looking up again, trying not to get distracted by the butterflies, for they, too, were attracted to the morning glories.

"What did she say?"

"She said each flower unfurls only once, has one life to live, then it closes and dies, to be quickly replaced by another."

"I never heard her say that before," he said. "Thank you for sharing that with me."

I laughed, and so did he, and at the same time that I glanced down at his left hand, I think he was looking down at mine. When he saw that I had no ring on my fingers, he said, "I've been meaning—after reading your book—to visit the Red Mangrove Overlook. I don't know if you have plans or not, but if you don't, I would love some company."

Like a little girl, I reached down and picked one of the heart-shaped leaves, feeling joy from the flowers and giving praise to the Lord for giving me my life. It didn't take me long to know what the spirit of God was trying to tell me through those flowers, that like the morning glories I had one life to live, and that this is my life!

I stood up again, aware that I had forgotten about the morning glories when writing my book, and that I should write another, a sequel to this book about flowers. Then again, what more can one say about flowers that hasn't been said already? Maybe I should write one about leaves instead, starting it with sea grapes!

"I'd love to see the Red Mangrove Overlook," I said to Liam. "Would you believe I've never been there?"

THE END

P.S. I do know a few things to be true about life. Not everyone is born with a green thumb. It's why God created wildflowers. And no, I don't believe life changes with a knock at the door. But rather, one has to open the door, or go out knocking oneself.

Christine Lemmon was born in Chicago, Illinois. When she was eight years old her family moved to Saugatuck, Michigan, where together they worked their family businesses. Her schooling was in Holland, Michigan, where she also graduated from Hope College, a private liberal arts college.

Christine lives on Sanibel Island with her husband and three children. Ideas for her novels come to her while bike riding, hiking through preserves, and watching sunsets with her family.

You can visit her at:

www.christinelemmon.com

Become a FAN of
Christine Lemmon
Novels on FACEBOOK
JOIN TODAY